THE PROMISE OF COUNSELING

The
Promise
of
Counseling

C. W. BRISTER

1817

Published in San Francisco by

HARPER & ROW, PUBLISHERS

New York, Hagerstown, San Francisco, London

FIRST EDITION

Designed by Jim Mennick

Library of Congress Catalog Card Number: 77–20453
International Standard Book Number: 0–06–061052–2

78 79 80 81 82 10 9 8 7 6 5 4 3 2 1

To My Wife

GLORIA NUGENT BRISTER

For Promises Kept and Promises to Keep

Contents

Preface

THIS book is addressed to people who care, both in the context of Christian congregations and in the larger community of faith. It informs the novice, who is beginning counseling as a learner; the professional, experienced in the tensions and traumas of pastoral work; and the layperson, who engages daily in caring conversations. Counseling is examined from the viewpoint of biblical faith, Protestant theology, and modern behavioral science. Readers will discover practical approaches for helping troubled people in particular circumstances.

Counseling is one of several skills, including preaching, leading, and teaching, that should be constantly updated in pastoral practice. Creative caring conversations are not optional; rather, they are fundamental in all effective human relationships. Counseling deserves to be done well. Thus, we shall search for certain footing in this challenging task by contrasting pastoral care with secular counseling approaches and learning from actual counseling situations. The names, locations, and circumstances of persons mentioned in case histories have all been changed. Where people are quoted in case histories, it is the substance of what they said, not their actual words.

This book appreciates, yet does not repeat, basic counseling approaches already available to ministers and specialized skills from psychotherapy. Rather, I have sought to clarify a responsible evangelical approach to pastoral counseling. Doc Gibbs, in Thornton Wilder's *Our Town*, says at the time of his son's marriage: "Everybody's got a right to his own troubles." But there is something more. Each of us has a right to share his or her troubles with a discerning listener, involved at a deep level of common humanity.

The Promise of Counseling speaks a new word to Christian helpers. One works, not in the present moment alone, but in light of divine dimensions. The passages we share with fellow passengers on spaceship earth involve a time frame of galactic dimensions. Our conversations foreshadow eternity. Pascal was right: "The present is never our end. The past and the present are our means; the future alone is our end." The fresh thrust of *Promise* opens life's bitter–sweet, pain–joy, and shadow–sunrise to the magnificent reality of resurrection history. The unremitting tension that is the essence of life has been touched with hands from a kinder world. We occupy a visited planet. Helpers and helpees are not alone; we share life's struggles and victories in the light of eternity.

No book springs full grown from the mind of an author. There are the seminal years, conception, a gestation period, and the life burst. The circle of my indebtedness is wide. An invitation from the International Baptist Theological Seminary, Buenos Aires, Argentina, to deliver their annual lectures inspired this project. I am deeply grateful to former President and Mrs. Jack Glaze, members of the faculty, and to President Daniel Tinao for giving me that opportunity. Portions of the lectures were also presented to audiences at Baptist seminaries in Cali, Colombia, and Santiago, Chile. My brief guidebook, *Life Under Pressure: Dealing with Stress in Marriage* (Nashville: Sunday School Board, 1976), provided background and ideas for chapter 10. A sabbatical leave from teaching tasks at the Southwestern Baptist Theological Seminary, plus a generous fellowship grant from the Association of Theological Schools in the United States and Canada have afforded ideal conditions for writing.

Warmest thanks to the following friends who have read all or major parts of the manuscript and provided helpful suggestions: Seward Hiltner, Princeton Theological Seminary; Thomas H. Cole, Memorial Hospital, Houston; Terry Swift, Houston Baptist University; Edward E. Thornton, the Southern Baptist Theological Seminary; Albert L. Meiburg, dean, Southeastern Baptist Theological Seminary; Nathan L. Stone, pastor, Manor Baptist Church, San Antonio; my son, Mark A. Brister, Instructor of Preaching at Southwestern Baptist Theological Seminary; Charles F. Kemp, Brite Divinity School; Robert S. Glen,

M.D.; and Charles W. Tow, M.D. The editorial staff of the Religious Books Department of Harper & Row has assisted me at each stage of preparation.

I express lasting gratitude to my wife Gloria, my constant companion and capable consultant for thirty-one years, and to my students who have been a continuing source of inspiration and illumination.

All scripture quotations are from the Revised Standard Version unless otherwise indicated.

C. W. BRISTER

Fort Worth, Texas

Introduction:
The Basis for Human Caring

THE problems of living know no boundaries of race, age, sex, social class, or nationality. There are universal needs for self-worth and survival, social-role identification and group affiliation, religious faith and meaning, life purpose and vocational usefulness. Developmental concerns, such as the birth and naming of children, rites of initiation into adulthood, marriage, aging, illness, and death are collective experiences of the human family. For purposes of discussion, growth concerns may be distinguished from crises provoked by acts of nature (destructive storms), economic disasters (factories closing and worker layoffs), social upheaval (liberation movements), calamities (airline crashes), social dilemmas (divorce and child abuse), and situational crises (diagnosis of cancer). Such concerns and crises may become overwhelming burdens for persons and families.

When life's normal routines are interrupted people may need help of varied kinds in order to survive. Human survival presupposes interdependence, knowledge of needs, and investment in life-giving processes. *Care*, which may be understood as a response to humanity's hurt and search for wholeness, is our term for such investment. Care implies concerned attitudes and helpful actions by a person or group on behalf of another individual, group, or cause.

THE MEANING OF CARE

Considering the apathy, anarchy, and anomie of today's culture, to speak of care seems absurd. Only when we understand the world's ambiguous moods—suspended somewhere between chaos and kindness —can we speak meaningfully of care. Christian concern presupposes knowledge of God's love, a feeling of personal worth, the assumption that life does matter, and an atmosphere of risky investment. Care is founded on and motivated by agapelike love.

Care is the fundamental capacity to cherish another person to the full range of his or her existence so that one acts willingly on that person's behalf. Care implies both profound feeling and thoughtful action in behalf of a person, group, or structure affecting life. Paul Tillich used the term *concern*, often with the adjective *ultimate*, to connote human tenderness in a tough world.

For Martin Heidegger, care (*sorge*, in German) is the source of selfhood, of being and willing. "When fully conceived, the care-structure includes the phenomenon of Selfhood."[1] Care reinforces a person's uniqueness as a human being. An individual's constancy of identity, potential for self-actualization, and sensitivity to act in another's behalf are ensured by care. Viewed thus, care is not merely a religious duty; it is a human obligation. Such helpfulness should not be the responsibility of ordained ministers alone. All of God's people are called to care. It is because of the Christian person's loyalty to God that he or she engages in caring activities (Gal. 6:1–5).

Concern takes many forms: a missionary's surgical suite in Bangalore, India, where few words are spoken; a mother's prayer for her children; a check contributed in a local United Way campaign; classes in English as a second language; child-care provisions for working mothers; leisure programs for retired persons; and so on.

Care implies cooperative effort. In a land of rugged individualism, with a penchant for heroes and heroines, we are faced with limits and interdependence. No person can achieve fulfillment solely through someone else. The biblical emphasis is on individual responsibility within community structures. On the other hand, both the Bible and life itself remind us of the shared dimensions of human growth, pain, and providing care. Following an automobile accident, for example, victims may be injured too seriously to help themselves. Ambulances must be called, physicians notified, and emergency rooms readied for hospital patients.

But caring is also personal. When care takes group, social, or legislative forms, it is sustained because certain individuals are behind it. One writer in this era of coalitions, task forces, and mass movements has referred to the individual carer as "a pathetic figure in our time." Such logic just isn't true. Cooperative relief programs, community agencies, and global resources will not be effective unless someone cares. Care, the wellspring of all the conversations this book proposes, is rooted in personal response to God and respect for human personality.

Granted, certain levels of human accountability—like respect for life and protection of the environment—must be legislated. Justice demands from the human community what love freely offers. Legal bases for the preservation of life and enhancement of mankind's habitat are essential. Without some self-imposed guidelines, man, in this power-centered and tyrannical age, might succumb to the temptation to destroy himself.

COUNSELING ENTERS THE PICTURE

Because God cares for the earth there are people who care. Caring implies ministering to human growth whatever comes. All people are involved in both giving and receiving help. A helper one day may be the person needing help the next because of an accident, illness, or stress. Here is an attorney, for example, who is influential in local and state politics and has helped many clients. Swiftly, on a single afternoon, the tables were turned when his teenage daughter was killed in a tragic automobile accident. A strong family undergoing stress was forced to open its wounds to sensitive friends and the healing spirit of God.

Counseling, correctly understood, is a conversation or series of conversations between a concerned individual or group and a competent carer, using certain disciplines, all with helping intent. Counseling may be viewed primarily as a secular process, between a client or patient and an interviewer or practitioner, employing scientific techniques for guidance or healing. Given a theological perspective, like that presupposed here, clients are concerned congregants or religious seekers. Counselors are pastors or lay befrienders, usually under pastoral supervision, deeply committed to the Christian faith. One's religious tradition, value orientation, theological stance, and ethical impulse serve as a support system for counseling practice.

This book is addressed primarily to Protestant ministers serving as pastors of local congregations. There are references to parish priests, though Roman Catholic thought is not discussed. Seminarians have been at the center of my thinking. Ministers certified as psychotherapists, clinical psychologists, and marriage and family counselors will discover a theological foundation for their work. Psychiatrists, psychologists, and social workers will find in case discussions religious language and concepts to assist them in understanding the religious ideas of certain clients. An auxiliary audience is formed by lay befrienders, whether appointed officials or volunteers, who wish to understand counseling as a ministry of the church and to enhance their caring skills.

You may wonder who needs counseling. Helping conversations usually arise in stressful situations, beyond the range of the expertise or the control of a person or family. Counseling may be needed in connection with some psychosomatic disorder, like sexual dysfunction; following a medical examination that detects cancer; during alienation and divorce of a husband and wife; after depression and hospitalization; following a coronary attack, when one's work-style must be altered; after sentencing for homicide, robbery, or rape, when social skills must be enhanced; when war is over and one's guilt for mass killings is overwhelming; or when alcohol or drugs become unmanageable. A helping interview often makes a difference following a young person's academic failure, breakup of a courtship, or an experience of social rejection. Several sessions may be required to assist young parents whose child is victimized by Down's syndrome (mongoloidism), or a woman who becomes depressed following abortion for an out-of-wedlock pregnancy.

Novelist John Cheever captured in *Falconer*, a modern Cain-Abel story, a paradigm of the complex, painful confinement that many Americans face. The protagonist is a forty-eight-year-old college professor, Ezekiel Farragut, who, though a socially prominent Episcopalian, is a drug addict. He killed his brother and, upon sentencing, was confined in a grim, forbidding prison. During one visit, his wife Marcia asks: "When do you think you'll be clean?" "I find it hard to imagine cleanliness," Farragut answers.[2] Imprisonment to Cheever represents not only a place of confinement but of atonement and purification, offering a period of suffering in order to reenter a state of innocence. Counselors dealing with the anxieties of human limitations will recognize that the home Farragut lost is located in the life of the spirit.

A pastoral counselor is seldom afforded the luxury of specializing in therapeutic endeavors. One appointed to lead a congregation must have the skills of an able administrator and be an effective communicator of good news. The pastor represents God, a congregation, and a historic tradition to persons seeking help. While working privately with counselees, a pastor must avoid privatism, underhanded methods (such as secretly recording conversations), and the perils of sexual promiscuousness.[3] He willingly assumes the mantle of ordination and uses the perspectives of a theological education in diagnosing and relieving disorders of the soul.[4] Such issues will be investigated in later chapters.

THE CARING CONVERSATION

Seldom can we orchestrate a counseling conversation. Voluntarism —a willingness to change and receive help—is part of the secret of counseling. Assistance is less something a pastor arranges than it is an attitude of availability. Without composing the drama, a scenario begins.

Here, for example, is a report of a helping dialogue between a minister, Mike Neely, and a friend whom he "bumped into" one day. This is the substance of Neely's visit with a young woman, whom I will call Misty Weber. She came from a sophisticated family with strong conservative Protestant roots. Now active in Transcendental Meditation, Misty had tried for years to sever ties with her parents and her previous religious identification. Born when her parents were middle-aged, she was fifteen years younger than her only brother. Misty's father died in his seventies after a long illness, but she had never worked through the grief process. A heavy valium user, she remained tranquilized and anxious about her widowed mother.

A few months after Misty's father died, her mother collapsed at the airport after a vacation trip. It was disclosed that her mother had a heart problem and that her life expectancy was rather tenuous. Still, she continued her full schedule of activities and enjoyed foreign travel. Misty had never negotiated her own identification apart from her mother, lived in the same city, and, though married, called home every day.

Misty and her husband Norm were scheduled to leave on a trip to Europe within a few days. Her mother was helping to pay for and plan the itinerary for the journey. Misty became convinced that her mother would die while she was in Europe. With this background in mind, here is the substance of her conversation with Rev. Mike Neely. They met casually one day and talked as friends in an informal setting.

MIKE: Are you ready for your trip?

MISTY: I could be ready to leave within the hour. I have been planning and reading and mother has been helping me get everything ready.

MIKE: How is your mother?

MISTY: She is doing beautifully, but I worry about her a lot. I worry about leaving her and going on this trip.

MIKE: Your mother is encouraging you to take the trip isn't she?

MISTY: Oh, yes! I couldn't have managed getting ready without her, but I'm afraid something will happen to her if I go.

MIKE: What exactly are you afraid of?

MISTY: Well, I've had a few dreams lately that she is going to die while I'm away.

MIKE: Have you talked to your mother about this fear?

MISTY: I couldn't talk to her about that! It might upset her, and I know it would upset me.

MIKE: From what I have observed, your mother is quite aware of her own finiteness. . . . She's made two trips abroad in the last year. I don't think your mother would feel ill at ease talking with you about the subject of death.

MISTY: You may be right. The doctors told mother that she may have only a couple of years to live. Yet, she looks better than she has in years and she just returned from that trip with my brother. I just feel very uneasy and uncomfortable with the subject of death. I don't know what I would do if something happened to Mother and I were not with her.

They talked about Misty's feelings of guilt, dread of death, and her obligation to go with her husband to Europe. Mike encouraged Misty to discuss the matter with her mother.

MIKE: If you are going to have a decent, enjoyable trip, you should talk with your mother and resolve your anxiety.

MISTY: I suppose you are right, but I don't know how I can approach the subject. Mother is coming over tonight to help me get some things ready. Maybe we can talk about it.

Upon reflection, Mike doubted that Misty would talk with her mother about her anxiety. To further complicate the problem, there is the Freudian view that Misty's fear could be interpreted as a subconscious death wish for her mother. Dreams of her mother's death force Misty to feel guilty and responsible should anything happen.

What good did the chance conversation in the park do? Mike felt he could be helpful as a friend to someone he cared about. He willingly became vulnerable by identifying with Misty's concerns, thus demonstrating the meaning of grace. Out of her need and trustful disclosure Mike experienced the ability to be a pastor to someone. Ministerial relationships are possible, he observed, while relating informally outside the church's walls. He discovered what Daniel Day Williams, in *The Minister and the Care of Souls,* called the "principle of linkage." Any life experience, like a forthcoming trip, may cause an individual to confront questions at the spiritual center of existence.

How could he have improved the encounter? When Misty said, speaking of her mother, "It might upset her, and I know it would upset me," Mike could have helped her share her fears and dealt with her confused feelings. Mike could have suggested that they continue the conversation after her trip, thereby fulfilling the promise of counseling.

THE PROMISE OF PASTORAL COUNSELING

To promise is to propose, pledge, offer, suggest, or assure someone of something so that the parties involved may expect eventual fulfillment. Mutuality between counselor and counselee is implied in such a pledge, along with covenant keeping. The basic pledge is one of caring for oneself and for others, because God cares.

In pastoral counseling the parties participate in a series of promises. They need to trust each other and speak openly about things that matter. They must trust the healing forces of life and seek freedom to grow. Through such trusting and confiding there is hope of finding pathways to a fulfilling life. The counselor wisely refrains from pledging more than he can honor—of time, skill, or solutions. The person seeking help does not offer more than he can deliver by way of change or growth. They share "the bread of faithful speech" and face the future with eyes of faith.

Promising involves recognition of several dynamic realities, mainly theological in nature, by both counselors and counselees. These will be outlined in the paragraphs that follow.

1. *There is the promise of presence—of being with the other person or group.* In all pastoral care, the church provides the context in which God's healing power is experienced. All parties pledge to turn to each other with individualized attentiveness. Mike, for example, temporarily suspended his own concerns and listened attentively to Misty's story. A helping group agrees to care for each member present: through faithful attendance at all sessions, active listening to what is being said, considerate sharing of feelings, protection of confidences, confrontation of duplicity, and encouragement of integrity.

2. *When people turn to a Christian pastor they share the promise of a faith perspective.* Because pastoral counseling is theistic, there is recognition of the powerful, healing presence of God. By turning to a minister, people signal that they want his guidance. Otherwise, they would have turned in another direction for help. They have sized up a situation and feel a need for pastoral care. They may wish to confess some sin, failure, or fault and to be rebuked or forgiven. They may search for strength to face another day, grace in time of need, or consolation in sorrow. They may desire a clarification of values, seek moral guidance, or the will to change behavior.

This means that the promise of Christian faith is significant to persons seeking help. They should not be sold short or referred quickly away. The pastor must be a theologian, who can apply doctrinal concerns to real life situations. Along with understanding human nature, the pastoral counselor knows that Christology lies at the core of his care. Jesus Christ brought love, power, and justice into life by identifying with human needs. The pastor must do so, too.

3. *Pastoral counseling is related firmly, if mystically, to the providence of God.* The promise of pastoral counseling involves assurance of God's care during all of life's passages. Promisors and promisees remember the biblical dictum: "Our times are in God's hands" (Ps. 31:15). Pastoral

counseling should help people discover how to live with their limitations, deal with doubts, and cope with disappointments, as well as how to overcome them. The philosophy "This too shall pass" is not always reliable. There is solemn mystery in God's judgments which are altogether good (Rom. 8:28). Providence provides a sense of history and destiny for true believers. They travel, not alone, but together toward destinations to be discovered.

Divine providence implies God's right to have his way with man. The Bible reflects a paradox between human freedom and destiny. "A man's mind plans his way, but the Lord directs his steps" (Prov. 16:9). A person is free to choose and live his own life: he "plans his way." Yet, God reserves the right to have his way with man; he "directs [man's] steps." One's counselees are both free and accountable before God. Life, ordered and sustained by the Father, has eternal dimensions.

4. *Pastoral counseling promises the professional skills of someone serving "in Christ's stead."* True, people may turn first to a minister because one is nearby. This is particularly true in rural areas where ministers serve as a first-line contingent of counselors. Also, some people turn to the church because its aid is relatively inexpensive. However, the minister's availability relies on the financial and spiritual support of an entire congregation. In many cases, the work of a church requires a large staff and massive financial backing.

The Christian pastor is viewed as a specialist in matters of the human spirit. People expect one with a theological education to understand personality development and predictable crises of life. Paraprofessionals, such as deacons, elders, and presbyters, who serve in helping capacities, are assumed by congregants to have training in caring skills. If referral is indicated, church members trust a minister to know what colleagues to contact in related professions. In Misty's worries about her mother, for example, the minister had to analyze her symptoms in a diagnostic manner. Was her concern merely the idiosyncrasy of a chronic worrier? Were Misty's dreams and premonitions unconscious death wishes, which created a phobia toward travel? The minister had to make some on-the-spot assessments.

5. *Pastoral counseling involves personal accountability, which the counselor and counselee pledge concerning hope and responsibility toward each other.* Remember the four previous factors affecting the

outcome of counseling: presence, a faith perspective, God's providence, and professional competence. Each factor points to an idealized outcome for the conversations. In addition, the counselor must assess what the counselee hopes for and aid in testing its validity.

Philosopher Gabriel Marcel helps us to distinguish between hoping and wishing.[5] One wishes for things: instant satisfactions, magical solutions, impossible dreams, and events that are unrealistic. There is a vast difference between the wishful counselee who expects healing, a job, acceptance, or a magical outcome and one who hopes. One who has hope realistically confronts life's events, and willingly examines reality with a counselor. The hopeful divorcee, for example, knows a mate has been lost, that both partners were responsible, and that the single life lies ahead. That person does not wish magically for a dead marriage to be reborn. Hope lies at the heart of biblical faith, and defers to God's transcendent purpose, ample provision, and sustaining power. Hope sees "through a glass, darkly" but, at least, it has eyes of faith.

How does a counselor inspire hope in spite of dire circumstances? Not by argument, for hope is more relational than rational. Not by avoiding the tragic, for hope confronts life's pain. Hope is inspired within a community of believers; yet, each person hopes through God for himself. Such personal accountability is a freeing experience for both counselees and counselors.

6. *The promise of counseling views human development as a dynamic process.* The dialogue of concerns and crises moves from the familiar here-and-now toward the unfamiliar future. Participants in the process sacrifice safety for the search. They are "becomers," as Gordon Allport suggested in *Becoming: Basic Considerations for a Psychology of Personality.* To believe these promises involves taking the risk of pain and growth while trusting in God. The concept of divine promise and human expectation will be expanded in chapter 4.

Most of us are where we are because some person befriended us and helped us find the way. A competent spiritual guide needs reliable theological signposts in order to show fellow men and women the way.

A THEOLOGICAL CRUCIBLE FOR COUNSELING

For purposes of discussion, we can speak of biblical, dogmatic, historical, philosophical, systematic, pastoral, and applied branches of theology. While this book is about counseling and is not a formal theological treatise, it is rooted in an integrative, dependable doctrinal position. The reader is justified in asking how certain terms are used, and whether or not an integrative method, critically arrived at, exists. It may help to present the foundations for both my own ideas and for criticism of notions of other scholars.

THEOLOGICAL IDENTITY

I view pastoral counseling as a ministry of the church, in its effort to make the Gospel explicit in life circumstances. Just as Christian congregations commit themselves to evangelism and social concerns, so teaching and healing actions are anticipated in the New Testament (see Matt. 10:8, 28:19–20; Acts 5:42, 10:38; Eph. 4:11–13; James 5:16).

My theological identity is rooted in the radical wing of the Reformation, aligned with the Puritan stream of the Free Church tradition. Since they advocated the primacy of separation of church and state, my spiritual forebears have been identified more with confessing believers' churches than with classical Protestantism.[6] Like other Christian leaders, I am convinced of the Bible's accuracy, authenticity, and authority as God's inspired Word, and of its reliability as a guidebook for faith and practice. While decidedly evangelistic, members of my communion are not Evangelicals in the precise American usage of that term.[7] Baptists have remained independent in ecclesiology—aware of, yet aloof from, the bitterly fought liberal/fundamentalistic controversies of this century. I appreciate Christian outreach concerns among all persuasions, and advocate Christian proclamation by every possible means. Part of our strength is found in Dean M. Kelley's ultimate criterion for success in the religious enterprise—providing meaning that makes life whole.[8] It has been in areas like pastoral counseling, hospital ministry, clinical pastoral education, and Christian chaplaincy where Baptists have joined ranks with other groups to advance the kingdom of God.

THEOLOGICAL METHOD

The title selected for this section: "a theological crucible" (rather than rationale or basis) reveals my own openness to truth and heuristic concerns. Theology—the study of God and of human life before God, interpreted within a historic community of believers—is dynamic, not static. The grist for theology is faith, blended with hope. Christian faith is a life-style, an existential attitude, not merely a belief system. Theology implies a body of knowledge, evolved through the ages by devoted scholars from all branches of the Church. Such evolving theologies have been tested by norms in the Scriptures and stated in historic creeds (see Rom. 10:9; 1 Cor. 15:4; Phil. 2:11). Theological wisdom comes in the course of living, yet the life of faith is guided and strengthened by what doctrine we know.

Non-Catholic theology has experienced varied faces, fads, and fortunes the past two centuries: Friedrich Schleiermacher's concern for feelings; Hegelian rationalism; Albrecht Ritschl's moral values; Ernst Troeltsch's scientific religious history; Sören Kierkegaard's paradoxical ideas; Karl Barth's focus on the Word of God; Rudolf Bultmann's demythologizing project; the process thought of Alfred North Whitehead and his revisionists (John B. Cobb, Schubert M. Ogden, and Daniel Day Williams); the radical and secular theologians like Dietrich Bonhoeffer, Paul Tillich, John A. T. Robinson, and Harvey G. Cox; third-world inspired liberation theologies from Orlando E. Costas, Kosuke Koyama, and James Wong; and theologians of hope, like Jürgen Moltmann and Wolfhart Pannenberg.[9] The pendulum of theological fortune swings freely according to philosophical moods, social conditions, world movements, personal and family life-styles, and pressures from the scientific community. While certain Evangelicals offer an alternative for persons without a convinced persuasion, there is no one agenda for biblical people.[10] The term *evangelicalism* is "a battle-torn flag that has waved over many different Protestant encampments ever since the Reformation," as church historian Sydney E. Ahlstrom of Yale has said.[11] "The Protestant Faith" or "The Baptist Way of Life", for instance, are arrived at more by general consensus and deft descriptions than by common agreement and mutual dedication.[12] The Apostle Paul reminds us that "we have this treasure in earthen vessels" (2 Cor. 4:7). Thus, the ultimate test of theology is God's Word.

My beginnings were in revelational and apologetic (not propositional) theology, reflected in the writings of men like E. Y. Mullins, W. T. Conner, and later, Frank Stagg.[13] While my enthusiasm for biblical theology runs deep, I appreciate certain contributions of process thought. Moltmann's trilogy of central Christian themes, *The Theology of Hope, The Crucified God,* and *The Church in the Power of the Spirit,* has alerted me to God's promise and man's hope in a desperate era of history. While he has been more influenced by Hegel's speculative logic than I might wish, Moltmann has opened faith to the future. He is also in touch with science and the political process.[14] His work, taken in entirety, answers critics, like Lutheran theologian David P. Scaer,[15] and develops new theological ground, which will strengthen Christians for years to come.

PASTORAL THEOLOGY

When it comes to pastoral theology many thinkers follow John Macquarrie's logic, reflected in the "Applied Theology" section of his *Principles of Christian Theology.* Macquarrie, who is identified with both secular and process camps, wrote: "Indeed, the very fact that we have chosen to set up a third division of this systematic theology and to consider in it some matters that traditionally belong to dogmatic theology . . . , indicates that we do not consider these questions of 'applied' theology to have the same centrality as . . . the doctrines of creation or of the work of Christ."[16] I, too, wish to begin with basics. Yet, the Church, its ministry, and its mission in the world are crucial questions. The work of ministers and laypersons, in the Holy Spirit's presence and power, yields wisdom that is doctrinal in nature. While the understandings gleaned from pastoral work are a *product* of God's Word, rather than a *part* of it, they are doctrinal in nature.

Pastoral theology implies reflection on caring activities, resulting in constructive theological statements. There are various methods for doing pastoral theology:

1. *Historic analogy,* or deducing conclusions from given premises, was modeled by Clebsch and Jaekle in *Pastoral Care in Historical Perspective.* [17] They discovered four basic patterns of ministry in Christian history—healing, sustaining, guiding, and reconciling—that require contemporary forms of expression.

2. There is an *idiosyncratic approach,* like that in *The New Shape of Pastoral Theology,* which sees doctrinal implications in each practitioner's speciality.[18] Yet, there is no all encompassing concept linking the bits and pieces.

3. Seward Hiltner, in the fifties, proposed a *perspectival method* of viewing all that a pastor does from the shepherd's standpoint. His *Preface to Pastoral Theology* marked a watershed in methodology, and has influenced my thinking.[19]

4. For centuries there has been an *anectodal method* of drawing

conclusions from individual counseling cases, which resulted in a generalized model for pastoral care. This method is detectable in Richard
Baxter's *The Reformed Pastor,* published in 1656; Wesley's journals;
and in William E. Hulme's *Pastoral Care Come of Age.* [20] Such contributions are both helpful and partial, often torn between a classic biblical
and biographical narrative model of counseling.

Labels tend to distort rather than clarify one's view. If I gave a name
to the way I practice pastoral theology, it would be *revelatory encounter.*
This involves recognizing God's presence and action in caring conversations with people. The late Jewish philosopher Martin Buber held that
through human encounter and interaction, through the community of
"I" and "Thou," there emerges a reality beyond both person's lives, a
"glimpse through to the Eternal Thou." Pastoral theology articulates
God's presence, with and beyond ourselves, which provides a pattern for
human relationships and a chance for forgiveness when we lose our way.
In examining the stuff of human interaction, we learn about existence
and the transcendent Reality within and beyond us.

In counseling, I employ a disciplined eclecticism that draws on
various sources of wisdom in the practice of ministry. In theologizing,
I prefer inductive processes by which universal ideas emerge from caring
praxis. John Patton is correct: "Counseling methods are most appropriately evaluated in terms of the quality of relationship and character of
humanness revealed in the counseling process."[21] Relationship is the
key to all effective pastoral work.

To summarize, I have tried to establish a basis for human caring by
defining care in a Christian context and depicting counseling as one
aspect of ultimate concern. It was noted that people care because of
God's providential care for the earth. The possibilities of a caring conversation were illustrated in the dialogue between Misty Weber and
Mike Neely. Indeed, Neely's counseling notes and critical reflections
demonstrate, in part, the process of revelatory encounter which I advocate for shaping pastoral theology. Linking human hope to divine promise is the central theme of this book. A theological crucible for sharing
counseling and shaping faith, based on my own Free Church tradition,
opens the discussion that ensues. The following chapters point toward
ways Christian promise and hope function in the counseling process.

I

MEETING GOD IN HUMAN NEEDS

I

When People Need Help

HELPING is a human affair. Men and women have helped one another to stay alive, touch the wellsprings of their creativeness, face the difficulties of life, and grow in spite of everything. For centuries, parents have been their children's first priests. Friends, like David and Jonathan, have encouraged each other and "strengthened [each other's] hands in God" (1 Sam. 23:16). Where would a society be without its network of helpers: teachers, healers, consultants, advisers, social workers, union representatives, and advocates? Spiritual guides, like ministers, priests, and rabbis, have been at the forefront of human sensitivity, lending their skill and strength to enrich people's lives.

The literature of counseling, unfortunately, is neither clear nor comprehensive. Each subspecialty of professionals, such as psychiatrists and social workers, is concerned with its own unique approaches. There are many appeals for help, tangible and intangible, in our highly technological culture, but no unified theory for helpers. This book bears a sense of urgency since crucial times breed both quacks and heroes, frauds and geniuses, murderers and magnificent people.

Christian pastors are distracted by the multiplicity of methods for dealing with troubled people. Some pastors have turned away from the pulpit, with its power to provide moral guidance and induce faith, and have selected counseling as a subspeciality. There is a temptation for ministers to turn away from outreach and incorporation of members into the congregation—a historic function of pastoral care.[1] Instead, as Don Browning has said, "Care is now more readily seen as something done by ministers to help people in a situation of emotional conflict and crisis."[2] Browning blames this shift, in part, on professional pluralism in our increasingly secular society. He sees people coming to church more for emotional support and spiritual comfort than for ethical direction and courageous action.

My *Pastoral Care in the Church* discusses how the church and its community provide a comprehensive context for pastoral care.[3] The full breadth of a Christian congregation's concerns for its members is described. Caring practices, like reconciliation, righteous discipline, mutual encouragement, and social action are illustrated. Here, my purpose is not to ignore the importance of moral guidance, but to clarify counseling in a biblical perspective. This book attempts to distinguish levels and modes of helping and to clarify roles of Christian counselors for both professionals and paraprofessionals.

There is a maze of therapies in the land. One healer develops a new approach, writes a book about the concept, gets research grants to fund a center, and launches another school of healing. Such an individual feels that everyone should beat a path to that clinic's door. We now have behavior modification therapy, integrity therapy, rational emotive therapy, transactional analysis therapy, human potential therapy, Gestalt therapy, reality therapy, primal scream therapy, hypnosis therapy, conjoint family therapy, and so on. Small wonder that pressured ministers throw up their hands in frustration, perhaps rejecting all forms of counseling or becoming pastoral specialists, who limit their practice to "religious psychotherapy." Still, the call for help comes.

CODE BLUE—A LOVED ONE IS IN JEOPARDY

I have a good friend who directs the pastoral care department in one of America's finest hospitals. He and his colleagues work each day, alongside physicians, nurses, and technicians, in a healing center that cost seventy-five million dollars. Its surgical suites, radiology center, laboratories, and cardiac-care and intensive-care units are linked by a complex communications network.

The chaplains and other personnel carry beepers, and are paged when critical incidents arise in the hospital. A "code blue" message pages a special team that includes a doctor, nurses, electrocardiogram and lab technicians, and a chaplain to the room of any patient in suddenly critical condition. A "code blue" signal notifies the chaplain that some loved one is in jeopardy. God's representative is needed to confer with relatives, medical personnel, and, perhaps, persons in grave crises.

An average pastor's days may seem quite ordinary in comparison to individuals carrying beepers and on call for emergencies. On the other hand, one's mind and emotions should be ready to handle life's unexpected events. One's parishioners may send their own "code blue" signals for help. Consider the following incident.

One Sunday evening prior to the worship service, a woman dressed in a negligee stumbled unceremoniously into the study of a minister acquaintance of mine. Her long blond hair was tousled and her words to him seemed thick-tongued. "He's going to kill me!" she shrilled.

The minister was out of his chair and at her side, touching her arm to calm her. She was breathless and trembling violently.

MINISTER: Who's going to kill you, Marjorie? [*He recognized the disheveled woman as a neighborhood resident, a talented musician, and the mother of two preadolescent daughters.*]

MARJORIE: Bill! Bill! You've got to help me. He has a gun; he told me he would shoot me if I left the house. [*She sank into a chair, sobbing.*] He locked me in the bedroom, but I managed to crawl out a window. If he finds me, he'll kill me!

MINISTER: What would make Bill want to do that? [*He really did not know the family well. He knew only that Bill Hammond was a druggist, who operated his own pharmacy in a nearby shopping center.*]

MARJORIE: He's crazy! I haven't done anything to him. He might hurt my girls. You're going to have to stop him!

Thus a helping relationship was initiated. Two deacons went with the minister to the Hammond home, while some women stayed in the office with Marjorie. Bill was at home. He had not even noticed his wife's absence. He was watching television and assumed she was still trapped in the rear bedroom. He explained that he had caught his wife stealing drugs again from the vault at his pharmacy. No prescriptions were available from a physician to cover her dosage. He had no way of accounting for the missing pharmaceuticals and would be legally jeopardized if his wife's addiction were discovered. Bill explained that the gun, the locked bedroom door, and the threat on Marjorie's life were last resort measures. He was at his wits end and was trying to terrorize her into changing her behavior. He admitted that a shortcut would not work. Through further conversations, after his showdown with his wife that Sunday night, Bill Hammond admitted that they both needed help.

Psychiatric hospitalization was arranged for Marjorie, with the assistance of the Hammond's physician, and care was offered for their daughters. Things did not turn out well for the family. The parents had long histories of alcohol and drug abuse. (Both Bill and Marjorie were members of a local chapter of Alcoholics Anonymous, but were in poor standing.) Marjorie received temporary relief from her physiological and emotional dependence on drugs during her hospital stay. But it was a long battle. The Hammonds' spiritual resources were thin. After their ordeal, the Hammond family worshipped occasionally but appeared closed to support from the church community.

Working with families like the Hammonds helps pastors to distinguish between pastoral care and counseling. An unstructured conversation, like the hurried one with Marjorie that Sunday night, may be the forerunner of formal counseling sessions. A pastor finds the relationship evolving from an initial caring contact to extended counseling, during which the mutual functions of counselor and counselee are clarified. When the task of each participant is clearly defined, through role induction, both can strive toward a common goal.

Whether or not the pastor sets out to be a counselor, the necessity of doing counseling soon settles upon him. When people cry, "Help," one must be ready to face different kinds of predicaments, including:

- how to deal with persons who are considering divorce
- how to counsel a sexually deviate individual
- how to advise a family with a teenage behavior problem
- how to comfort a person dismissed from a job, bereft of friends following a move to another city, or shaken by the death of a loved one
- how to cope with one's aging parents
- how to distinguish psychosomatic illnesses from other diseases, and from emotional disorders
- how to talk with a child with a learning disability
- how to confront a manipulative parent or parishioner
- how to understand a depressed person and help him face it

- how to form an alliance with physicians and health care professionals for purposes of referral or consultation
- how to deal with suffering and how to help people accept it
- how to support a person following a serious accident
- how to reassure cancer patients who may be dying
- how to help persons live at peace in these times of change, social upheaval, and personal uncertainty
- how to deal with the frustrations of daily living

The list could go on endlessly, for persons are complex and the situations they experience are varied. Add to this list, however, one's own personal need:

- to make sense out of life, and deal with one's moods
- to provide leadership for a congregation
- to cope with daily demands at home, work, or school
- to study and stay abreast of professional disciplines
- to be able to share one's inner self honestly with others

When someone risks telling them a personal story, ministers need care as well as proficiency in providing counsel.

THE DECISION TO RISK

Deep inside every person lives his or her own story.[4] Sometimes that which lies folded secretly within the depths of one's most private self has to be shared. The catalyst for releasing one's secret may be joy or anguish, pressure or pain, ecstasy or anger, understanding companionship or intolerable loneliness. The timing may be entirely spontaneous or carefully planned. The setting may be a casual fireside, high in the mountains during a vacation; or it may be in a psychotherapists's office.

But in all cases, the decision to risk oneself with another human being must be made. The process of risking oneself involves both the person being helped and the helper. On a human scale, a carer's investing himself with another person or group needing help is akin to the Incarnation. That signal and unique event involved God's risk in being made flesh in the person of his Son (John 1:14, 16). Christ made clear the love that God has for us. God's person, who has been helped, responds by offering to help someone else who decides to take the risk of sharing.

The conversation may at first take the shape of superficial revelation. The deeper one's feelings of anxiety the more insistent the need to share one's story. Counseling begins when a person senses that essential issues are at stake, and shares such concerns with another individual in order to obtain help. When a sense of ultimate significance in the discussion is appreciated by both speaker and listener, religious counseling is in process. By *ultimate significance* I imply that the conversationalists recognize, tacitly or by agreement, that they are talking in the presence of God. Faith assumes that, while searching for answers, seekers are guided by "the true light that enlightens" every person who longs to see (John 1:9). The compelling conversation thus becomes a revelatory encounter.

It is an art to be able to listen carefully, with deep respect for the storyteller and redemptive intent for his life. It is also a skill that can be cultivated. Such ministry to pain, confusion, human growth, and aspiration requires wisdom of the heart, head, and hand. The pastor talking with Marjorie, for example, had to assess quickly what had driven her to his study, as well as a wise way of helping her home.

Counseling does not mean merely sharing one's opinion or taking control of another person's life. It is more than just giving advice or quoting Bible verses to troubled people.[5] Listening and responding to someone's story grants that individual the freedom to act, hopefully with responsibility. The process of caring for someone who hurts, and helping a person think more clearly and act more appropriately, is akin to religious experience. The Bible speaks of help being given to one "that is in misery, . . . whose way is hid" and of life returning to one "bitter in soul" (Job 3:20–23). Such change and growth in human personality occur, not merely as humanistic longing, but in relationship to the purpose and power of God.

Counseling, viewed traditionally, is the work of specialists devoted to the psychological theories of Freud, Jung, Adler, Sullivan, Erickson, and others. You may feel that it's not for you, that it's foreign territory, and that such problems should be left to psychiatrists. But there are not enough licensed therapists to go around. Many people do not require long-term psychotherapy to gain inner strength. They may need rather moral guidance, forgiveness, or clarity of purpose.[6] A part of God's assignment to each of his people is to share the good news of his acceptance through Jesus Christ (Matt. 28:19–20; Rom. 12:1–21; James 2:17).

Counseling, helping other people to do life, appeals to the best within each of us. True, not everyone is competent to counsel. Persons who wish to counsel others need consultation with or supervision by caring specialists. Periodic consultation with medical or other specialists should be arranged by counselors and be funded by congregations or counseling centers as a matter of policy.

WHO ARE THE CARE-GIVERS?

The power to change lives through counseling is not a universal gift. *Power,* which comes from the Latin root *potere,* means "to be able" or to possess the potency to support, influence, persuade, encourage, or challenge other persons. When it comes to helping individuals through consultation, clarification, and counseling, many pastors and laypersons feel powerless. Care-giving is not for everyone. Yet, a world without the richness, liveliness, and immediacy of personal counseling would be grim indeed. Fortunately, counseling's significance has been recognized in churches, schools, hospitals, industries, and the helping professions.

Giving and receiving help is a costly business. I have demonstrated the risk one takes when inviting a helper into the privacy of one's life. Yet, the care-giver also pays a price to accompany a disturbed person's journey. Here, we shall distinguish the pastor's risks from the lay volunteer's role in helping. The risking a pastor must do in taking the keys to the innermost rooms of a counselee's life is greater than that of a layperson who counsels.[7] A pastor's identity, vocation, and destiny in a given community are linked to his pastoral effectiveness. Counseling is a major aspect of his role. The layperson takes risks in caring, but usually from an amateur's rather than a professional person's perspective.

PASTORAL RISKS IN GIVING HELP

The risk a pastor takes involves the image of his own adequacy, exposure to his sexual and aggressive impulses, sensing limited responses to his proclamation, and occasional feelings of impotence in prayer and leadership. History reveals a long line of religious healers in various cultures—the shaman, exorcist, *curandero,* witch doctor, reader of palms and tea leaves, and astrologist. Magical power to cure human ailments, alter history's course, and predict future events has been attributed to such diviners. From the days of the apostle Paul, people have had more faith in Christian ministers and expected more from them than is reasonable.

Pastors are encouraged to seek strength in the Scriptures, but not to play God. Perhaps you recall a visit by Paul and Barnabas to Lystra in the first century (Acts 14:8–18). Following a miracle of healing, the people shouted: "The gods have come down to us in the likeness of men!" People brought oxen and garlands to the gates, offering sacrifices to their guests, whom they called gods. Paul and Barnabas must have struggled momentarily with the image of their own adequacy and of God's providence. Then came their honest admission: "We are but men." That is a confession every care-giver must make.

Ministers are particularly susceptible to the temptation of deceiving themselves into accepting the burden of divinity. When lives are broken we want to fix them. When home life collapses we want to glue the pieces together again. When divisions appear in a congregation the pastor must be a peacemaker. When faced with a compromising sexual temptation, he is expected to deny both his godliness and manliness and "play dead." A preacher's words are to elicit a hearer's response, yet some sermons fall like stones into the ocean and sink without a trace. The sensitive pastor may feel helpless in praying for an inoperable cancer patient, an incurable stroke victim, or a transsexual who has been socially rejected.

People turn to pastoral counselors much like the Lyconians faced Paul and Barnabas. They hope the "gods have come down in the likeness of men." But a counselor cannot walk on the water; he is no miracle worker. Sooner or later someone expects more than the pastor can deliver. Then, the apostles' prudence becomes self-evident. The burden of divinity is impossible for ministers. Its load is crushing. Partly for such reasons, counseling should be shared among Christian workers. Some lay persons, including teachers, social workers, and physicians, are skilled counselors. For strong biblical reasons, as well as common sense, God's people may serve as priests to each other.

TRAINING VOLUNTEERS IN GIVING HELP

Many pastors wish to equip lay befrienders for ministry, but lack appropriate models in the area of counseling. The pioneering work of California psychiatrist Warren L. Jones, in training mental health center volunteers in first aid for acute crises, has provided some valuable lessons:[8]

1. Interested, concerned people can help others make it through a crisis.

2. Identification with the role of counselor, while not easy for a volunteer, can be reinforced by participating in repeated case conferences. At such conferences, a professional counselor models the role each helper should take, demonstrating how to follow the client's initiative with firm, encouraging questions and assessment of emotional resources. Through multiple presentations the volunteer learns to apply simple procedures under varying circumstances.

3. The helping person's ability to collaborate involves intuition, ingenuity, and experience in recognizing signals of need. He is not expected to change careers in midstream and attend medical school in order to learn to assist people who hurt. The concept of providing emotional first aid relieves the worker of the need to be a professional expert.

4. The helper learns to marshall therapeutic resources, after identifying specific needs, and learns to rely on a team of health care professionals for consultation. Such experiences put to rest the criticism from certain quarters that volunteer caring represents only a palliative endeavor.

How might a layperson, trained by a pastoral specialist in crisis intervention, respond in a given situation? We might imagine a Sunday school teacher taking the role of a care-giver with a class of fifteen-year-old girls. A member of the class, whom I will call Betty, took an overdose of sleeping pills because she felt misunderstood by her parents, her boyfriend, by everyone. Fortunately, her suicide attempt was abortive. It was a cry for help, shared with a friend her own age, who felt compelled to notify Betty's parents. She was rushed to a hospital emergency room and her life was saved.

"But, will she not destroy herself unless she gets some help?" asks

Betty's concerned teacher. Possibly so. A wise teacher may decide to become a priest to Betty. She should at least have an opportunity to talk with someone who cares, not to hear a sermon against suicide, but to muster strength to go on with life. Her parents and school friends are already involved. To help her may require the skill of a clinically trained minister or therapist. Conjoint counseling for the whole family may be indicated. The fact that a teacher listens with love and support will assure Betty that she is befriended. That someone wants to understand how she feels should enhance her will to live.

What do you do when talk is not enough, when insight doesn't come, or when willpower is weak? The limits of volunteer assistance become obvious. A team approach by professionals is often essential. This suggests another issue Christian counselors must face.

DIVINE PROVIDENCE AND DILEMMAS OF LIVING

When people care deeply, questions arise about God's providence and the dilemmas of living. Why does God permit thus-and-so to happen? Has he limited himself? Are there satanic forces in the universe more potent than God's power? At times the brightest and best of helpers become stumped and fail. Then who's to blame? Or is scapegoating even a relevant question when we face evil and suffering?

The matter of human hopelessness came up one day in the time of Jesus Christ. After the majestic experiences of his transfiguration, Jesus, with three disciples, faced an epileptic boy at the foot of the mountain. The boy's father explained from the edge of the crowd that the other nine disciples had been unable to help the boy. The Lord asked, "How long has he had this" offending spirit, to which the father replied, "From childhood . . . but if you can do anything, have pity on us and help us." "If you can!" repeated Jesus. "All things are possible to him who believes" (Mark 9:14–29; Matt. 17:14–21; Luke 9:37–43). Jesus then healed the lad and presented him to his father.

Later, in private, the disciples asked: "Why could we not cast it out?" God's Son replied: "This kind cannot be driven out by anything but prayer." Jesus laid great emphasis on faith and prayer. A person of genuine faith refuses to set limits on God's power.

There is a sense in which, from a human viewpoint, a sufferer may lie beyond help. Yet, faith holds that a "God who is active and available in the midst of every crisis and present in every tragedy is a God who can change the world. The uncertainty is not whether God is with us . . . , but whether we will join God in the struggle," writes Howard Burkle.[9]

Helping is a complex process. Often a team effort is required for diagnosis and treatment, while family members and friends pray for deliverance. Obtaining medical assistance in such instances may be viewed as an act of faith itself. Jesus taught his disciples what all true healers ultimately believe: "From the most High comes healing." Human assumptions, diagnoses, resources, and treatment have value to the degree that they recognize and represent a divine purpose. The Bible reminds us that healing rests, not on the counselor's competence alone, but on an eternal promise. Alongside our best human efforts lies the incomparable, restorative love of God.

To summarize, human needs come in many forms, as varied as mankind. Christian care anticipates an interest in and response to all persons without distinctions of race, sex, social class, age, or religious belief. We are free to care because God cares and his spirit is with us. Healing requires trust by both counselors and those seeking help. It costs to care. Only "wounded healers," Henri Nouwen reminds us, care as a life-style.[10] My own discovery of God's care and confidence in counseling form the theme of chapter 2.

Discovering God's Care: A Personal Odyssey

HAVE you ever listened to a speaker and wished that you could see behind the mask to the person? Ralph Waldo Emerson told the graduating class at Harvard Divinity School in 1838: "The true professor can be known by this, that he deals out to the people *his life*—life passed through the fire of thought." I would add: life passed through the fires of experience, feelings, and convictions. An effective teacher needs the capacity to inspire persons, not merely to inform them.

During a visit to the home of Karl Barth, in Basel, I asked him: "What do you think of psychiatry's view of man?" Puffing on his pipe, he replied with a smile: "I try not to think about it." I am unable to dismiss life's passages with the same ease that Barth bypassed the behavioral sciences. The following suppositions are basic to my experience, guide my caring actions, and anchor my hope in God. My assumptions and actions as a counselor have been shaped by the fragility of life and the force of time.

DEATH AND THE SEARCH FOR IDENTITY

Daniel Day Williams, who was a friend to many of us who studied with him, once said, "For a person to begin the search for himself is like facing death."[1] My quest, a road I would never have chosen for myself, was jarred into motion by family tragedy.

A child has the illusion that earthly existence is eternal. He wears no watch; his view of time is pretechnological. Childhood is the closest thing we know to eternity, where time does not matter. Adults chop their lives into bits and pieces of days, hours, and minutes; time is everything. The most important aspect of my childhood was the sense of intimacy I shared with my parents. Our closeness was shattered one May morning in 1935, when my father was crushed to death in a freak truck accident. Just when we thought that we might escape the Depression's undertow, the world appeared at an end for my thirty-year-old mother, seven-year-old sister, and myself.

Feelings of rejection by heaven—a cosmic "put down" by the loss of a parent—are some of life's hardest emotions for a child to handle. A youth's sense of self-esteem and the value of others can be distorted by death. Rationally, I felt that I was as good as anybody else. But emotionally, I felt different from all the other children whose dads were still around. And psychic difference can be painfully lonely.

Since children view life through a limited peekhole of experience, decisions made early may seem too demanding or become distorted. Vows made to oneself, to God, or to significant others may be unrealistic. In adulthood, their consequences may be minor or major, according to the wisdom, stupidity, or pathology of the vows. At nine, I decided to become a man. I accepted the conventional wisdom of adults, who advised, "You must be a man and help your mother and sister." Yet, in my young heart, I faltered in my faith, and the lamp of hope flickered. Now, I understand more of living with the "kindness and severity of God" (Rom. 11:22). But it took years for life to convince me that I would ever see "the goodness of the Lord in the land of the living" (Ps. 27:13).

Yet, there were serendipities and surprises along the way. The earth's dispossessed and disenfranchised citizens became my spiritual kinfolks. To this day my sympathies lie with the underdog and the loser in any contest. One of the reasons why I became a Christian minister and believe in counseling is to help persons on the losing side of existence to become winners by God's grace. And there was another surprise. My heavenly Father soon took on added significance.

WE ARE MADE FOR FAITH

Death teaches us that life is either closed in a zero or opened to
faith's possibilities because of Jesus Christ's resurrection from the dead.
It was he who taught us, "With God all things are possible" (Matt.
19:26). During adolescence I discovered what faith and doubt are all
about. Now, I am convinced with the apostle Paul that "whether we live
or whether we die, we are the Lord's" (Rom. 14:8). That conviction
gives me a sense of both deep security and great freedom.

The more I believed in God the more human I could become.
Growing into adulthood I discovered that Jesus of Nazareth was a "man
of like passions" with us (see John 2:13–17). The more I learned of him
and surrendered to his spirit, the more real I could become. My defensiveness, in time, was laid to rest.

This trust in the heavenly Father did not come easily for me. My
goodness since childhood had depended on following rules and living up
to expectations. Approval was earned as a reward for good behavior.
Years later, through clinical pastoral education, I discovered that if I
could be honest with God, I could be more authentic with people.
Because I experienced understanding and acceptance in my sin-bond-
age, I can accept counselees today. No person is good or wise enough
to earn God's love. Acceptance is a gift, which becomes explicit in
human relationships.

CARING LOVE CAN PREVAIL

One's spirit can be paralyzed by tragedy. It is true that hurt people
can hurt others. But the strength to care and a social conscience may
also be shaped by suffering. Such was my experience. In a world of
demonic powers, broken communication, discredited government officials, raw violence, and disadvantaged members of society, love provides
an exclusive, saving possibility (Luke 10:27).

The power of love to prevail is illustrated by emigrant Bel Kaufman,
author of *Up the Down Staircase*, in a thank you letter to her former
English teacher in Newark, New Jersey:

You had asked us to write a composition in a class about one of Hardy's heroines
. . . , but I had neglected to read the book assigned. Caught off guard, writing

frantically against the clock, I described [someone else]. I anticipated failure, disgrace, worst of all—your disappointment. Instead, you gave me a minus for being unprepared and an A for something uniquely mine. Your scrawled comment in red ink on my paper read, "This isn't Hardy's character, but you've made yours very real." Startled into gratitude, I became aware of my own possibilities. You *recognized* me.[2]

Love recognized this shy, uneasy, intense foreigner, whose new language lay clumsily on the tongue. Love dignified her teacher with respect. Love is more than a feeling; it involves caring. Love blesses, affirms, and provides a person room to grow, as well as to fail. Love touches, strokes, receives, gives, validates, and shares with others. Indeed, agape love never fails (1 Cor. 13).

Interestingly, the New Testament polarizes love and fear, rather than hate, as emotional opposites. "There is no fear in love, but perfect love casts out fear. For fear has to do with punishment, and he who fears is not perfected in love. We love, because he first loved us" (1 John 4:18–19). Love then is not a Mount Everest that one dreams of conquering, assaults willfully, endures alone, to achieve the summit in a final effort. A true lover leaves what John Claypool called "tracks of a fellow struggler" rather than one shining triumph. Love loses some and wins others. But love never really fails because our fragile, partial, wayward human loves are part of the majestic, mysterious, cosmic love of God, the source of all true loving.

Pastoral counseling at its best requires wise, patient caring. Daniel Day Williams, author of *The Spirit and Forms of Love*, wrote: "We cannot know the love of God except as it is first given to us in our brokenness."[3] Such love walks hand in hand with a sense of the tragic. It is neither smug nor condescending. Christian love cannot be learned all at once; it grows with passing of time. A counselor's care can be thwarted, tested, or rejected. Thus, love implies perseverance and wisdom, not gullibility, in pastoral encounters.

Love's shining ideal passes judgment on every broken relationship, beckoning us toward reunion. God provides both love and justice, which prevail despite man's imperfect love. He is the waiting father in the story of the prodigal son (Luke 15:11–32), longing for reunion with his creation. That is the good news of Christian hope for people who care.

HOPE PROCEEDS WITH THE DAY'S WORK

I have written of the gift of life, my sense of the tragic, of living between belief and unbelief, and the power of love. One thing remains. I believe that life truly "abounds in hope" (Rom. 15:13). Without hope the counselor's skill is lost, growth is impossible, alternatives are absent, vision shrinks, and self-esteem dies. The basis for hope is nothing less than the promise of God.

GOD'S PLAN OF THE AGES

Biblical faith begins with a promise of redemption from sin. The Old Testament views God's promise of salvation through his covenant with Abraham (Gen. 12:1-3). Generations passed, and the chosen people experienced tough times. Still, "God heard their groaning, and God remembered his covenant with Abraham, with Isaac, and with Jacob" (Exod. 2:24). God had promised Abraham that he would have innumerable descendants (Gen. 12:2, 15:5, 17:6-7); that God would give him a land (Gen. 12:7, 15:8, 17:8); and that through him and his kindred all the families of the earth would be blessed (Gen. 12:3, 18:18). God repeated the promise to Isaac (Gen. 26:24) and Jacob (Gen. 28:13-15). Later, at Sinai, the nation of Israel received this covenant (Exod. 20). God never forgot those pledges, but in return he expected obedience. Israelites in exile dared to believe that their shattered covenant would come true.

The hope of eternal salvation, fulfilled in the mission of Jesus Christ, is God's plan of the ages. Despite human sin and perversity, he hears man's cry. "It is I who answer and look after you," he promises (Hos. 14:8). Christ on the cross believed that his kingdom would prevail. In risen splendor, he promised the apostle John on Patmos, "Behold, I make all things new" (Rev. 21:5). Thus, God in Christ accepts man's brokenness, hurt, and failure, and points him toward a future full of hope (1 John 3:2). The promise of new beginnings undergirds and informs the work of the wise pastoral counselor.

DIMENSIONS OF HOPE

I related the promise of counseling, in the Introduction, to six great realities: the caring person's faithful presence with an individual or group, a faith perspective, the providence of God, the counselor's professional skills, the participant's personal accountability, and a view of life as unfolding process. I will examine aspects of hope that help strengthen counseling's promise:

1. *A pledge of assistance to any person depends on the Ground of hope, expectation, and assurance who is our life.* God has declared himself to us through the words of Jesus Christ, who promised, "Because I live, you will live also" (John 14:9-11, 19). This promise connects the counselor and counselee within the circle of divine concern.

2. *Hope helps point us toward the future as a friend.* So much of living is bound up in the past—its irony, ambiguity, deceit, darkness, and disappointment. Pastoral counseling helps relieve that melancholy legacy that has festered for so long. Yet, confident of God's help, it points each sufferer toward the future. It is not easy to redirect one's life, and turn it toward another dream. But God's persons, possessing both memory and hope, can face toward the future as well as the past.

3. *There is the hope of discovering a pathway to responsible living.* At best, the struggler may have the ability to grow. If a family or group is involved, they may pledge together to make a go of life. But persons in prison, the severely handicapped, and those where help must cross major barriers can still believe this same promise. It is a challenge to health and salvation.

4. *The participants in the process are not alone.* The church, a community of faith, surrounds them in fact or possibility. Mutual ministry involves clergy and laypersons alike. The professional identity and integrity of the minister should be recognized. A minister's education and involvement in the church's life and work add much to the promise. Ministers have given their whole lives to become skilled at speaking the "truth in love" in order that persons "grow up in every way into . . . Christ" (Eph. 4:15).

But the counselor's care should not exclude other approaches. Consultation with a professional specialist may be desirable during part or all of the process. On the other hand, the need for complementary functions among ministers and laypersons should be recognized. There should be commitment to team efforts, both in the congregation and in the community. Interdependence among helping persons is presupposed in effective counseling. A team approach recognizes the need for mutual respect and support. While clergy and lay persons may not be associated as professional colleagues, they are members of the same body and are "workers together with God" (2 Cor. 6:1; see 1 Cor. 12:20, 27).

5. *Those involved in counseling are engaged in an intentional ministry.* Intentional ministry implies a spirit of availability but not constant activity.[4] "I have discovered that, along with my teaching and writing," a psychiatrist confessed, "I can be responsible for only five patients at any given time." While atypical of a practicing psychiatrist's case load, that was his work style.

This leaves one's role as a helper open to some negotiation. Even a professionally certified counselor may not be able to see all clients desiring an appointment on a given day. Likewise, pastoral counselors will have to say no to some requests and opportunities.[5] They should provide all the care they can muster, but guilt should not be placed on anyone who cannot give help at a particular time. The mere fact of being needed or fear of disapproval are inadequate motives in ministry.

There is also a need to retreat from involvement, to rest and repair one's own body and soul. Some helpers are one hundred percent "on call." Still, they cannot be vulnerable to human cries, brutality, and suffering 168 hours a week. Only God "never slumbers nor sleeps" (Ps. 121:4).

The time comes when the counselor himself needs care. There was a minister, for example, whose wife left him. In the process of obtaining a divorce, he was at emotional ebb tide. It would have required massive denial for him to pretend that he was as secure as ever. He needed help, and for the time being was not a fit helper. The promise of counseling takes into account the human need for periodic renewal and retreat from involvement. Through study leaves, retreats for spiritual growth, work rotation, and days off, a negotiated understanding of one's responsibilities can be made. This is not an invitation to irresponsibility, but to accountability in the best sense of that term.

Christian counselors believe:

1. No failure need be final.
2. Life beckons us toward growth in spite of circumstances.
3. Much of life is spent in a weary round of study and work. Yet, chain reactions of creativity happen within the ordinary routine. Life surprises us with joy.

4. No one is true to all his loyalties all the time. One is expected to live up to the best he knows and seek forgiveness when he fails. We need both vision and pardon.

5. We must learn to trust the dark. Obvious answers to our questions are rare. Often the light we seek is not on the face of the question but in its shadow. Yet light does come!

6. Hope keeps us on the job, inspires zeal when spirits sag, and stretches our aspirations toward new goals.

All this is possible because we live in the presence of eternity. God "has put eternity into man's mind" (Eccl. 3:11). Once man catches sight of this vision, life never returns to its original dimensions. Life keeps growing and testing and stretching toward the ultimate dimension of "the measure of the stature of the fullness of Christ" (Eph. 4:13). That is why I believe in pastoral counseling.

Each of us is unique, and this book encourages us to share each others' stories. I believe that "the measure of man's life is not his freedom from inner struggle, but his discovery of how the whole of life, including its dark side, can be brought into the service of growth in love."[6] Unless would-be helpers acknowledge their own idolatries and wrestle personal demons to the ground in defeat, they cannot be free to help at all.

3

Counseling Inside Out
and Outside In

THUS far we have investigated certain counseling risks and responsibilities in meeting human needs for survival and growth. Pastoral counseling was identified as a series of conversations, between a competent counselor and a concerned individual or group, in which theological and behavioral resources are used to facilitate personal growth and interpersonal competence. In such counseling, ministers and laypersons share human concerns in Christ's stead. We have discussed the basis for human caring, the role of counseling in the church, as well as its promise.

In counseling, pastors sense constant interaction and tension between theological and scientific perspectives. Because pastoral counseling is both art and science, a faithful counselor correlates biblical wisdom and psychological insights in an effort to strengthen persons for life, death, and destiny. Wayne Oates said the pastor "works in the boundary situation between the great continuities of the 'deposit of faith,' on the one hand, and the seeming discontinuities of scientific discovery and theory, on the other hand."[1] The competent counselor refuses to function with restricted vision of either empirical hypotheses or biblical truth, arrived at by historical-critical interpretation. Both sources of wisdom must be included in his perception. Given this tension, I shall next examine the counseling situation today, and propose guidelines for pastoral practice. If my case seems overstated, it is made merely to challenge ministers to function with both theological and psychological integrity.

Counseling, properly conceived for pastors, should be characterized by: (1) theological richness and congruence with Christian tradition; (2) goals of personal growth and interpersonal competence for counselees; (3) appreciation for, without restriction to, changing secular models of therapy; (4) openness to minorities and all sectors of society; (5) awareness of social systems that shape and shackle life; and (6) a vision of spiritual wholeness rooted in the promise of Christian faith. The remainder of this book serves as a commentary, with case studies, on these criteria. Now, as a reminder, we shall discuss why people turn to the church.

WHY PEOPLE TURN TO THE CHURCH

People turn to the church because it is there. The church represents a local group of Christian believers working together as a congregation. Each communion and each parish is unique, according to its historic doctrines and imposed duties. There may be no conventional pastor in a conventional building with conventional services. Still, indispensable activities are occurring: public worship is maintained; the Gospel is preached; pastoral care is offered; and channels are opened for the practice of Christian discipleship. The building and its other visible symbols bear witness to the church's stubborn survival and saving purpose. Its human representatives are found daily in the midst of life, wherever people gather to work or play.

People turn to the church because of what it is and stands for—a fellowship of true believers, learning to live appropriately as citizens of two worlds. People turn to the church because of its Savior, Jesus Christ, and the eternal life he offers. Men and women come to church because they desire to worship God, to honor him in all the systems and structures of their lives. There, they hope to find meaning, usefulness, courage, clarity of vision, and strength through fellowship.

The pastoral counselor's concern is with the one and the many, those gathered and still scattered, the local group and the universal task. His ruling obsession, contrary to some laymen's opinions, is not with one congregation alone, running its own holy business and fostering its own comfortable advantage. The Christian pastor's fascination is with the world that God so loves he gave it his Son—the whole of that world, known and unknown, black and white, urban and rural, Christian, Jewish, Buddhist, and Moslem. The church's task, through Christ's commission, is to go into all the worlds of human living and make disciples of all nations (Matt. 28:19–20).

Christian counselors perceive that the place to begin this global assignment is up close, in the particulars of one life or one family. The ministry must be specific or else it is a fraud. Frequently, the universal is unattainable except through a combination of localities and cooperative efforts.

People turn to the church in order to make sense out of life and to discover strategies for living. People are searching for "keys to the kingdom" of self-understanding and fulfillment. They want to know how to plan ahead, make decisions, enjoy sex, overcome prejudice, buy the right product, get married, handle depression, endure divorce, manage time, negotiate life's passages from youth to old age, face singleness, be successful in sales, cope with anger, be open, use power or endure powerlessness, refashion broken relationships, face illness and death, or meet grief. They want to survive rapid social change, liberation movements, environmental concerns, energy shortages, and threats of violence and nuclear holocaust.

How does a local parish minister involve himself, beyond the pulpit, in this quest? Consider the following vignette, not as an anecdote, but as depiction of the Gospel's explicitness for strugglers.

An attractive young woman named Judy stood on a bridge one day contemplating suicide. Life had fallen in upon her. Feeling frustrated and utterly forsaken, she searched the river's swirling waters below. Suddenly, she glanced up and noted a cross high atop a church steeple. Afraid of dying, and determined to give herself one more chance before ending it all, she made her way to the church office and requested a conference with the minister.

The pastor's secretary interrupted his study schedule with these words: "There's a girl here who asked to see you. She said she wants to know what is under that cross. Will you see her?" Because the pastor cared, he spoke with Judy, saw her turn in a new direction, and was able to relate the experience with gratitude and relief. A deeply depressed college student had showed up at the pastor's door; after counsel, she departed reinforced for life.

Such incidents, in slightly differing detail, occur constantly in our complex world. People seek help, often from the church, and pastors try to assist them. Life propels God's servants into counseling situations, whether they are ready or not. They, in turn, are searching for methods to help, for counseling rationales congenial to authentic biblical faith. Many of them wish to obtain supervision or professional consultation in the helping process. Thus, we shall examine the counseling situation today, and propose procedures appropriate to church contexts.

LIFE AMONG THE COUNSELORS

Professor Thomas Oden, while lecturing at Fuller Theological Seminary, asked for a full self-disclosure by pastoral counselors of their own distinctive religious presuppositions.[2] He questioned the dominance in Christian counseling of medical specialists who provide models, both inappropriate for the clergy and ineffective in the cure of numerous character disorders and neuroses. Here, I attempt to comply with Oden's challenge of self-disclosure.

The term *counselors,* in this context, includes four principal groups who attempt to communicate complex, at times confusing, messages to one another. The first includes ministers who have received some education in pastoral care, perhaps supervised clinical experience. The second is pastoral specialists, such as chaplains, clinical supervisors, pastoral counselors, and teachers of pastoral care. The third is the expanding group of skilled persons in the so-called helping professions—psychiatrists, psychologists, and social workers. The fourth includes volunteer paraprofessional workers, who function as listeners and nurturers in varied settings. Many members of these groups communicate with those in other groups in roles of consultants, authors, guest faculty members, and supervisors, sometimes using specialized jargon and alien suppositions. Too often, the communication has been one way: from medical mentors down to ministers.

When a pastoral care colleague from another school heard that I was writing this book, he protested: "Do we need another book on counseling at this time? Perhaps those of us in the field should get together periodically and decide where we need to go in the creation of new literature." As a member of a number of professional organizations, I am certainly committed to the principle of consulting with colleagues in one's field. Thus, his question could not be lightly dismissed. What justification is there for another pastoral counseling volume? Can any new ground be broken? Aren't counselors overwhelmed with case studies, research reports, and biased books already? Such reservations should be faced head-on. I propose to answer the above queries by considering life among the counselors. What help has actually been received by pastors from specialists in recent years?

1. *Much available literature used by religious counselors is theologically threadbare.* Counseling trainees in each new generation are introduced to the seminal thinking of Carl R. Rogers.[3] Exposure to his client-centered therapeutic procedures still serves as a corrective to any would-be helper's insensitivity and manipulative control of counselees. Granted, he emphasized unconditional positive regard, careful listening to each client in the therapeutic process, and knowledge of what it means to become a person. Still, Carl Rogers worked and wrote in a scientific context.

Late in his career, Rogers, at one time a student at New York's Union Theological Seminary, shifted to group work. While on staff at the Center for Studies of the Person in LaJolla, California, Rogers became heavily involved in the encounter group movement. In his *Becoming Partners: Marriage and its Alternatives,* the former child therapist became an advocate for homosexuality and free-forming sexual liaisons between consenting adults.[4] In an effort to circumvent moralizing about sex, he advocated national adoption of laws permitting any form of cohabitation shared by adults. The state of California did pass such a law. Rogers's alternatives to marriage are a far cry from the Bible's view of family life. Rogers's work, and that of his revisionists, Charles B. Truax and Robert R. Carkhuff, and his critics, William Glasser, proponent of reality therapy, and Hobart Mowrer, advocate of integrity therapy, all spring from a humanistic perspective.[5]

Howard Clinebell's *Basic Types of Pastoral Counseling* has the virtue of summarizing nearly a dozen types of therapeutic methods available to ministers.[6] It is one of the most widely used books on pastoral care in America, and my students have found it helpful for years. It proposes "reality practice" exercises at the close of each chapter to improve clinical effectiveness. On the other hand, Seward Hiltner has criticized Clinebell's book as being "virtually devoid of any theological reference or connectedness."[7] That assessment is open to challenge, since one chapter focuses on counseling in religious-existential problems.

There are, however, notable examples in pastoral counseling literature of books with a theological perspective. In 1961, Seward Hiltner and Lowell Colston published *The Context of Pastoral Counseling,* a careful comparative study of counseling in clinical and church settings.[8] From the beginning, Hiltner's work has had a decidedly doctrinal flavor. That was also true of David Roberts's *Psychotherapy and a Christian View of Man,* Edward Thornton's *Theology and Pastoral Counseling,* and all of Wayne Oates's major works.[9] While cognizant of depth psychology, aware of the primary writings of pioneer analysts like Freud and Jung, and working in professional dialogue with psychiatrists, each of these specialists wrote with ministers in view.

2. *Much of the pastoral counseling literature assumes a medical model of illness, diagnosis, and treatment.* Therapy is performed in a one-to-one relationship with a client in a formal office setting. A predominantly white, middle-class context is presupposed. True, little was written by ministers about diagnosis per se, with the exception of a note in Charles Kemp's *A Pastoral Counseling Guidebook.*[10] Specificity of evaluation first appeared in the work of psychiatrist Edgar Draper, *Psychiatry and Pastoral Care,* and in that of psychologist Paul Pruyser, *The Minister As Diagnostician.*[11]

Much of the early bias toward a psychotherapeutic model was naturally passed to pastoral counselors from their medical mentors. Clinical pastoral education itself emerged, not in local parishes, but in general and mental hospitals where treatment was the only available mode of care. Pioneers like Seward Hiltner, Carroll Wise, Anton Boisen, Russell Dicks, and Wayne Oates were influenced by clinical training experiences and association with physicians.[12] Reading their earlier works, one becomes enmeshed in the scientific axioms, personal history-taking, and treatment models of various psychotherapies. Without such guidance a generation of ministers would have been impoverished in one vital aspect of their daily work. These pastoral theologians have fortunately become greater persons than the systems they devised. Their more recent writings take seriously the changing theological climate and the context of pastoral work.[13]

Interestingly, it was not a pastoral specialist but a devotee of "third-force" humanistic psychology—Abraham Maslow, father of the human potential movement—who turned our attention toward building on strengths and assisting the strong to live life better. Maslow wrote: "Freud supplied to us the sick half of psychology and we must now fill it out with the healthy half. Perhaps this health psychology will give us more possibility for controlling and improving our lives and for making ourselves better people. Perhaps this will be more fruitful than asking 'how to get *unsick.*' "[14] He challenged counselors to see the positive potential and creativeness of people rather than their crippling liabilities alone.

Blacks have helped white counselors to understand what W. E. B. DuBois called *The Souls of Black Folk.* Due to a history of racial discrimination in the United States, many black Americans have been crippled by notions of racial inferiority. Eric Lincoln wrote in *My Face Is Black:* "Self-hatred has scarred the Negro personality like some corrosive acid. No sane man can marvel that this is so, because for all his life in America the Negro has been hated for being black and he has learned from his haters to hate himself."[15] I have done some formal office counseling with black men and women, where the challenge of whiteness and blackness speaks nonverbally yet powerfully. Edgar Ridley has correctly suggested that the black community's concern for sociopolitical liberation may eclipse its need for pastoral care.[16]

On the other hand, as Charles Kemp noted in *Pastoral Care With the Poor,* advocacy is needed by the poor, blacks, and disenfranchised citizens of the nation's cities.[17] Rather than just formal, talk-oriented therapy, counseling with the poor takes place everywhere—in homes, on porches, in hospital corridors, and at street corners. Unless counselors understand the "hidden language of the poor," they may miss essential meanings of many statements. Indeed, consciousness-raising among various groups will continue to change the shape of the church's ministry.

3. Counseling as presented to ministers by specialists has been too crisis-centered, rather than growth-directed.[18] Furthermore, certain efforts at clarification, between theology and psychotherapy, were so esoteric and abstract that they created more confusion than guidance.[19] The pastor's chief concerns were viewed as fire fighting operations with life's burdened, guilty, anxious, angry, confused, and deeply troubled people. Counseling was viewed more as a lifesaving activity, during emergencies and crucial situations, than as a day-to-day function.

This is not to say that crucial situations do not count in pastoral practice. That is far from true, as the presentation in chapter 9 will show.

Using Christ's analogy of the man who owned a hundred sheep and temporarily left ninety-nine, in order to seek one that was lost, a pastor must do crisis intervention (Luke 15:3–7). A pastor faces both growth concerns and developmental crises with his people. Special needs call for occasional crisis intervention. Still, one's search for wholeness provides the backdrop and overarching concern while a crisis is being resolved. The counselor's ultimate goal moves beyond crisis intervention to salvation and health.[20]

4. *A frequent criticism leveled at counseling pastors is that they sacrifice a major portion of the ministry trying to fulfill the roles of psychologists or psychiatrists.* Many of counseling's critics are ministers intimidated by intricacies, subtleties, and complexities that appear to lie beyond their comprehension and control. Church growth advocates sometimes claim that counseling parishioners feeds the pastor's ego, giving him a feeling of self-importance. They feel that time spent in counseling is one of the reasons for spiritual decline in many of the churches. They employ not only the fear tactic of imminent church decline, but point threateningly to the peril of sexual involvement with persons experiencing sex aberrations.

5. *At least some helpers present their ideas more as trendy faddists than as constructive carers.* I alluded in chapter 1 to the welter of therapies abroad in the land. Spokespersons continually emerge from various corners to advocate the next therapeutic modes, usually in opposition to the constructive endeavors of their predecessors. Third-force psychologists, for instance, appear opposed to Freud. The truth is that anyone in a helping profession who hopes to understand human nature owes a major debt to Freud and his revisionists. Behaviorists appear polarized against ego psychologists; reality therapists have no patience for transactional analysts; integrity therapists and conjoint family therapists are alien; and value clarificationists are not always cordial to Gestaltists.

Given the kaleidoscope of choices, and the gullibility of would-be adherents, the stage for faddism is set. Pastoral counselors should be guided by criteria like those mentioned earlier, in an effort to resist zealots and to move counselees toward spiritual wholeness.

THE SITUATION TODAY

Recognizing such circumstances, what is the situation facing today's pastoral counselors? It is not ignorance or a lack of information that has shaken Christian shepherds. Vast floods of unassimilated, uncomprehended theories and unexamined experiences plague us. Counseling specialties proliferate at the same time that pastors seek a unifying perspective. The average minister knows enough about the Bible and life, human nature and culture, salvation and alienation, ethical ideals and moral corruption, and hope and despair to offer people an encouraging word from the Lord. Let him consider the following questions and draw his own conclusions.

Is there vocational ambiguity among some counselors today? Consider certain leading pastoral counselors of this century and the problems they faced in achieving a unified perspective on the ministry. Fosdick often described his preaching as "counseling on a group scale."[21] Another significant pastor, John Sutherland Bonnell, presented his counseling as preaching on a one-to-one basis.[22] Edgar N. Jackson, a longtime Methodist pastor, narrowed the focus of his published concern primarily to grief work. Before retiring to a Vermont farm as a Christian mystic, he directed the therapeutic activities of a psychiatric clinic. This list, which reflects a wide range of vocational foci among pastoral counselors, could be greatly expanded.

I know ordained ministers who are also physicians and practicing psychiatrists. A successful psychiatrist once enrolled in our classes at the Southwestern Baptist Theological Seminary. He said that he was clarifying his vocational identity and that he might become a minister. I have clergy friends, with extensive psychological training, who hold faculty appointments in psychiatry departments of reputable medical schools. Numerous ministers have dropped out of pulpits, sought specialized behavioral science education (frequently after personal or family psychotherapy), and become licensed as psychotherapists, clinical psychologists, or social workers. My concern is not with giftedness, nor diversity, but with ineffective correlation of theological-psychological disciplines, and the consequent vocational ambiguity.

A South Carolina pastor related that he was spending forty to fifty hours a week in private counseling. I surmised, correctly as time proved, that he would not be a pastor much longer. A few clergymen across the country are resigning church-type settings and joining health care professionals in family practice. With health insurance controlled by medical personnel in many places, such liaisons are understandable.

There are professors of pastoral care in theological schools who hold advanced degrees in behavioral science. Some have professional affiliations with the American Psychological or Orthopsychiatric Associations or the American Society of Group Psychotherapy. Some of their students wish to become clinical psychologists. With mixed models among their mentors, blurred identification occurs among certain young counselors.

Is there loss of theological center, or confusion about pastoral care's true focus? Karl Menninger, dean of American psychiatrists, called for theological fidelity in *Whatever Became of Sin?* With an encouraging openness, Menninger braved criticisms from mental health and clergy professionals alike, and suggested that many helpers now ignore the concept of sin.[23] Mankind's misfortunes are now attributed to selfishness, alienation, schizophrenia, egocentricity, and so on. People want a "no-fault" theology, equivalent to no-fault casualty insurance, in which no one is to blame. In order to justify his admonitions for ministers to become better disciplined within theology, Menninger cited the words of Benjamin Rush, the first American psychiatrist. In June 1788, Rush addressed American clergy of all faiths on the subject of morality.

It has been my experience in working with psychiatric consultants in pastoral care training programs that they expect theological competence from pastoral counselors. They desire and deserve responsible theological input in the healing, growing process.

It is not just that certain pastoral counselors are plagued with blurred identities and lack of biblical-scientific clarity. Have not some church executives, who focus on evangelism, church economics, and growth, lost sight of a God who cares for individuals? There appear to be efforts in some quarters to discredit all counselors dedicated to facing the complexity of human need. While I shall document this concern explicitly in chapter 4, here is an example of anticounseling mentality.

A church executive wrote to more than four thousand pastors under his care, warning them of the perils of counseling, particularly with women. He told of a pastor in a metropolitan church who refused to talk with people who had domestic difficulties unless they would kneel together in his office and confess their sins to God. He said that when the pastor introduced this policy, the number of conferences was drastically reduced. That is understandable.

I have cited the need for a high view of God's grace, adequate to forgive sin, and I strongly support genuine repentance. But I deplore the implication that talking with persons about things that matter is a bother. The church executive implored his readers to minimize counseling and to get on with "the ministry of the Word." But pastoral vision implies that strengthening one person or family in Christian fellowship will enhance the faith of an entire congregation.

BEYOND THE PRESENT CONFUSION

I have implied that in this century pastoral counseling has been subverted more by its friends than by its foes. It comes as no shock to specialists in this field that some proposed remedies, like that of Jay Adams in *Competent to Counsel* and that of his psychologist father, Hobart Mowrer, in *The Crisis in Psychiatry and Religion*, have lost touch with crucial historic Christian concerns.[24] Lawrence Crabb's effort at biblical-scientific correlation in *Basic Principles of Biblical Counseling* proved ineffective. A more disciplined analysis of the issues in theocentric and psychological thinking may be found in Gary Collins's *The Rebuilding of Psychology*.[25]

Still, there are correlational thinkers who drop the plumb line of historical, theological, and psychological reality to test our therapeutic structures. I refer to works like Don Browning's *The Moral Context of Pastoral Care*, Thomas Oden's *Game Free*, Seward Hiltner's *Theological Dynamics*, Wayne Oates's *Pastoral Counseling*, William Oglesby's *The New Shape of Pastoral Theology*, and John Biersdorf's *Creating an Intentional Ministry*.[26] While by no means exhaustive, this list is indicative of pastors, theologians, and helping professionals who are sympathetic to both scientific and biblical realities.

When we move off course, there are calls to return to basic foundations, some of the clearest from behavioral scientists. For example, Paul Pruyser, of the Menninger Foundation in Topeka, has said: "I am convinced that a great many persons who turn to their pastor for help in solving personal problems seek assistance in some kind of religious or moral self-evaluation."[27] This gifted psychologist is saying that ministers who rely only on behavioral science miss the *richness* of theology and *oughtness* of ethics in counseling. Pruyser wrote in *The Minister As Diagnostician* that people do not wish to appear pious in turning to a minister. Still, they want to see some aspects of their faith applied to themselves.

To summarize, we have seen why people in deep need turn to the church in the first place. True believers are essentially those who have hope, and who willingly stake their future on Jesus Christ. I have discussed how counselors who work among spiritual searchers occasionally seek clarity for themselves. Pastoral counselors should attempt to live within the tension of theological truth and empirical evidence, represented by the finest scholarship of correlational thinkers. I have hope that we shall move beyond the present confusion, and counsel in light of biblical reality, as well as individual and social concerns. In chapter 4 we turn to the place of religious values in counseling.

II

THE SEARCH FOR
PURPOSE IN COUNSELING

4

The Uniqueness of Pastoral Counseling

A QUARTER century ago, Liston Pope, dean of Yale Divinity School, predicted that pastoral counseling would fade in significance because it was a passing fad. Time has proved him wrong. Counseling is here to stay as a way to share one's faith with estranged, beleaguered, and distressed persons in congregations and communities. Few avenues of Christian ministry are so rewarding as reaching out to persons under stress with pastoral warmth, perceptiveness, and support. Seeing persons work through serious emotional and spiritual concerns, then move on to growing discipleship, rewards a helper's faith and caring efforts.

Most ministers want to help people cope with personal problems and negotiate life's difficult passages. They are interested not merely in philosophical theories of evil and suffering, but wish to care wisely for life's sufferers. But ministers are not always prepared to deal with the existential growth pangs of the counseling movement itself, to answer its critics, to perceive its need for commitment and performance, or to reduce infighting among those pleading for special causes.

In a quarter century of working with seminarians, I have discovered that we must search for common ground before we talk much about counseling methods. Intergenerational perspectives differ; vocabularies differ; theologies differ; ideas about ministry differ; emphases and prejudices differ, as do vocational objectives. One cannot assume that every minister desires to counsel effectively. Some wish only to preach or study and to be left alone. Some young ministers are afraid of ecclesiastical systems, established pastors, their own emotions, criticism, and above all, failure. They are hesitant to open up to others, thus exposing their clay-footedness, and losing face. They dread being asked to provide a gift, such as love, faith, and hope, which they may not possess.

Still, the hesitant learner asks: "What distinguishes pastoral counseling from psychiatric, educational, and social work counseling?" This is more than merely a question of technique, since counseling methods are open to all, and therapeutic models move in and out of fashion. Authentic pastoral counseling differs from other approaches on theological and perspectival grounds, rather than on methodological grounds alone. Young pastors are exposed to conflicting messages in their search for answers and their struggles for a unified ministry.

CONFLICTING MESSAGES AND A UNIFIED MINISTRY

The church's historic task has been threefold: proclaiming the gospel *(kerugma)*, creating a faith-love fellowship of baptized believers *(koinonia)*, and caring for persons both in- and outside the congregation *(diakonia)*. Competent pastors are sensitive to the church's total task and care for the flock of God with these broad goals in mind. At one end of the spectrum the counseling pastor works preventively and educationally. He proclaims the gospel to instruct persons in courageous living, convict of sin, challenge in kingdom advance, and call for responsible social action. He helps to construct values, interpret ideals, provoke change, make decisions, mediate differences, and inspire hope.

At the other end of the spectrum the counseling pastor works supportively and therapeutically with every conceivable kind of concern and crisis. The cases from the average pastor's file range from borderline schizophrenia to attempted suicide, from a victim of poverty to an arrested prostitute, from a belligerent youth to a deranged sex pervert. People who have permitted themselves to sink to the depths of despair turn covertly to a minister at a social gathering, grab him in the hallway after worship services, or monopolize his time on the telephone in the wee hours of the night. A minister may feel trapped between a desire to send them away and a need to see them healed.

The ministry is a calling that absorbs considerable time, and demands all the skills that a gifted person can bring to it. That is why the pressure created by conflicting messages bothers the sensitive counselor so much. These messages come from persons both inside and outside the field of counseling.

First, consider the criticisms of people altogether opposed to pastoral counseling. With a clever bit of art work the cover of a leading evangelical journal depicted a seminary graduate whose head was divided sixteen ways. Each part represented one aspect of a congregation's expectations: bus driver, parent, social worker, supervisor, servant, counselor, leader, preacher, public relations expert, teacher, manager, peacemaker, scholar, administrator, economist, and prophet. The issue's lead article, "The Impossible Dream: Can Seminaries Deliver?" pictured the "impossible possibility" of ministers getting it all together in the parish.[1] Pastors and laypersons faced the question and, with one exception, all either opposed counseling or omitted it from their discussions. One pastor wrote: "I question how valuable a course in counseling is until [one] has the chance to counsel." A woman said: "The pastor must resist the temptation to counsel instead of preach." She opted for the ministry of the Word and sacraments as his primary tasks.

A wealthy layman, who has contributed much to the cause of missionary church construction in South America, was critical of seminaries. "They go into counseling a great deal which I have a good deal of skepticism about. . . . While I know that every pastor has a lot of work in this direction, I have serious doubts that the seminary can really teach him enough to be very valuable here."

While their arguments were all negative, they demonstrated that in fact a Christian pastor does counsel, and must do it well. One who ignores these vital questions fails to acknowledge the spirit of Christ in ministry. The fundamental weakness of their logic is that one aspect of pastoral work is assumed to exclude all others. Jesus Christ linked both prophetic and pastoral concerns in his ministry. Can modern pastors do less?

A far more positive message about perceptive counseling is conveyed in the *Readiness for Ministry* research report of the Association of Theological Schools in the United States and Canada (ATS). In national surveys of several thousand church executives, laypersons, theologians, seminarians, and parish ministers, sixty-four core clusters of qualities and skills for clergy were distinguished. "The sixth-ranked dimension [of what persons look for in a pastor] describes the minister as a perceptive counselor, as one who reaches out to persons under stress with . . . sensitivity and warmth that is freeing and supportive."[2] Four pastoral qualities and skills related to counseling ranked in the top fifteen clusters; whereas, preaching ranked twenty-fifth in importance. That does not imply that one's public ministry is unimportant. Rather, it stresses the major importance attributed to a pastor's private ministry to persons under stress.

The second conflicting message that distracts idealistic young ministers comes from specialists within the pastoral counseling movement. There is a chaplain supervisor, certified by the Association for Clinical Pastoral Education (ACPE), for example, who objects to the notion of doing pastoral counseling. "I consider myself as doing psychotherapy when I see an individual or a family."[3] Consider his logic. "A student studies speech in the seminary in order to learn sermon delivery. Is that called pastoral speech or public speaking? Speech is speech. Counseling is counseling, though what a pastor does parallels the guidance movement more than the psychotherapeutic process." John Patton, of the Georgia Association for Pastoral Care, followed similar logic when he wrote that the method of pastoral counseling "suggests a psychotherapeutic understanding . . . in that it focuses on transference . . . as the major issue in method."[4] I am suggesting that, on the contrary, pastoral counseling has a rich heritage, theological consciousness, and uncommon perspective, which make it unique.

An entire issue of the *Journal of Pastoral Care* confronts the issue of whether ministers perform psychotherapy much like mental health specialists or merely do pastoral care.[5] Dealing with the theme, "Pastoral Counseling at a Crossroad," advocates of religious counseling as one aspect of the national health care delivery system (qualifying for fee payment through insurance) debate those who argue that the ministry is not a health profession. Claims by specialists that they are one arm of America's health care delivery system, and counterclaims by traditionalists for theologically based pastoral care rapidly become tangential to the main point. Debating, while essential for clarification of identity, can digress into a diversion from caring tasks. Yet, one can defend such discussions. The process of clarification through debate is a valid model for seminarians who hope to become effective pastors.

Perhaps a more helpful approach would be to consider fidelity to one's role as minister during a series of pastoral conversations. Such a focus permits the pastor's rationale, relationship, and rituals to speak for themselves.

PASTORAL FIDELITY IN CARING CONVERSATIONS

Imagine a Sunday morning worship service in a Christian congregation. The pastor, Rev. Stan Shipp, had delivered a rousing sermon on sexual standards. Far back in the sanctuary sat a youth, Bob Shirley, who had violated his value system and hurt another human being. He was trapped in a web of remorse and confusion. Waiting in the background, until everyone had congratulated Rev. Shipp on his stirring message, Bob asked if he could see him soon about an urgent matter.

They agreed to meet at 5:00 P.M. in the pastor's office, and Bob arrived on time. Stan Shipp's style involved reaching some kind of contractual clarity early in the first counseling session. The initiative was Bob's to share as much as he desired; the pastor would listen to him faithfully. Then, after mutual discourse for about one hour, the next steps would be agreed upon. Since the pastor saw counseling as one aspect of his ministering activities, no fees were involved.

Bob was twenty years old and was a professing Christian when this conversation transpired. He had been reared in New England, had traveled while in military service, and, following a visit home after his discharge, had settled in another part of the country. As Rev. Shipp would learn, Bob was jolted by the morning's sermon on sexual standards. He felt the need to confess his sins and obtain the blessing of God.

REV. SHIPP: You said this morning that you needed to talk with me.

BOB: Yes, Mr. Shipp, but how to begin. [*Pause*] I was saved in July, a year ago, when I was down here the first time. The following September I started dating a sixteen-year-old girl. I saw her the other day. She told me that she had a baby and that I was the father. It really floored me when she said it. I denied it to myself, but when I saw the baby I felt like it was the truth. I don't know what to do. I really feel guilty. I'm living with the Warricks. They think I will be a good influence on their teenaged son. [*Pause*] Now, look what I've done!

REV. SHIPP: Do you have reason to believe the child is yours?

BOB: Yes. We had been dating and making out. One night we got carried away. I wanted to use something but she said that it hurt her, so I didn't. About six weeks later she told me that she thought she was pregnant. I took her to the doctor and she was. She said I was the father. I did not know for sure then.

REV. SHIPP: Had she had intercourse with other guys?

BOB: Yes . . . but, I feel real guilty about it. I don't love her. She doesn't love me. I'm engaged to another girl back home. I love her. We are supposed to get married this summer. I don't know what to do. The Warricks would put me out if they knew.

REV. SHIPP: You seem pretty upset.

BOB: I am. What should I do? I called my fiancée. You and she are the only ones who know about this. She said that she would forgive me. But I can't seem to face it myself. I mean, how can I be a Christian and have done this? I can't ask God to forgive me. It will take more than that. I feel like I have to confess it to the world before God will listen to me. Isn't that so?

REV. SHIPP: No, you don't have to do that. God has not rejected you or the girl. You can both ask him to forgive you. And he will.

BOB: I don't know. I don't think so. I feel so guilty. If it was only affecting me it would be different. But it will kill my parents if they find out. The Warrick's son will wonder what kind of a person I am if he finds out. And I feel like I ought to do something for the baby. After all, it is my kid.

REV. SHIPP: You feel like you must do something for the baby even though you may not actually be the father?

BOB: Yes, there is a baby out there. That is not something I can overlook or just forget. [*Pause*] I am supposed to be a Christian with a good influence. Now, I've done this!

REV. SHIPP: Your problem is serious. You feel guilty. You are worried about being hypocritical. You are worried more about the other persons who will be affected by this than by what will happen to you.

Bob's anxieties were compounded by the fact that he had been born out of wedlock twenty years before. He had been placed in an orphanage when he was four. His own parents did not love him enough to keep him, so he had been reared by adoptive parents. As a child, he had vowed to "always care for" his children, if he had any. If he and his future wife should be unable to have children, he vowed to adopt some. Now he had possibly fathered an illegitimate child. His past abandonment as an orphan, his present predicament as an unwed parent, and his future hopes for marriage and a home of his own almost blew his mind. His conversation with Rev. Shipp continued.

BOB: Isn't God going to punish me for this?

REV. SHIPP: Well, you might say it that way. But see if you can look at it from another angle. You did this act. Now, you ask God for forgiveness and accept it, after realizing that you were wrong. God is offering his forgiveness to you right now. As you accept his forgiveness, you will still be living with the consequences of what you did. God did not intend for you to get this girl pregnant, if you did it, but he can use these circumstances to carry out his will for your life. He can still work with you and through you. He wants to.

Bob had come to church that morning confused. "I was about to explode," he confessed, adding, "I felt if I could talk to anybody whom I could trust it would be you."

Bob was searching for a job and Stan Shipp introduced him to a company where he was immediately employed. In a few days, Bob voluntarily explained his predicament to his host family, the Warricks. They, in turn, introduced Bob to their attorney, who helped establish that no paternity could be legally verified. The girl had been sexually involved with several men at the time she and Bob had had intercourse. Legally, he found a reprieve. At a deeper level, Bob came to terms with God, himself, the Warricks, his fiancée, and the world. The unwed mother, as is often the case, failed to receive effective pastoral care.

While human complexities are not always as easily resolved as Bob Shirley's concerns were, pastoral care was effective in this instance. Are there identifiable elements in pastoral counseling, then, that distinguish it from other therapeutic endeavors? Admittedly, there are features common to all therapies.

COMMONALITIES IN ALL FORMS OF COUNSELING

In describing common factors in psychotherapy, Hans Strupp wrote that the commonalities in counseling "are far more impressive than their apparent differences, which may be no more than relative emphases."[6] Common aspects include "hope, expectation of change, trust, an emotional relationship, the facilitation of emotional arousal, catharsis, receiving information, the social impact of the healer" and so on.[7] In every counseling interview or potential helping relationship there are at least four common factors: a counselee, a counselor, a troublesome situation (concern, decision, or crisis), and a time frame.

Psychologist Gordon Sixty has depicted these common features, plus degrees of concern, with most participants working from *d* to *a* in reverse order.[8]

1. Counselee
   a. Counseling is welcomed
   b. Counseling is desired
   c. Counseling is needed
   d. Counseling is essential
2. Counselor
   a. Is available
   b. Wants to help
   c. Ought to help
   d. Must help
3. Situation
   a. Self-improvement
   b. Problem prevention
   c. Problem resolution
   d. Crisis intervention
4. Time Frame
   a. Long-term basis
   b. Intermediate term
   c. Short-term
   d. Now

The perspective of counselor and counselee is a fifth dynamic ingredient common to most counseling situations. According to Sixty, any counseling situation may be diagrammed to denote the interaction between the subjectivity and the objective reality of both participants.

		Counselor	
		Subjectivity	Objective Reality
	Subjective Feelings		
Counselee			
	Objective Reality		

From the counselee's perspective, he may feel in a state of tremendous crisis. The objective reality of the matter may be of minor consequence. Many things that people fear never actually happen. Research by Eysenck has demonstrated that as many persons are helped through spontaneous remissions as by psychotherapy.[9] Eysenck's studies have been challenged, however, on two points: there is less danger of complication and less pain of isolation when one receives therapy. For Bob Shirley, in the above conversation, counseling through crisis intervention seemed essential.

The counselor knows objectively that facts and feelings must be ferreted out. Further, perceptive hunches must be tested, intuitive notions checked, and diagnostic opinions formed. Objective reality for the counselor is revealed by the counselee's subjective emotions (both repressed and overt). The caring counselor has empathy; he feels subjectively for and with his parishioner. While the counselor must be warm and genuine, he must not fall prey to subjective responses alone.

Pastor Shipp, above, was understanding and brought unhurried affection to his task. With appropriate humility, Rev. Shipp asked Bob to discuss the painful guilt he experienced over sexual misconduct. Still, Rev. Shipp maintained an objective perspective on the problem, and helped Bob accept God's forgiveness of him.

All persons who do counseling share some common features: (1) a healing *relationship*, which is morale-building; (2) a *rationale* that offers an explanation for the person's symptoms and how they may be relieved; and (3) *rituals*, accepted by both helpers and those being helped as a means for restoring a person's health, meeting his needs, or enhancing relationships. In his comparative study of psychotherapy and religious healing, Jerome Frank, of Johns Hopkins University Medical School, suggests that the primary function of all therapies is to combat demoralization.[10] A helper observes symptoms that are direct expressions of demoralization, such as discouragement, sense of failure or loss, a feeling of helplessness (inability to change one's attitudes or circumstances), bewilderment, confusion, and lack of courage. Frank suggests that all "therapeutic schools, whether they use individual or group approaches, can be classified with respect to whether they conceptualize the causes of the patient's problems as lying primarily in the past, present, or future."[11] Some healers assume that all problems lie buried in the past. Their psychodynamic therapies (or rituals) aim at relieving unresolved inner conflicts and arrested development resulting from destructive early life experiences. Others, like behavior therapists, view the person's distress as the result of maladaptive behavior in the present. Their treatments are aimed at changing responses to conflicted persons and situations through systematic desensitization and behavioral readjustments. Existential therapists stress rituals aimed at the patient's view of the future, which confront life's meaning, purpose, and desired experiences.

A vast literature, typified by Robert Harper's analysis, *Psychoanalysis and Psychotherapy: 36 Systems,* has been developed on therapeutic theories and techniques. There are almost as many rationales and rituals as there are healers. Pastoral counseling cannot neatly avoid this body of knowledge any more than it can dodge all of the theologies which have arisen through the ages. But counseling is slippery ground at best. Helpers in other fields need to know those things that are unique to pastoral counseling.

DISTINCTIVE ELEMENTS OF PASTORAL COUNSELING

Pastoral counseling may be identified in various ways:

1. according to its *context* in a religious setting, where the person being counseled senses God's presence and talks privately with God's representative

2. according to its *subject matter,* where certain materials are dealt with and other topics are minimized

3. according to its *depth,* with disorders of thinking and behavior, and unconscious conflicts often left to psychiatrists and pastoral specialists

4. according to its *methods* or rituals, so that counseling is considered pastoral if the helper employs certain religious procedures (like hearing confession) or performs certain religious rites (like absolution)

5. according to the counselor's *pulpit functions* and *continuing relationships,* after therapy, as an ordained minister

6. according to a pastor's *preventive orientation,* as well as therapeutic concerns, and *goals* as an enabler, confessor, encourager, and growth facilitator

7. according to counseling's *identification* with the unique theology and ethic of a Christian community

8. according to *resources* used—like personal faith, pastoral blessing, the Bible, and prayer—in ministering to human needs.

Given such criteria, we may conclude that *counseling is both Christian and pastoral when two or more individuals, who acknowledge the value of God's action in their lives, communicate, at dynamic levels, about things that matter in the context of the community of biblical faith.*

Let us reexamine Pastor Shipp's fidelity to the law of his own inner being, to God, and to counselee Bob Shirley in light of these criteria. The two men met, each from a perspective of faith in God, in the context of a Christian community. Without knowing Bob, the pastor prized him as one for whom Christ died, reflecting a basic reverence for human personality. Rev. Shipp validated the role of minister in their convenantal relationship. He brought all of the wisdom, both theological and psychological, at his command to bear on Bob's demoralized condition. God-talk, acknowledgment of sin, repentance, acceptance, and amendment of life were relied on as appropriate resources. The true test of Bob's growth through counseling was not simply new insight, but changed behavior as a man of faith.

Earlier, I alluded to the soul-searching within the counseling movement concerning the uniqueness of pastoral care versus psychotherapy. In light of its identity crisis, the American Association of Pastoral Counselors (AAPC) commissioned Morris Taggart, of Houston's Marriage and Family Consultation Center, to conduct an extensive membership information project. He asked hundreds of AAPC certified pastoral counselors to complete a twenty-page questionnaire focusing on two questions: (1) "Does there exist within the profession a 'body of knowledge,' a point of view, a way of understanding human events . . . which, although found among members of other professions, is somehow represented 'institutionally' within this particular profession?" And (2) "Does there exist within the profession a set of professional competencies, related to the body of knowledge, for which there is a clearly visible educational process?"[12] Taggart's survey focused primarily on the second issue, with the intent of supporting claims that pastoral counselors are competent health care professionals, but I will address the prior question.

It is my thesis that pastoral counseling does indeed bring some distinctive elements into the therapeutic community. Counseling by

Christian care-givers, both ordained clergy and lay volunteers, contributes a new consciousness, with distinct goals and unique expectations, to the therapeutic process. Pastoral counseling should not be viewed as a distinct profession (unless a practitioner is educated, certified, and employed full time as a counselor); it is a ministry performed by a Christian pastor along with other activities. A commitment to one's unique calling as minister spares one appellations from other professional communities like *quasi, pseudo,* or *crypto.* An authentic pastoral counselor wears no prefix implying ineptness; he is a caring specialist.

A NEW CONSCIOUSNESS

In addition to bringing a pastoral perspective to all that one does in ministry, a counseling pastor brings a new consciousness into the therapeutic process when he is faithful to his theological education and disciplines. Wayne E. Oates, a major shaper of thought in this field, supports pastoral counseling's uniqueness.[13] The pastor's competence arises from his expertise: specific knowledge of biblical teachings, perception of human history and the unique Judeo-Christian contributions to history, data of comparative religions and the pluralistic forms of American religious systems, awareness of ethical issues and social trends (as well as the effects of social class on ethical decisions and actions), use of prayer and religious resources, and wisdom in negotiating life's passages from birth to death. Members of the so-called helping professions will grant the pastoral counselor "equal time," in case conferences and diagnostic evaluations if he consistently speaks with the theological expertise of his vocation.

He appreciates the diagnostic value of the religious views of persons, and has a clear understanding of their religious histories. The woman from southern Georgia, who sprinkles voodoo powder on her doorstep, as a magic charm or fetish to keep other women away from her husband while she is at work, can be understood in light of her background in sorcery. Bob Shirley, in the passage above, wanted to confess "to the whole world" because he had learned that opening his wounds for all to see might atone for his sin. Rev. Shipp had to remind him that Jesus Christ died "once for all, the righteous for the unrighteous, that he might bring us to God, being put to death in the flesh but made alive in the spirit" (1 Peter 3:18). To crucify oneself is, therefore, not only unnecessary but idolatrous. It is the pastor's task to wean counselees from their idols, and then to comfort them in the loss of their false gods through the "God of all comfort" (2 Cor. 1:3).

The pastoral counselor is conscious of the God-man dialogue of existence. Instead of a mere dialogue, recognition of God's presence creates a trialogue with the counselor and counselee. He is also conscious, whether working with individuals, families, or groups, of the social fabric of a supportive Christian community.

In this connection, Edward E. Thornton wrote of "the uniqueness of *each event of meeting* between a pastor and a person in need."[14] The new consciousness of participants in counseling lies in the internal dialogue, within which one decides to risk the truth or run from it, to face reality or deny it. The focus is not the helper's need for superiority or continuity with tradition, but the counselee's need for spiritual wholeness. By centering on these issues, the counselor transcends ego needs and zeros in on one's idolatrous self or the self before God.

A UNIQUE EXPECTATION

I shall return to the unique goals of pastoral conversations in a subsequent chapter. It remains here, however, to return briefly to my basic thesis of *promise* in counseling. It was not until I had proceeded deeply into this study that I recognized the link between biblical Exodus and Easter and deliverance from human bondage through hopeful expectation. There is a repetitive phrase in the Scriptures: "And the word of the Lord came to" so-and-so. With that word, which people felt internally rather than heard audibly, life was transformed. Old Testament men and women lived with the expectation of hearing from God and seeing the promised Messiah. Just so, counselees in existential darkness turn to Christian counselors, hoping for light from heaven. They expect something to happen, in the process, so that a new word is spoken, and new meaning and strength is injected into their lives.

Thomas H. Cole, an Association for Clinical Pastoral Education (ACPE) chaplain supervisor who counsels as a specialist, reported his clients' most frequently cited response after therapy: "I see things differently now." Sensitive to the notion of promise, Cole affirmed: "It is as though a *new word* had been spoken in the counseling process, not a literal word (there are thousands of words), but new wisdom given as a result of hoping for a breakthrough."[15] In this sense, pastoral counseling becomes a revelatory encounter. Faith is rewarded with revitalized hope for life.

"When everything falls apart," as it did for the ancient psalmist numerous times, the only alternative to futility is expectancy (Ps. 11:3, TEV). "What would become of us if we did not take our stand on hope!" exclaimed John Calvin in reflecting on Hebrews 11:1. Hope proves its power in helping us cope with suffering, evil, and death. A counselor is one who holds out reasonable hope to life's strugglers. One who hopes, through Christian eschatology, comes to regard himself "as an open question addressed to the future of God."[16] God's promised care does not disregard any situation. Life may open a person or family to "pain, patience, and the 'dreadful power of the negative'," as the neo-Hegelian theologian Jürgen Moltmann has said.[17] The person of promise does not ask that all questions be answered nor that all problems be solved. Rather, he lives between the tensions of hope and the ambiguities of freedom in life. A true believer takes life's pain in stride, strengthened by the spirit of him who raised Jesus Christ from the dead.

There are several reasons for viewing pastoral counseling as expectation:

1. God reveals himself in the language of promise and in biblical history marked by promise. Moltmann, in his *Theology of Hope*, distinguishes the God of promise from the nature gods of epiphany religions, surrounding Israel in the new land.[18] God maintains his faithfulness "all the day long," as one who "neither slumbers nor sleeps." His people are always within his presence and live in a constant spirit of expectancy.

2. God's promise of salvation brings forth faith in strugglers, causing the authentic carer to rejoice. Thus, the Christian counselor does much more than "search for a pearl in an outhouse," as the dean of a respected theological school once said. The counselor's words carry the force of promise, and life offered within the church, as a community of hope, is essentially one of expectation.

3. Promise holds out the hope that there is always the possibility of change. Think of the toughest situations that you can bring to mind: a teenager who is mentally retarded, children (like Bob Shirley) who were abandoned by their parents, a mother dying of brain cancer, a paraplegic out of work, a political prisoner, or a family forced to move in order to retain employment. In each instance, "the word of the Lord"

can be sensed through counseling's insight and inspiration. A word of encouragement will foster constructive attitudes, enabling persons to face life. With God's help, there is a way out.

To conclude, pastoral counseling reflects a perspective, springing from a unique commitment, rather than one unique ritual. Pastoral counselors use varied methods to facilitate both individual growth and group procedures, including marriage enrichment groups, conjoint family groups, and growth groups directed to specific needs. Much of pastoral work is preventive and educational, rather than therapeutic in a medical sense. It is aimed at life's enrichment. In order to deal wisely with peoples' lives, the pastor must understand human nature, and therefore elements of psychology.

5

What Psychology Can We Trust?

PSYCHOLOGY is usually defined as the study, prediction, and control of human behavior. Scientific psychology goes back to the 1870s when Wilhelm Wundt, of the University of Leipzig in Germany, established the world's first psychological laboratory. Many laypersons stand in awe of this field, attributing almost magical powers to its understanding of behavior and its effects on all aspects of life. It is many fields in one—experimental, clinical, social, industrial, religious, and research—using varied techniques to advance the welfare of mankind.

Here, I presuppose a transpersonal, theocentric psychology, which acknowledges God's reality and man's universal religious quest. Transpersonalism represents a new "fourth force" in psychology, akin to humanistic psychology, which assumes that persons possess a spiritual dimension. Therapists help persons "to live their daily lives in ways which foster spiritual fulfillment."[1] Since people form the pastor's working world, he must ask, "What psychology can we trust?"

THE PASTOR'S WORLD IS PEOPLE

I know a minister who was interviewing staff members in a large, metropolitan church in order to arrive at competencies needed by ministers in the modern world. He and the minister of childhood education were interrupted by a knock on her office door. There stood a darkhaired woman, nearly forty, with sensitive features. "I'm sorry, Josie, I cannot see you now; I'm talking with Dr. Richardson."

"Dr. Richardson?" came the quizzical response. "I know a Dr. Richardson!"

"Did you know him in the hospital?" replied the minister of childhood education. "No," came the response, "I knew him a long time ago."

Quite unexpectedly, while Richardson had been searching for professional data to feed into a curriculum development project, Josie and he had met once more. The hurt in her dark eyes was unforgettable. Memory took him back almost a quarter century, to the months when she had attended a church where he had served as pastor. Her mother was an amputee and a diabetic patient. Her stepfather was a tough man of another religious persuasion. Josie Compton, who suffered from a learning disability, came to the minister's attention through a Sunday school teacher, who reported that her teenage student was depressed, perhaps suicidal.

Because of some genetic defect, Josie was slower than other fifteen-year-olds, and was a candidate for special education in the public schools. Her clothing was not stylish, and her speech was halting. She needed love and was incredibly lonely. Her stepfather had taken advantage of Josie's sexually developed body, slow mentality, and emotional deprivation. He had committed incestual acts with Josie, forcing himself on her with her ill mother's knowledge and apparent approval. Josie's values were so strong that violating her Christian conscience was making her ill. She had numerous symptoms of depression—sleep loss, anxiety, ashen complexion, crying, loss of appetite, and fantasies of self-destruction. Given the seriousness of the situation with her unhealthy family, Josie was removed, for her own sake, and placed in a state psychiatric hospital. She was a resident there for several years. In the meantime, Richardson had resigned from that pastorate, changed jobs, and had lost track of her. Now, after twenty-two years, he and his former counselee were briefly reunited. She now lived alone in another city, was active in the single adult department of her church, worshipped regularly, and enjoyed limited volunteer service with a children's group.

Seeing Josie Compton emphasized the significance of time in pastoral work. Her psychic scars had not completely disappeared. Still, time had been her healer. One is reminded of what T. S. Eliot said in "Burnt Norton":

Time present and time past
Are both perhaps present in time future,
And time future contained in time past.

Josie's adolescence, which Erik Erikson calls the critical period polarizing identity formation and role confusion, had left its legacy of grayness on her spirit.[2] The incest taboo forbids intergenerational and sibling copulation in most cultures of the world. Once that taboo is violated, life seems to crumble. Nothing matters. Death itself, of oneself or others, does not appear as forbidding as intercourse with one's own kin. Some girls so violated by fathers or brothers have become lesbians, prostitutes, or almost permanent wards in psychiatric hospitals. It takes considerable effort—shifting dependency needs, defiance of selfdestructive wishes, and a desire to rejoin the human community—to escape incest's undertow.

Now in middle adulthood, Josie's earlier experiences still cast a shadow on her life, but they will not predetermine her future. By God's grace, she is not a helpless psychotic in a hospital's back ward. Because of temporary medical and milieu therapy, she did not end up a brooding neurotic. Josie is a functioning person, not entirely healthy, but heroic and living courageously in spite of her suffering.

To acknowledge the shaping forces of one's childhood and youth is not to yield to Freudian determinism. Rather, as Tennyson once wrote: "I am a part of all that I have met." A person cannot jump out of his or her historical skin. Development is a *given* like one's biology; but life's chances are more open-ended. Human personality never completely escapes what psychiatrist Hugh Missildine calls the "inner child of the past." That does not, however, invoke a fatalistic curse on a person's later life that can never be broken.

Fortunately, society provides its correctives to family-induced curses, enabling individuals like Josie to experience achievement and meaning, not simply anxiety and pain. Erikson wrote in *Childhood and Society* "of the way in which societies lighten the inescapable conflicts of childhood with a *promise of some security, identity, and integrity*. In thus reinforcing the values by which the ego exists societies create the only conditions under which human growth is possible [emphasis added]."[3] That is what growth counseling, from a Christian perspective, is all about. Pastoral counseling faces the curse of a person's past with what Myron Madden called "the power to bless."[4] Given God's promise of help, there is sunlight and shadow, along with many loose ends, in the normal course of living.

This leads us to acknowledge that personality is a complex system that cannot be trussed up in some "conceptual straightjacket," as the late Gordon Allport once said. By "system," I infer *a complex of elements in mutual interaction.* While systems may be open and closed in physics, personality theorists hold to some kind of open system. Charlotte Buhler has set forth four criteria of open systems to understand personality: (1) *material and energy interchange*—implying stimulus input and response output; (2) *homeostasis*—one's effort to maintain physiological and psychic equilibrium; (3) *increased order over time*—emphasizing personality's goal orientation and thrust off a homeostatic balance in a forward direction; and (4) *transaction with the environment*—which recognizes one's biological reality and genetic givens along with interactions with people and circumstances in history.[5] The first two criteria emphasize stability (being) rather than growth (becoming), and are thereby limited. These first two are biologic in the sense that they recognize in personality two features clearly present in all living organisms. The latter two focus on uniquely human capacities for identity formation, goal setting, growth motives, and time management.

There are numerous advantages of viewing personality as a living system, as part of a family system, and in a cultural system. The student is free to draw on all the theories available in an eclectic fashion, without avoiding the fragmentation of focusing on one approach. The concept of system is congenial to philosophy and theology, since one can relate contemporary findings to the cosmic order.

Josie Compton reminds us that ministers are enmeshed in personal relationships, like fish in water. Human nature is the crossroads of one's theology and pastoral practice: sexuality, culture, ethnic origins, attitudes, values, decision-making powers, bondage, freedom, rebellion, alienation, vocation, marriage, sense of responsibility, anxiety, sin, parenting, aging, creativity, crises, conversion, illness, maturity, and death. One's views of God and persons are intertwined like vines and branches. Such realities have propelled ministers into controversy over psychology.

THE CONTROVERSY OVER PSYCHOLOGY

"Yes, I agree with you," nods the minister. "People making, family making, citizen making—that's my business! But, really, what psychology can I trust? I am so busy ministering that I have little time to stand back from my job to analyze it, reflect upon it, and try to formulate concepts about human personality and the counseling process."

Ministers and others who wish to understand and use psychology in their professional work have long been troubled by controversies among behavioral scientists. The language of behavioral scientists is esoteric in nature. Freudian analysts talk of oral, anal, genital, and latency periods of human development; of defense mechanisms, like projection, displacement, denial, conversion hysteria, and undoing; and of behavior symptoms, like aggression, anxiety, passive-dependency states, and paranoia. Transactional analysts have turned away from Freud's personality structure—id, ego, and superego—and developed more popularly understood ego states called *parent, adult,* and *child.* Behaviorists, like B. F. Skinner, hold that man is an animal shaped by his environment. Personal change, according to Skinner, requires not insight, but operant conditioning and behavior modification. According to behaviorists, behavior can be altered through a system of rewards and punishments. And humanistic psychologists, like Abraham Maslow, speak of self-actualization, meta-motivation, and the "farther reaches of human nature."

Psychology supplies not merely a lens for viewing personality formation. Freud looked heavily to physiology, his specialty. Gardner Murphy has prepared *Personality: A Biosocial Approach to Origins and Structures,* a massive study that takes Freud's biosocial concerns seriously.[6] Further, Freud founded psychoanalysis, a therapeutic school that makes certain assumptions about life, diagnoses what has gone amiss, and attempts to restore a vital balance (homeostasis) through stages of psychoanalytic practice. Since it is a total way of viewing and living life from a humanistic perspective, ministers must try to understand Freud.

Is it any wonder that psychology is "totally out of the question" for many religious workers? They are intimidated by white mice and rhesus monkey medical experiments, humanistic assumptions, sexual preoccupations, and conflicting conclusions of behavioral scientists. Many people fear what they fail to understand. Others actively oppose psychology as a tool of the devil. Some helpers merely say, "Let's wait until the psychologists themselves straighten out their various systems!" It is a fact that almost any pastoral practice can be supported by citing the appropriate behavioral scientist and dogmatic theologian.

Over the years, a body of reasonably reliable facts has been accumulated. Some formulations, particularly those of classic psychoanalysis and behaviorism, must be modified in light of biblical wisdom about persons. Research findings continue to be reported in books and journals like *Counseling Psychology* (published by the American Psychological Association), the *Journal of Pastoral Care* (published by the Association for Clinical Pastoral Education), *The American Journal of Psychiatry* (the official publication of the American Psychiatric Association), and the *Journal of the American Medical Association.*

My own position is a disciplined eclecticism, avoiding playing pick-and-choose games with various systems. Rather, I carefully assess different theoretical frameworks, contributors' biases and methods, and maintain footing on slippery ground in light of biblical truths. I am indebted particularly to Harry Stack Sullivan's contributions to interpersonal theory, Gordon Allport's Gestalt wisdom and theory of becoming, the work of developmental theorists like Erik Erikson and Theodore Lidz, "third-force" psychologists like Abraham Maslow, and existential formulations by Kierkegaard, Heidegger, Jaspers, Sartre, Binswanger, Frankl, Tillich, and others.[7] Existentialism can be theistic or atheistic, despairing or hopeful, empirical or mystical, depending on the theorist.

Rather than developing another school of psychotherapy, like O. Hobart Mowrer's "integrity therapy," or becoming a disciple maker for an iconoclastic, manipulative position, like Jay Adams's "nouthetic confrontation," I advocate a carefully gathered consensus of findings that may be useful to ministers and educators.[8] Given this background, I propose to address the confusion of the variety of theories by raising some basic issues about human nature.

COMING TO TERMS WITH HUMAN NATURE

Suppose one of your minister friends was arrested for driving while intoxicated, following an accident; or one of your laymen embezzled $100,000 from the bank where he was an officer; or the wife of one of your best pastor friends flew to Los Angeles for cosmetic surgery and, at age fifty, started dating men ten years her junior.

What are the proper questions to ask about the behavior of such people? Shall we assume that each person mentioned was immoral, irrational, and is irreparably doomed? Both psychologists and theologians face such basic questions as whether people are inherently good or evil, basically rational or irrational, motivated by free will or determinism. How would the psychologists reply?

Sigmund Freud wrote in *Civilization and its Discontents:*

> Men are not gentle, friendly creatures wishing for love, who simply defend themselves if they are attacked, but . . . a powerful measure of aggressiveness has to be reckoned as part of their instinctual endowment. The result is that their neighbor is to them not only a possible helper or sexual object, but also a temptation to them to gratify their aggressiveness . . . to seize his possessions, to humiliate him, to cause him pain, to torture and to kill him.[9]

Freud depicted the individual as essentially a predatory animal. Given the death drive in the unconscious, which Freud called *thanatos,* man wreaks havoc upon his own family and plunders his neighbor's possessions. Freud's negative view of personality is reminiscent of Genesis 8:21: "The imagination of man's heart is evil from his youth." There is much evidence of the dark, shadowy side of man's nature in our civilization. The news media feed and flourish on aggression, robbery, rape, homicide, and senseless crime.

But despite this evidence, there is another aspect of human nature: people are neutral and malleable, capable of working in new directions. Studies by anthropologist Margaret Mead and others have shown that many people in the world are gracious and kind. Mead described a tribe in New Guinea that assumed "all human beings . . . are naturally unaggressive, self-denying . . . concerned with growing food to feed growing children."[10] The late Abraham Maslow discovered a similar lack of social aggression among the Northern Blackfoot Indians: "These are not a weak people by any means. The Northern Blackfoot Indians are a prideful, strong, understanding, self-valuing group. They are simply apt to regard aggression as wrong or pitiful or crazy."[11] Such findings led psychologist James Coleman to observe that man is a "highly educable animal who is neither good nor bad by nature but has the potentialities to develop in either direction."[12] The shaping influences of family and cultural values largely determine whether a person becomes kind or cruel, selfish or generous, good or evil.

A third view is that people are essentially constructive, creative, kind, and capable of growth. Interestingly, the Judeo-Christian faith, while acknowledging man's innate waywardness if left to his own urges, also teaches that man was created in God's image. The New Testament speaks of "the true light that enlightens every man" who enters the world, and Jesus emphasized that "the kingdom of God is within you," that is "in your midst" (see John 1:9; Luke 17:21). Acceptance of this view has risen and fallen through the centuries of enlightenment, romanticism, and today's ruthless realism.

Several twentieth-century psychologists have advanced a positive view of human nature. Carl Rogers wrote: "The basic nature of the human being, when functioning freely, is constructive and trustworthy."[13] And the late Gordon Allport, of Harvard, introduced his work on *The Nature of Prejudice* with these words: "Normal men . . . like to live in peace and friendship with their neighbors; they prefer to love and be loved rather than to hate and be hated."[14] He felt that the weight of mankind's approval was on the side of peaceful cooperation, not war.

Let us return momentarily to the minister arrested for driving while intoxicated; the embezzler, who was also an active church member; and the pastor's errant wife. Was each free to obey or defy the law, or are people predetermined in their actions? Further, were they acting wisely and rationally, given the facts of life? Or were they driven by some unnameable, malicious force to violate their Christian value systems? One's response to these queries depends both on one's theology and one's psychological perspective.

THE ENRICHMENT OF PERSPECTIVES

Let us return to Josie Compton's case. Where would a pastoral counselor turn for help in understanding her predicament? Were he to function from a "bits and pieces" approach, he might read up on depression in a medical textbook on psychiatry, like that by Charles Hofling, M.D., and wonder if Josie suffered from loss of a love object, grief over value violation, or the like.[15] He might turn to a nontechnical source, like Wayne Dyer's *Your Erroneous Zones,* and then try to convince Josie to pull herself up by her own bootstraps. Dyer holds that one can do almost anything one decides to do.[16] His self-therapy approach is highly idealistic at best, and could be extremely dangerous.

A much wiser approach would be to turn to an authority in the field, like Juanita H. Williams, who directs women's studies at the University of South Florida. The topics in her *Psychology of Women: Behavior in a Biosocial Context* include biology, socialization, life chances, and personality.[17] Her well-tempered feminism provides a corrective to the sexism of other books in the field. Or our mythical minister could look into the classic two-volume work by Helene Deutsch, M.D., *The Psychology of Women.*[18] He should consult with a social worker assigned to family service in a local or regional mental health–mental retardation center.

Let us assume that along with any bits and pieces of information he might gather, our pastor friend counsels with a holistic perspective. He understands major schools of psychological thought, the strengths and limitations of various therapeutic methods, and he functions responsibly in consultation with a physician. His knowledge of people would help him set limits on what he would attempt with Josie.

Neither psychoanalysis nor behavior therapy appear appropriate in counseling a victim of incest like Josie. Behavioristic psychology focuses not on one's unconscious drives, but on behavior. Through operant conditioning, theorists like B. F. Skinner, Joseph Wolpe, and others have attempted to modify human actions and reactions.[19] Behavior is changed through positive reinforcement of appropriate actions and aversion, or repressive therapies, on undesirable behavior. Humanistic and existential psychology should prove more fruitful for understanding the transcendent dimensions of pastoral counseling.

Humanistic psychology, represented by the late Abraham Maslow, James Bugenthal, and Carl Rogers, evaluates conscious concepts, attitudes, and behaviors.[20] Such scientists place a high value on human personality. Their therapies seek to help individuals predict and control their own lives. In Josie's case, with suicide a possibility, a stable, trustworthy environment, outside the home, was needed. Humanistic treatments aim at restoration of a degree of self-esteem. In time, with her needs for survival, esteem, and love met through a therapeutic community, Josie would be pointed toward self-actualization and resocialization in a new environment.

The existential model of personality originated in philosophy and literature rather than in science. As with other schools, there is not a single close-knit system of thought, but rather certain common themes and concepts. It has been said that Albert Camus humanized existentialism, Jean-Paul Sartre popularized it, Viktor Frankl dramatized it, and Rollo May formed it into a therapeutic technique.[21] A basic theme in existentialism is that the individual's unique *essence* is a given, but that what one makes of it—one's *existence*—is a personal responsibility. The existential question for Josie is not so much, "How did I get into this mess?" but "What will I do now that I am here?"

Trapped by incest and mental retardation, Josie agonized with what Viktor Frankl, of Vienna, called "existential frustration." She needed validation that her reactions made sense when viewed in the context of her unhealthy family and environing circumstances. A counselor would not try to convince Josie that her disturbance was "all in her mind." Rather, he would help her to believe that life's struggle is worthwhile, that there is victory for the human spirit, and, through the promise of hope, point her toward more satisfying relationships and a meaningful niche in society. Like the rest of us, Josie needed what Bruno Bettelheim called *A Home for the Heart.*

Transpersonal psychology also complements what pastors do in counseling. Through scientific studies and their *Journal of Transpersonal Psychology,* its supporters are concerned with life's ultimate values, capacities, and potentialities. Therapists guided by this "fourth force" are concerned with self-transcendence, cosmic awareness, mystical experience, and the sacralization of everyday life.

Pastoral counselors will work responsibly, in light of the most appropriate theological and psychological resources, when confronted with counselees like Josie. The following paradoxes and polarities of human nature have been sifted from my own experience and empirical observation.

PARADOXES AND POLARITIES OF HUMAN NATURE

I believe that pastoral counselors should be disciplined within the Judeo-Christian faith and tradition of their particular religious heritages. Biblical revelation provides the symbolic archetype and ideal model of life at its best. All philosophical approaches to human nature, phenomenological descriptions of behavior, and pastoral observations from caring contacts with people should be tested by biblical realities.

Further, I believe that differences in personality theories and counseling techniques may become strengths in ministering to deeply troubled people. Disciplined eclecticism does not discredit all the gains from careful research and the accrued wisdom of behavioral science. Psychology should inform pastoral diagnosis and practice in a dynamic interchange with biblical views. The responsible pastor tests all proximate perceptions of personality in light of one ultimate truth—the knowledge of the glory of God as it was revealed through Jesus Christ.

I encourage you to use the strengths that result from working within a special set of spiritual loyalties. Be sensitive to the transcendent dimension; be faithful to a biblical perspective. These loyalties may be stated in the form of twelve propositions. They provide paradoxes and polarities of human nature with which many psychologists, I think, would agree.

1. *Personality is both free and determined.* It is created in the image of God, fashioned for fellowship with the Creator, and acquainted with disobedience, sin, and grief. Men and women are sinners, yet not without hope because of the forgiveness offered freely through the death and resurrection of Jesus Christ. Thus, the image of God is marred but not destroyed by human evil.

2. *Personality presupposes both body and spirit.* A person is destined to die, yet fashioned to live forever. Biological death does not imply psychic death in light of Christ's resurrection. For one who concludes that this life is all there is, time is everything, physical culture and health are the ultimate values, and death is the final loss of meaning. Counseling's promise holds out the hope of eternal life. (See John 3 and 4 for Christ's offer of rebirth and eternal life.)

3. *Personality is both dependent and independent.* We are designed for fulfillment in marriage and responsible social relationships. The Bible's ideal proposes one partner, of the opposite sex, for life. However, the single life is an equally acceptable alternative in Scripture. Persons need faith commitments, companionship, and collaboration in social groups, whether single or married.

4. *A person is both male and female.* People have both self-fulfilling (masculine) and self-giving (feminine) tendencies. In the Judeo-Christian tradition, women counted themselves "blessed" if they had a fam-

ily, children, and a homemaking career. Men headed home life. In the
biblical view "anatomy is not destiny" (biological determinism), but it
influences significantly one's life-style. Since "in Christ there is neither
male nor female but one new humanity" (Gal. 3:28; Rom. 12:5; Eph.
4:13; 1 Peter 3:8), a loving egalitarianism is the ideal. Concerning
sexuality, all are equal at the foot of the cross. Jung's symbolic approach
of the *anima,* the personification of the feminine principle in man, and
animus, the inner masculine part of the female personality, is in accord
with biblical views of sexuality.

Paul K. Jewett's study of sexual relationships from a theological
perspective, *Man as Male and Female,* exposes the faulty logic of persons who are zealous for a divine "chain of command" in masculine and
feminine relationships.[22] Men are not lords and saviors over their wives
and children, but one new humanity with them in Christ. The apostle
Paul taught men and women to "be subject to one another out of
reverence for Christ" (Eph. 5:21–33). Jewett records the conversation
between Nora and Torwald, in Henrik Ibsen's *A Doll's House,* where
Torwald reminds his wife that she is his possession (like a doll to enjoy).
Nora responds, "I don't believe that any longer. . . . I believe that before
all else I am a reasonable human being, just as you are—or—at all events
—that I must try and become one."[23] A person's right to be "a reasonable human being" is one that no woman should be asked to surrender
in marriage.

Along with Ernest W. Burgess and others, I advocate a companionship model of marriage, which is democratic and flexible, rather than
one that is authoritarian and autocratic. Relying on love and mutual
respect, compansionship stresses the autonomy of the individual and
mutuality in decision making, personal fulfillment rather than duty and
subordination, and assimilation of ideas rather than accommodation to
one's spouse's views as a means of resolving conflict. An elaboration of
my views on marriage and the family may be found in *Life Under
Pressure: Dealing With Stress in Marriage.*[24]

5. *A person, in theological terms, is both sinner and saint.* One
struggles with aggression, hate, rebellion, and alienation. Yet one is
attracted to life's highest values—affection, friendship, work, play, faith,
hope, and love.

6. *A person both receives and is responsible for sharing God's gifts.*
The Old Testament begins with a man and a woman, rebels lost in a

garden. The New Testament closes with persons redeemed in a garden, with God as the source of light, and a tree of life, "the leaves of which are for the healing of the nations" (Rev. 22:2–5). The New Testament promises the faithful: "All things are yours, and you are Christ's, and Christ is God's" (1 Cor. 3:21–23).

7. *Human existence provokes both anxiety and hope.* An individual may know the terrors of war, rejection by family, and the violence and inhumanity of the social order. There is what Tillich called an existential threat of nonbeing. Still, man is the creature who places faith in God. Hope keeps one alive at work and at play, and living with radiant optimism.

8. *Personality is both patterned being and in the process of becoming.* Persons can both believe in and lose confidence in themselves. They *are* and are underway, regress and progress, "top out" and "bottom out" along life's journey. Rather than viewing human existence deterministically, Christian workers view persons developmentally. Persons can learn and grow.

9. *Personality is motivated by conscious values and unconscious drives.* We know that "the Lord looks on the heart," for from its secret depths come "the issues of life" (1 Sam. 16:7; Prov. 4:23; Matt. 15:19). Man's motives "answer to man"; yet his heart "cries out for the living God" (Prov. 27:19; Ps. 84:2). Paradoxically, one may achieve what Sidney Simon calls "values clarification" and violate affirmed values at the same time.[25] No one is loyal to all his loyalties all of the time.

10. *Persons live on a continuum of sickness and health.* We ascribe to God the ability to "keep man from falling" into harm (Jude 24). Still, tissue is vulnerable to malignancy; bodies are invaded by germs; accidents do happen. Relationships are contaminated by insecurity, pride, anger, and aggression. Still, God is on the side of health and salvation.

11. *Humanity's goal is both personal survival and social productivity.* Man needs to befriend himself (love himself, in the best biblical sense) as Freudians teach. People need what humanistic psychologists term self-actualization, and existentialists call "the will to find meaning." Counseling's promise helps one move beyond disgust and despair to productive living.

12. *Personality is simple, yet terribly complex.* Thus, Christian counselors should avoid labeling people as sinful, neurotic, depraved, paranoid, or compulsive. Such labels fail to capture the richness of a Christian view of people.

These polarities of human personality are indicative of life's creative tensions.[26] We are drawn toward each extreme, but to neither to the exclusion of the opposite pole. These aspects of personality place human existence under stress as individuals grow "toward the measure of the stature of the fullness of Christ" (Eph. 4:13). Such stressors create tensions that occasionally call for counseling.

To conclude, Christian counselors need to take a holistic view of human nature that is transpersonal and theistic, rooted in the Bible, yet aware of scientific truth. No developmental concern or crisis is "simply spiritual," any more than it is merely social, physical, or emotional. We have thus acknowledged a diversity of approaches without losing sight of the common aspects of personality. While I doubt the feasibility of integrating psychology and Christianity, as Gary R. Collins advocates in his excellent essay, "The Rebuilding of Psychology," I am convinced that they should be considered together.[27] The basic issues of human nature are not the exclusive domain of any helping group. Psychology and theology need each other. This leads us to a consideration of psychiatry's offer to help, and its mutual concerns with religion.

6

Psychiatry's Offer to Help

PSYCHIATRISTS in many communities across America are offering to help their counseling colleagues. Practitioners from various health care backgrounds are forming alliances for education, consultation, professional, and political concerns, as well as for delivery of therapeutic services. Many of these helping persons have had to become surrogate parents for hurt, abused, often angry adolescents. Through milieu therapy, a team of counselors may become an extended family for someone confused or oppressed by life. What have psychiatrists, social workers, and psychologists to offer to humanity's search for wholeness?

My own view of psychiatry has moved from fear to respect with the passing of time. Years ago, I visited a Cherokee Indian reservation near the Great Smoky Mountain National Park. Along with turkey feathers, tom-toms, and the trinkets sold to tourists, I was intrigued by a large earthen oven built on a hillside. A guide explained that years before, when one of the Indians became ill, he was placed inside the heated oven-mound and left until the fever was gone. It looked more like a prison for punishment than a place for treatment.

I mention the oven because, initially, I viewed psychiatrists and primitive witch doctors as being somewhat alike. Their treatment methods and results seemed similar when, in the 1930s, our alcoholic neighbor was periodically placed in a straightjacket and locked up in a "psycho ward" to sober up. The guarded gates at the entrance to the state mental hospital in my hometown were foreboding. There was a great gulf between the barren, locked wards, where hundreds of patients waited to die, and the doctors' nice houses and well-groomed yards. As a young observer, psychiatric hospitalization implied to me an individual's loss of control and low self-esteem. Worst of all, the hospital patients didn't make sense, giggled at the wrong things, and had scarey eyes.

To me, the psychiatrist was like L. Frank Baum's classic Wizard of Oz, who lived in the Emerald City, and held out hope to Dorothy and her friends on the yellow brick road. They believed that the wizard would give the Tin Woodman a heart, the Lion some courage, and the Scarecrow a brain. Perhaps you remember how the story ends. When Dorothy and her companions finally arrived in the Emerald City, they discovered that the wizard was without expertise, a fake. When Dorothy discovered that they had been deceived, she accused the impostor of being a very bad man. The wizard replied, "No, Dorothy, I am a good man but a very bad wizard."

Today, we have a hard time thinking of psychiatrists as good people who marry and divorce, succeed with some patients and fail with others, enjoy golf and soccer, and go to church or synagogue. Many think that all psychiatrists are atheists, when, in fact, many are devout believers. They seem too interested in sex, but, in fact, they are interested in sex for about the same reasons as you and I. We may assume that they are the only ones around who are sane, but some healers are emotionally ill themselves. Psychiatrists need faith; yet, many of them have difficulty dealing with a patient's religious beliefs and behavior. What has been the nature of religion's relationship to psychiatry?

PSYCHIATRY AND THE SEARCH FOR WHOLENESS

A historical examination of the relationship between religion and psychiatry is as confusing as it is edifying. In 1408, for example, the first European asylum for the mentally ill was established by the church in Valencia, Spain. Cures for mental illness were sought at shrines of special patron saints. Martin Luther regrettably advocated the drowning of mentally retarded children, and many people linked mental illness with demoniacal possession during the sixteenth and seventeenth centuries. Treatment appropriate to that diagnosis involved exorcists and religious torturers.

The late William Temple once said, "Religion's first word is a word against bad religion." An examination of John T. McNeill's *A History of the Cure of Souls* shows that pastoral care has sometimes fallen into superstition and stupidity.[1] Religionists, like therapists, may be considered as wizards and magic makers. Small wonder that Sigmund Freud, a disenchanted Jew in Catholic-dominated Vienna, questioned the value of religion as he observed it in analysis. His correspondence with Reverend Oskar Pfister, however, and his detailed studies of religion, *The Future of an Illusion, Totem and Taboo,* and *Moses and Monotheism,* dramatize how seriously Freud studied aspects of religious experience and expression.[2]

In the past, religious and psychiatric practitioners have been suspicious of one another, protective of their special territories, and critical of weaknesses without knowing each other as persons. There too often has been a cynical attitude when a minister or therapist has met personal or professional setbacks (such as sexual involvement with a patient or a physician's suicide). Some folks have gloated over psychiatrist Karl Menninger's confession:

> I used to believe that psychiatry was the great hope for America. But now I feel it's failed, and I don't know why. People in analysis don't seem to get better. Perhaps psychiatrists have become too arrogant, without enough love or compassion for their work.[3]

The truth is Menninger never gave up on psychiatry or religion. He worked to improve the education of professionals in both fields, and spoke supportively to his colleagues when appropriate.

Man's concern for the health of his soul goes back to ancient times. He has always had healers, endowed with special powers for treatment.[4] The tribal shaman of Asia was a healer who used trusted rituals to cure the sick, fight evil spirits, and to change life events. The witch doctor in many African societies performed healing rites through the use of hypnotic suggestion, casting of lots, herbal medications, and animal sacrifices. The guru (from Sanskrit, meaning venerable) of India has served for centuries as a spiritual guide, and has recently gained new popularity. The Latin American *curandero* used magic, folk belief, and empirical experience in therapy. Spiritual guides have had considerable influence in many cultures.

Psychiatry has deep roots in antiquity. In the 1930s, psychiatrists started using electrical shock therapy. Yet four thousand years earlier healers in Greece and Egypt did essentially the same thing using electric eels. Drug therapy came into vogue in the 1950s, helping to empty the back wards of American hospitals. A major tranquilizer used for this purpose has the same properties as a root used for centuries in West Africa and India. Dream analysis, developed at the turn of this century as the focal point of Freudian psychoanalysis, goes back four thousand years to Joseph's creative interpretation of dreams in the land of the pharaohs.

Sigmund Freud, born in Austria in 1856, began his medical career in a neurophysiological laboratory. He gradually worked his way from neurology through philosophy, then theology, to psychology. He observed that a "basic anxiety" pervaded the bodies and emotions of his patients. At first he saw anxiety as a specific thing, resulting from a particular conflict, a product of the mind's tendency to deal with conflict by forcing it aside. This force he named repression. People paid a dear price for remaining ignorant of what ailed them. Later Freud determined that anxiety is more pervasive than he had at first imagined; its presence is part of everyone's psychic makeup. His efforts to understand psychic defenses led him to speak of "the psychopathology of everyday life," and to examine the content of anxiety-producing situations in his own life. This, in turn, pushed him to examine the content of dreams —a fertile field for discovering clashes between the self and its environment. His *The Interpretation of Dreams* was completed in his forty-third year (1899), but the Psychiatric and Neurological Society of Vienna gave his ideas a cool reception. It was not until 1909, when he was fifty-three, that he was first invited to present his theories in a university lecture.

Freud had many followers, however, and as early as 1902 he started a study group called the Psychological Wednesday Society, which met in the waiting room of his consulting office. He wanted to attract followers so that his ideas would have wide institutional backing. Alfred Adler, Max Kohane, Rudolf Reitler, and Wilhelm Stekel met every Wednesday evening to learn what Freud had found in psychoanalysis. Those followers, plus thousands of others, discovered a theory of the world of the mind, a method of inquiry, and a therapeutic technique. Freud continued to develop his controversial theories until his death in 1939, following multiple operations for cancer the last fifteen years of his life.

Carl G. Jung, unlike Freud, declared his allegiance to Christianity, and the most important of his works dealt with religious concerns. "I find that all my thoughts circle around God like the planets around the sun, and are as irresistibly attracted by Him," he wrote in 1952 to a young clergyman.[5] Looking at religious questions from the standpoint of psychology, Jung stressed understanding and reflection, rather than faith alone. This made him appear as an outsider to traditional advocates of Christianity.

Though Jung and Freud did correspond, Jung's ideas about human nature developed independently of Freud, not in reaction to him. Jung's therapeutic concepts are more holistic than Freud's, and much more closely related to religious values. Rediscovery of Jung, like that in Henri Ellenberger's history of dynamic psychiatry, has some possibilities for establishing a closer link between psychiatry and religion.[6]

MUTUAL CONCERNS OF RELIGION AND PSYCHIATRY

Views are mixed as to the present state of psychotherapy and its relation to religion. Some observers hold that psychiatry is well on its way to replacing religion in the United States.[7] Others, sensitive to contributions from both fields, detect a variety of relationships.[8] In truth, there are numerous theologies, not one; and there are many schools of psychotherapy, not one. Unfortunately, there is too much naiveté among psychiatrists and pastors about each other.

Perhaps the greatest single contribution of psychiatry is providing therapists with a careful diagnostic procedure. People crave clarity concerning the symptoms that ail them, as well as a means of alleviating them. While ministers follow the biblical models of sin, guilt, forgiveness, salvation, and the grace of God, medical practitioners follow clinical models of diagnosis and speak of anxiety, hysteria, depression, acceptance, tension release, and courage. With the influence of modern medicine, ancient theological concepts like sin and virtue are being replaced by concepts of sickness and health.

Some psychiatrists have moved into the realm of private and public morals, as ministers have preoccupied themselves with other things. To quote psychiatrist E. Fuller Torrey of the National Institute of Mental Health: "In *The Scarlet Letter*, written in 1850, adultery is explained by the minister as due to evil inside the woman." Today, "it is explained by the psychiatrist as due to the woman's low self-esteem and attempts to get close to people. In the past 25 years more and more socially unacceptable behavior is explained in such terms, to the apparent satisfaction of more and more people." The power to define good (health) and evil (illness) is a heavy burden for psychiatrists to shoulder. They are uncomfortable in their emerging role of moral leadership.

Conversely, too few ministers are doing something about values. Some behavioral scientists have become so frustrated with the clergy's abandonment of moral leadership that some, such as Karl Menninger in *Whatever Became of Sin?*, have become religiously oriented. He lists various reasons why the term *sin* has fallen into disuse, the most discouraging of which is its abandonment due to collective irresponsibility. This, he says, is the broad and misty plain on which most of the horrors of our time take place: war, slavery, pollution, the callousness of corporations, and the oppression of women and minority groups.

Sin is properly defined by Menninger as a "transgression of the law of God; disobedience of the divine will; moral failure"; as "aggression against people"; or, by the word *hate*. But, like the prophet Amos, Menninger indicts in order to reform. "If we believe in sin—as I do— we believe in our personal responsibility for trying to correct it, and thereby saving ourselves and our world."[9] The psychiatrist feels certain religious attitudes damage his patients. He expects Christians to forgive sin, not merely to expose it. Of course, Karl Menninger speaks only for himself, not all psychotherapists. Many of his professional colleagues would suggest that he has grown soft in his old age.

Many psychiatrists would deny any responsibility for moral and ethical leadership. On the contrary, most schools of psychiatry emphasize that the therapist should not impose values on a patient. Despite their disclaimers, psychiatrist Jerome D. Frank holds that "all [therapies] are attempts to heal through persuasion."[10]

What about guidance in daily decisions and controversial issues? The American public hears far more about human problems—like abortion, drug abuse, violence, and sexual perversity—from television programs than from ministers. Some psychological experts (pushed to the fore by their financially shrewd agents and publishers) tell people how to treat their spouses, rear children, handle anger, manage time, keep in top shape, make love, and face death.

Those involved in psychological healing are not split only over beliefs and behavior. The cleavage runs deep concerning man's nature, predicament, and search for wholeness. Classic Freudians believe that man's aggression is inborn, a position close to the original sin experienced by Adam and Eve in Genesis. The analyst's task is to teach people to channel their aggression in socially acceptable ways. New York psychoanalyst Bruce Maliver says Freud described a well-adjusted person as one with a controlled, though persistent, depression. Freud offered little hope for the salvation of mankind.

New therapies—springing from the work of optimistic humanists like Carl Rogers, Fritz Perls, Eric Berne, and Abraham Maslow—hold hope for human liberation. Transactional analysts, Gestaltists, human potential advocates, and humanistic psychologists emphasize the importance of a deep regard for the dignity of each individual. On the other hand, followers of B. F. Skinner hold that therapists must go "beyond freedom and dignity" in modifying human behavior through educational rehabituation.[11]

The new psychological approaches not only duplicate old theological controversies, but they also clash over whether to concentrate on personal change or society's welfare. Psychologist Paul Pruyser of Topeka, Kansas, says: *"Do your own thing* is similar to Nineteenth Century pietism, that saving my soul is a personal issue with an utter blindness to the rest of the world." People following Gestaltist Fritz Perls's dictum, "I please myself first," have nothing to hold onto when pleasure gives way to pain, tragedy, and death.[12] Suffering persons cannot easily escape from their damaging contexts. Their healers must work to transform hurtful institutions as well as individual attitudes.

We see, then, that there are many therapies, not just one. New psychological trends threaten to overshadow current, even classic approaches. Just when it appeared that psychology was coming into its own as a responsible science, Seymour Halleck wrote *The Politics of Therapy,* Thomas Szasz published his *Manufacture of Madness: A Comparative Study of the Inquisition and the Mental Health Movement,* and a host of feminist authors attempted to show that most therapists, including Freud, are sexist.[13] Yet psychiatry can and does help pastoral counselors.

HOW PSYCHIATRY INFORMS PASTORAL CARE

Persons working on the boundary between psychiatry and pastoral care are sometimes too involved to gain proper perspective. If one travels far enough in the right direction in either psychiatry or pastoral counseling, he inevitably ends up in the other area.

Personality can be compared to a four-legged stool, where, if one leg is shorter than the others, the stool becomes unsteady. The self's "legs" include physical, spiritual, emotional, and intellectual factors. Some ministers fear that examination of one of these aspects of the human self, say the emotional, means abandoning the spiritual. Guilt and fear accompany any feeling of neglecting the theological base. But actually, working in both theology and psychiatry gives one a fruitful basis for interchange. Consider how at least some psychotherapists assist pastoral counselors and lay helpers.

1. *Psychotherapists may help ministers to understand human nature.* Two books mentioned in chapter 5, Gardner Murphy's *Personality: A Biosocial Approach to Origins and Structures,* and Juanita Williams's *Psychology of Women: Behavior in a Biosocial Context* concur with Freud that people are physiological beings. Whatever else one is, the individual is a physical being with physical drives and needs. Psychiatry understands that the denial of one's physical, animallike nature is a source of real anxiety. Modern chemotherapy is designed to alter emotional states by modifying biological systems. Physicians remind us that physiological processes are regulated by hormones, the chemical messengers produced by endocrine glands, and that nerves transmit impulses through fibers much like electric current through wires.

a). Psychiatry researches multileveled motivation. An ancient wise man wrote, "As a man thinks in his heart, so is he" (Prov. 23:7). Freud and his revisionists, like Erik Erikson, Heinz Hartmann, David Rapaport, and Erich Fromm, viewed the unconscious motivation of personality as the shadowy, impulsive id. One's needs and drives seek fulfillment, though they may be out of one's conscious thoughts. According to Freud, these unconscious drives can be controlled by insight and a strengthened ego. Jung, on the other hand, saw the unconscious as a rich source of human creativity. The therapist's job, according to Jung, is to break the chains that hold the patient in bondage, releasing him to freedom.

Later investigators further modified Freud's understanding, and demonstrated that striving could be for conscious and more noble reasons than satisfying "the pleasure principle" alone. Gordon W. Allport acknowledged the uniqueness of persons, and warned in *Becoming* against views that neglected individuality. Carl Rogers noted in *Client-Centered Therapy* that man has "one basic tendency and striving—to actualize, maintain, and enhance the experiencing organism." Humanistic psychologist Abraham Maslow noted in *The Farther Reaches of Human Nature* that human motives have primary, secondary, and tertiary value. If man's primary needs, like food, are met, then the person responds to secondary needs like safety, love, and belongingness, or tertiary beta values in the realm of the spirit. Existentialists, like Viktor Frankl, who wrote *Man's Search for Meaning,* hold that persons live for ultimate purposes, goals, and objectives, not merely unconscious drives.

b). Persons grow according to a specific ground plan of development. This was the major contribution of men like Robert J. Havighurst in *Human Development and Education* and Erik H. Erikson in *Identity and the Life Cycle.* [14] A developmental view of personality leads to a sense of age-appropriate behavior, from infancy to old age. It focuses on growth and time's changing demands on people. For example, the rebellious acts of the adolescent are appropriate for that age of development. A person's independence is seen as an affirmation of one's identity and worth, paving the way for interdependence with adults.

c). People possess inherent worth, creativity, and dignity. People are felt to have the right to determine their own needs and how they can best be met. Along with this right is the responsibility to provide each family member and fellow citizen equal opportunities for self-respect and self-determination. [15]

d). Both behavioral scientists and theologians hold that there is something in human beings with which a counselor can make an alliance. In this view sin is not denied. Persons mismanage life, whether observers call it sin against God or sickness of soul, but health, or a mature self, is possible. Psychiatrist Lewis R. Wolberg provides eleven measures of a healthy personality in *The Dynamics of Personality.* [16] *Maturity* implies the full development of all one's resources to capacity for a given age. The goal of spiritual-emotional growth is maturity—to be a healthy, fully functioning, free, growing person. Help, including guidance and counsel, is essential on the way to maturity.

2. *In addition to helping understand human nature, psychiatrists may help pastors with individual cases.* There are several ways in which this might occur:

a). They can consult, or collaborate with a pastor in counseling a church member whose problems are beyond the pastor's expertise.

b). Psychiatric consultation can be useful to the pastor, where emotional problems, entirely internal to the members of the church, can create disorder or difficulty.

c). Help is available for the pastor himself and members of his own family when facing trying personal conflicts.

d). Pastors may refer deeply troubled people for psychiatric evaluation and treatment (discussed in chapter 12). Religious concepts and practices, like love and prayer, may be used not only in the service of God but in mental illness as well. People who are emotionally troubled become false witnesses to the Christian message. Through an understanding of their psychopathology, it is often possible to help them become witnesses to the truth.

As an illustration of psychiatry's assistance in pastoral care, I cite a case of family conflict within a minister's household and how a psychiatrist helped the family overcome the difficulty.[17] To quote extensively from Robert S. Glen, M.D.:

On this particular occasion, the pastor came to see me personally and told me that he was having a great deal of trouble with his fifteen-year-old daughter. She was staying out late at night, not calling to say that she was going to be late and, in general, gave the impression of being an extremely rebellious child. The father was highly regarded as a pastor by his congregation. He devoted a great deal of time to his church duties, and he was very loving with his family. In fact, on the surface, it would be difficult to see that anything was wrong, except for the behavior of his daughter. . . .

It is necessary to see what might be going on in this family, or what might be going on in the daughter's life—unrelated to her family—to determine the reason for her behavior. Prior to making a moral judgment, an emotional understanding of this situation must first be developed.

About five years earlier, the pastor had been in a much smaller and less demanding church, and had been as well loved there as in his present one. It turned out that he was very anxious about transferring to this new church, because of the demand and challenge it presented, and because he realized he would have to double his previous efforts. . . . In the former church . . . he was able to give his family adequate time and love. When he moved to the new church, Jean, his daughter, appeared pleased with the new school and became actively involved in its activities. Seemingly, she had less need for her father than before. . . .

However, when Jean reached the age of fourteen and started dating young men . . . , she began talking to her father about seemingly inconsequential matters. Because these topics seemed minor to him, and due to the pressure of his work, he would cut [off] her conversation saying, "I will talk to you this evening." Of course, "this evening" never came. . . .

The pastor remembered one time that Jean said, "When I needed you, you did not have time, and now that it is bugging you, you have time." This, then, became the key to the situation. . . . Jean felt rejected by her father. She felt that he had no interest in her. . . . Formerly loving the work of her father, she now began to hate it. Simply because, in essence, it was destroying her chances of successful growth.

The pastor and I decided that what was necessary was to give Jean his attention, even when she did not expect it, and for him to initiate periods of time for her, recognizing that initially she would surely reject this.

Fortunately for all, the massive doses of love worked. His daughter changed her behavior, became happier, and again felt secure with her father and the family. Jean's needs simultaneously warned him that a similar problem was brewing with his wife. Being older, she was dealing with it more effectively than Jean, but she was also experiencing feelings of hurt and rejection.

3. *There are obvious limitations to relations between psychiatrists and ministers.*

a). Psychiatrists may wish only to give and not to receive help from the theological community. Kenneth R. Mitchell illustrates in *Hospital Chaplain* how a minister collaborated with a young psychiatric resident to help understand the deeply religious outlook of a hospitalized female patient.[18] The Christian pastor can care for the psychiatrist's spiritual concerns, personally and professionally, just as readily as he can receive therapy for a psychological disorder. The interchange should work both ways, as Paul Pruyser has convincingly argued in *The Minister as Diagnostician.*[19]

b). The understandings of persons from the perspective of pastoral care and psychiatry differ markedly. This would be particularly true if the therapist were steeped in classic psychoanalysis or Skinnerian behaviorism.

c). The chosen approach, whether psychiatric or religious, places limitations on treatment. Ministers, for example, do not prescribe medication for relief or remediation of symptoms. Nor do they prescribe elecroconvulsive shock therapy or perform psychosurgery. Most psychiatrists do not employ religious resources common to a church or synagogue.

d). The goals of each discipline limit the relationships. Most ministers proclaim salvation, while psychiatrists tackle troublesome behavior, pushing back the shadows enshrouding psychological suffering. Ideally, a holistic view of people should encompass both salvation and health.

PREVENTION AND HEALTH

From this discussion, it may appear that the whole world is bent on tyranny, suicide, alcoholism, incest, environmental pollution, crime, and violence in what economist John Kenneth Galbraith dubbed "the age of uncertainty." But that is only part of the picture. Prevention is still the best cure for the world's afflictions. We shall never know, this side of eternity, how many persons the church keeps well and fully functioning. It is not that religion anesthetizes peoples' feelings and insulates them from reality. Rather, faith opens persons to life's ultimate realities and gives them courage and hope to face all its hardships. Furthermore, the maintenance of mental hygiene and promotion of preventive programs lies at the center of organizations like the National Association for Mental Health.

To their discredit, healers and helpers have been far more fascinated by human perversity and treatment than by disease prevention. In part, they are motivated to alleviate humanity's hurt, like fire fighters drawn toward the flames. There is a natural curiosity about the unique, deviant, and bizarre, which piques the helper's imagination, challenging him to do battle against human ills. Also, there is a place to "take hold" in a person's perversity or a family's pathology. Individual or group relationships can be established in controlled settings, with the healer as ultimate authority. In preventive work, on the other hand, the counselor is forced into the public arena as an adviser, planner, politician, speech maker, and social moralist. It appears easier, and much more feasible financially, to work with paying patients and parishioners, rather than to stir public concern over mental health.

Dr. Kenneth Cooper of Dallas, founder of the internationally recognized aerobic exercise system, advocates a regular program for physical and mental fitness. He directs a preventive medicine clinic and aerobics center where people run, swim, bicycle, and keep fit through many activities. "It is amazing how the body forgives us, how it tries to compensate for misuse," says Cooper. "But then it can't go any further. *A man dies not just from disease, but from his whole life.*"

The apostle Paul spoke of the body as the "temple" of God's Spirit (1 Cor. 6:19–20). Individuals should take care of their bodies, and glorify God in all things. While the Christian mission is much wider than Howard Clinebell's description in *The Mental Health Ministry of the Local Church*, it includes wholeness of body and spirit. The church should help prevent alcoholism, crime, sexual promiscuity, and evil in every form to the limit of its ability. Still, as Karl Menninger once said: "There is some kind of a curious resistance in all of us to the idea of preventing anything and we act only when we are forced to do so."[20] I join the plea for prevention of disease, disorder, and demonic behavior, which Menninger proclaimed as a goal twenty-five years ago. Sermons can be preached, legislative programs can be authorized, and centers for preventive medicine can be established to move all of us nearer the goal of a better, saner world.

In summary, I have looked at psychiatry's development within the historic framework of mankind's search for wholeness. The mutual concerns of religion and psychiatry have been explored. I have explained and illustrated how psychiatry informs pastoral care, and pointed to a vast literature to help in ministering to deeply troubled people. Theology and psychiatry should work to the mutual benefit of both fields. We have gifts to receive and share that will help us all.

7

Goals of Pastoral Counseling

THE novelist Eli Wiesel once wrote that "God made man because He loves stories." A passage in Wiesel's *The Gates of the Forest* pictures God listening and responding to man's plea for help.[1] Set in the tradition of rabbinic Judaism, it reflects God's attentiveness to man's anxious longings and sincere desires.

When the great Rabbi Israel Baal Shem-Tov saw misfortune threatening the Jews it was his custom to go into a certain part of the forest to meditate. There he would light a fire, say a special prayer, and the miracle would be accomplished and the misfortune averted.

Later, when his disciple, the celebrated Magid of Mezritch, had occasion, for the same reason, to intercede with heaven, he would go to the same place in the forest and say: "Master of the Universe, listen! I do not know how to light the fire, but I am still able to say the prayer." And again, the miracle would be accomplished.

Still later, Rabbi Moshe-Leib of Sasov, in order to save his people once more, would go into the forest and say: "I do not know how to light the fire, I do not know the prayer, but I know the place and this must be sufficient."

Then it fell to Rabbi Israel of Rizhyn to overcome misfortune. Sitting in his armchair, his head in his hands, he spoke to God: "I am unable to light the fire and I do not know the prayer; I cannot even find the place in the forest. All I can do is to tell the story and this must be sufficient." And it was sufficient. God made man because He loves stories.

God's willingness to communicate with his creation shines forth in this narrative. Also, the belief in man's ability to perceive truth directly from God is quite ancient. Mysticism is the universal source from which myths and legends of all human civilizations are fashioned. Early on, man sensed that he was more than one tiny organism floating in endless space on a sphere called earth. John Donne was right: "No man is an Island, intire of itselfe; every man is a peece of the Continent, a part of the maine. . . ." We need each other, as well as ancient Israel's "Wonderful Counselor" (Isa. 9:6). Indeed, God's power, what Tillich called "the New Being of the divine Spirit," makes effective pastoral counseling possible.

Protestant Christianity holds that not only are all persons their own priests before God, but we are also priests to one another. The tale of one rabbi going into the forest, lighting a fire, and saying a special prayer on behalf of his people has significance for strugglers everywhere. Religious counselors serve uniquely as mediators and teachers sent from God. When a burdened, nearly destroyed individual is "unable to light the fire," does not know "the prayer," or cannot locate "the place in the forest," he must share his plight with someone. Otherwise he shall die.

Counselees turning to Christian pastors are saying, in effect, "All I can do is tell the story and this must be sufficient." Fortunately, God has good ears. His representatives, caring persons, also listen and respond. Such help becomes sufficient precisely because the Father "loves man's stories." Not all counselees reach out to God with great faith, like the woman with "an issue of blood" who touched Jesus Christ in a crowd (Matt. 9:20–22). It helps to recall, however, that God's Son promised: "I am come that they may have life and have it abundantly" (John 10:10). With that life-giving objective in mind, the Christian pastor should develop goals for counseling.

THE SIGNIFICANCE OF GOALS

A minister I know served on the staff of a Christian counseling center while doing clinical pastoral teaching. He related to me the details of several sessions with a depressed, forty-five-year-old professional man, whose wife was an accomplished musician. She and their two daughters belonged to a local congregation, where they had gained not only membership, but quite a name for themselves. The man said of his wife: "She becomes president of everything she touches!"

The man was from a small town, had served in the armed forces since Uncle Sam helped to pay for his education, and had experienced considerable guilt over behavior that violated his values. Since youth he had hated his father because his father had been unfaithful to his mother. When the counselee and his sister were teenagers they had learned of their father's unfaithfulness, on a trip into town with him one Saturday. They had entirely lost confidence in him.

The counseling sessions revealed a passive man, so depressed that he doubted his own sanity. His active wife kept books on his professional earnings and provided him a token weekly allowance. She served as his office receptionist and billing clerk, and was also in charge of the family at home. The man felt trapped in the hopelessness of a substantial income, counterbalanced by large expenses, lack of faith, lack of serenity in marriage, low self-esteem, and a desire to escape from it all. Sex always seemed to be for him, not for her. A recent diagnosis of diabetes had placed him in the identical situation as his father, who had been a diabetic before his death. He was angry at what Providence had permitted, and sought a way out—even suicide.

Following the third session with the distraught man, the staff supervisor asked the counseling minister, "What are your goals in counseling this man?" It is important to recognize the significance of counseling goals in light of Christianity's redemptive objective. A counselor's goals are related to, and emerge from, actual conversations. They are not borrowed from a book, nor taken from one source and applied directly to a person's life. Goals emerge both from the counselor's capabilities and the counselees' needs, with a spirit of respect for individuality. Sensitivity to others is the path to skilled diagnosis and treatment.

WHERE DO COUNSELING GOALS COME FROM?

Since caring conversations lead helpers and those being helped in some direction and to some course of action, we must examine where counseling goals originate.

1. *The counselor's professional identity will set limits and offer guidelines for goals in counseling.* The pastoral counselor uses methods similar to other counselors, but his objectives are guided by the central beliefs of the Christian faith. A vocational guidance counselor is concerned with achievement tests, vocational interest tests, psychological aptitide tests, and the like, in an effort to help place people in the most

appropriate job niche. A psychiatrist is interested in tension reduction, interpersonal relationships, satisfaction of psychic needs, and psychological equilibrium for the patient and his family. In contrast, a minister brings the promise of God's presence to persons' seemingly insoluble problems. The hope that a minister inspires is related, not just to needs and drives, but to finding meaning in life.

A minister usually has established prior personal relationships with individuals in the congregation. Members of the congregation have heard sermons, prayers for the church family and all mankind, and many of them have visited personally with the minister prior to counseling. One can take the initiative and make oneself available to church members through writing and personal calls. A pastor symbolizes the reality of God, love of a congregation, faith of a religious tradition, an ethical way of living, and hope for human justice. Because of this symbolic power "there may be unconscious negative forces to be dealt with," as David K. Switzer wrote in *The Minister as Crisis Counselor.*[2] Not all religious experience has benefited all people. Unhealthy, counterproductive, and self-defeating religious ideas or behavior must be worked through and overcome.

Pastors are expected to intervene in certain situations like hospitalized illness, surgery, divorce, death, and grief. If one does not make oneself available during such crises, people will wonder why. On the other hand, were one to intrude on a family feud, a business decision, or a legal battle over child custody, one's presence might create more stress than it would relieve.

2. *Wholeness and strength of spirit are goals toward which people should develop.* Process theologian John B. Cobb, Jr. wrote correctly that counseling should be seen "as a part of the distinctive pastoral work of making Christian faith effective in the lives of people."[3] In *Theology and Pastoral Care,* he distinguishes between counseling as ministry to human need in general and counseling to make Christian faith effective. Therein lies the challenge of distinctiveness for pastoral therapists. It involves not merely the pastor's socially defined role, but also a proper understanding of God, sin and salvation, and understanding human development.

What of those persons who appeal directly to the Bible for a counseling model? William B. Oglesby, Jr., of Union Theological Seminary in Virginia, warns that there is no "specific instruction regarding process in counseling" in the Bible, "just as there is none regarding the construction of a sermon or the form of church organization and administration."[4] In a major evaluation of psychotherapy, compared with biblical approaches, Oglesby sees three main approaches for counselors: concentrating on *knowing* or insight, on *doing* or behavior, and on *being* or existence. He claims that the importance of each of these emphases is affirmed in Scripture, though knowing and doing are derived from being. *Being*, in Oglesby's view, is related to one's "heart," and is the essence of life. One is to keep one's "heart with all vigilance; for from it flow the springs of life" (Prov. 4:23). It is upon the heart that God looks (1 Sam. 16:7), and with the heart man believes and is saved (Rom. 10:10). Israel was instructed to "love the Lord your God with all your heart, and with all your soul, and with all your might" (Deut. 6:4).

In the New Testament, writes Oglesby, "the heart as the seat of *being* is primary, and from it come *knowing* and *doing*."[5] Jesus Christ in the beatitudes affirms purity of heart (Matt. 5:8), and Paul sees obedience arising from the heart (Rom. 6:17). The point of Oglesby's logic is this: both law and gospel, culminating in the incarnation, tell of God's search for and acceptance of sinful man. Jesus Christ came "to seek and to save the lost" (Luke 19:10). The cross is the supreme manifestation of God's search, which reestablishes broken relationships in the atonement. "He is our peace, who has made us both one, . . . that he might . . . reconcile us both to God in one body through the cross, thereby bringing the hostility to an end" (Eph. 2:14–16). From a biblical point of view, according to Oglesby, man's basic problem is neither lack of knowledge nor improving behavior, though good works are never ignored. "His problem is that he is a sinner who needs forgiveness and reconciliation, from which come both right *knowing* and right *doing*."[6] When pastoral counselors assist in making the gospel explicit in human situations, so that people become closer to God in being, belief, and behavior, they are on the right track. The goal of achieving wholeness and strength of spirit is being realized.

This returns us to promise, expectation, and hope in pastoral counseling. If Jerome Frank is right in assuming the curative effects of confidence in the healing process, we can assume that hope, generated by trust, is the ingredient on which wholeness of spirit depends. We are "saved by hope" (Rom. 8:24). Both the helper and the one who seeks help depend on a sustaining fellowship of believers who survive as "prisoners of hope" (Zech. 9:12).

3. *The church, ideally a community of faith, hope, and love, sustains the counselor's ministry.* This living system serves as an extended family of spiritual kinsmen, who are encouraged to "build up one another" (1 Thess. 5:11–14). Mansell Pattison, an experienced minister and psychiatrist, views each congregation as a supportive "social system that produces a whole, holy, person."[7] The ideal system is a wholesome fellowship that informs, corrects, supports, and cherishes each member. When dysfunction arises and repair is needed, helpers and helpess function in the context of that unique system. In the church "we exist *in* and *from* and *for* one another."[8] The Christian ideal of *wholeness* involves personal wholeness in a whole fellowship of faith.

The New Testament suggests that we are all joint participants in the body of Christ (Rom. 12:5). The ideal is for individuals to contribute to the richness of one another's existence. In that manner people become priests to each other, both during the predictable passages from one stage of life to another, and through the unpredictable crises that inevitably come. Human spirit requires a helping community, notwithstanding the claims of Heidegger and Sartre, who depict existence as an isolated, individual struggle. Unfortunately, many communities of faith enjoy little fellowship. John Cobb is right: "Christian history bears witness not only to the difficulty of attaining this ideal but to the tension between it and the strengthening of the individual spirit."[9] Idolatry, alienation, petty jealousies, social customs, powerful traditions, and family loyalties intrude on the Christian community. The emergence of strong personalities may yield, not brotherhood, but strife and conflict.

Still, ministers do not escape their roles as representatives of particular congregations, each with its unique reputation for love or conflict, hope or despair, fidelity or disobedience. Their character and limitations affect pastoral effectiveness. Pastors can usually rely on a supportive fellowship to undergird and share the tasks of caring. That would *not* be the case if one worked as a theological consultant or as an ordained therapist in a mental health center. There, one would be identified with health care professionals rather than a congregation.

One's administrative context—whether local church, pastoral counseling center, school campus, denominational agency, hospital, or missionary assignment—affects pastoral approaches with people. The fact that persons are called *clients* in one setting, *patients* in another, and *counselees* in a third shapes goals toward guidance, therapy, or growth.

4. *Goals must be related to the personal needs and expectations that individuals bring to counseling situations.* Not all counselees will require the same response. One person, for example, may need immediate help of a practical nature: medical, legal, financial, or even lodging for a night. Another person may face a family fight, infidelity of a mate, a change of vocational direction, or some dark night of the soul. A counselee may need forgiveness and a new sense of self-respect. Or a minister may visit a stroke victim who presents a barrier of silence during the conversation. What one says to a teacher, fired without justification from a job, is different from one's response to a retiree who anticipates freedom from work and needs creative ideas for new leisure.

Think of the goals that might emerge in a series of conversations with five different persons in the same week: a young child torn between his divorcing parents;[10] a brother who hates his sister and wishes her dead; a factory supervisor bypassed for a promotion to an executive position; a young man whose love has been spurned by a fickle girl; and a widow whose husband recently committed suicide.

The skilled counselor refuses to thread barren, prefabricated, empty clichés, or time-worn solutions into conversations. There is an old saying in rural America: "Each tub must sit on its own bottom." Likewise, a confused child, a shattered lover, an angry man, an outraged brother, and a crushed wife each merit an individualized response. Love in each instance implies, not an external act or a spoken word, but active participation in others' lives.

QUESTIONS TO ASK ABOUT COUNSELING GOALS

The following is a list of appropriate questions to ask about counseling goals, but it is meant to be suggestive rather than exhaustive.

1. What expectations does my counselee bring to this session? What is the stated reason for seeking counseling?

2. What is my immediate goal in working with this person? Is he in need of an improved self-image (stronger ego), encouragement, structure for chaotic feelings, confrontation concerning values, forgiveness of sin, or guidance in decision making? Does he seek deliverance from some

bondage, or acceptance, or a pastoral blessing to help him proceed in life?

3. In light of the Bible's emphasis on being, knowing and doing, what goals are appropriate for Christian growth?

4. In light of the counselee's emotional condition and spiritual resources, what goals are realistic and possible?

5. How do our agreed on, immediate objectives relate to the long-range goals of this person?

A counselee may feel temporarily better without getting healthy. It is not a realistic counseling goal to expect an individual to say he is "feeling better." But tension reduction and need satisfaction usually lead to better feelings, which may, in turn, free persons for psychic growth and responsible action.

Unrealized goals may become stressors that further erode the strength of entrapped individuals. Counselees should recognize that no one is loyal to all of one's loyalties all of the time. Counselees may not always conform to an idealized self-image or a culturally approved value system, or expect to find readily theological truth or emotional insight. For example, the willpower of an alcoholic may be weak. A person with repressed anger may have continuing difficulty with depression. A delinquent or criminal individual may experience remissions, behave irresponsibly and continually break the law.

Unlike most humanistic therapists, pastoral counselors participate with God and the person seeking help in a caring relationship. Pastoral counselors are not indifferent or aloof, though they try to bring objectivity and expertise to their task.

PURPOSES OF PASTORAL COUNSELING

What then does the Christian pastor hope to accomplish through counseling? Here, pastoral conversations are distinguished from administering church business affairs, meeting with commissions, preaching and administering baptism and the Lord's Supper, visiting newcomers in a city, and witnessing to outsiders. There is an interweaving of goals in one's public and private ministries, and an appropriate tension between them. Still, there are some unique purposes of pastoral counseling.

1. *Pastoral counseling puts people in touch with God.* Many persons who come for counseling live on the ragged edge of religious identification and commitment. For example, the counseling minister asked the professional man mentioned at the outset of this chapter, "Would you call yourself a religious person?"

"I guess you could say that I am somewhat religious," came his qualified response. "But I almost never go to church."

"It would help me to understand why you turned to a pastoral counseling center at this time," the minister responded, hoping that the client would clarify his intent.

"Well," he hedged a bit, "I've been to a psychiatrist already. I'm not sure that's what I need. Perhaps you can tell me whether or not I am really nuts and need to see a shrink." One of the crucial, though unspoken, reasons that counselees turn to a pastor is that they hope to get in touch with God. The man expressed this need thus: "I know that I should become active in some church."

The past experiences of the professional man in this case considerably influenced his life-style, yet his quest for support was related to the present and future rather than to the past. His orientation was toward the future, yet he lacked direction, specificity of goals, and the inner strength to move ahead. God is pictured in Scripture as going before his people, opening unrealized possibilities for existence, and empowering them to make decisions. According to theologian Cobb, the biblical God "has purposes for the world, and from the divine purposes persons derive theirs."[11] Though the client did not express it, he sensed the need to be related to divine direction.

Circumstances like this one demonstrate the possibilities of promise in human experience. The professional man whom my minister acquaintance was counseling had made promises to himself as a youth— about men, women, God, achievement, and revenge—which were patterned toward destruction. In counseling, we recognize that *promises can be perverted, not only when they are taken too lightly but also when they are undertaken too rigidly.* When life falls short of some promise, one does not merely shrug off criticism, promise more, and start again. Tension also comes with vows too rigidly taken.[12] One must be willing to accommodate to new circumstances when they arise, and to accept change. As part of his promise, God helps people accomodate to new circumstances and face new challenges.

Pastors who counsel half-believing, half-fearful strugglers represent the incarnate Christ, who brings God's direction, order, and might into daily existence. As counselor and counselee discern together "the mind of Christ," direction comes and new pathways are opened. They validate that "it is always God who is the call to growth and the giver of growth."[13] As helper and helpee understand life's bondages and freedoms, the more they sense God at work in the process. Such discernment relates more to the heart (being) than to the head (knowing). Yet, it is reinforced by living a life of faith, and strengthened by a fellowship of belief in the Scriptures. The wise counselor agrees with Cobb's conclusion: "Trust in God is the essence of all Christian life."[14]

2. *Pastoral counseling aids in discovering one's identity.* People must tell their own stories if they are to discover themselves, and understand their own history, handicaps, emotions, and gifts. A second, deeper look at life, beyond the primary experience of living it, gives people perspective over its passages, perils, and privileges. Each counselee deserves an opportunity to claim his people as his own, and to discover freedom beyond the fateful nature or curse character of the past. The counselee is a learner who narrates his story to a teacher sent from God, who interprets life's meaning and assists the counselee in gaining meaning from experience. One's identity and destiny are thus linked to a community of promise, expectancy, and fulfillment.

The decision to reveal one's hurt, sin, or hope to another person is in itself healing. A long journey begins with that first step. True, as a counselee said to me, "It is not easy to bleed in another person's presence." A person chooses to advance or to retreat, step forward or sink into despair. The struggle, while painful, reduces guilt and anxiety and helps release pressure. At best, the counselor's responses offer new freedom and better vision, or, at least, a fresh way of viewing an old situation.

3. *Pastoral counseling assists one in learning to live.* The essence of sin is mismanagement of life, missing life's meaning. A counselor is willing to spend time with a sincere learner. So many of life's decisions are made on the basis of insufficient information—great choices like one's vocation, marriage mate, and even life philosophy. Seeking light along one's way is productive. The search, learning to live, goes on in each stage of life, from childhood until death. Man eventually gives up his teachers (counselors), but he continues the search. Carl Jung held that, in effective therapy, the one seeking help can become his coun-

selor's mentor, and life's roles can be reversed to everyone's profit.

4. *Pastoral counseling assists in developing interpersonal competence.* What one learns with a "significant other" person, the counselor, must be practiced in everyday experience. The counselee does life on a "trial run" basis with transparency to God and his healer-teacher. Taking the risk of personhood with others is what counseling is all about. The goal of growth is that the person being helped will generalize from the therapeutic experience, then apply newfound wisdom and strength in the day-to-day business of living.

Many counselees are at odds with people around them—teachers, fellow employees, family members, and so on. Their attitudes, conversations, and actions may be counterproductive in personal relationships. Their life-styles create anxiety and conflict; desired goals are not realized. Most people, for example, do not know how to handle hostility. Anger can destroy them, cause them to damage themselves, or to injure others. There was a young housewife, for example, who in a fit of rage, resulting from numerous fights with her headstrong husband, killed herself. When he returned from work in the evening, he discovered his wife's body in their mobile home. He called his parents, told them of the bloody discovery, and said that he was going to shoot himself, too. When the police arrived, they discovered the pair of estranged lovers, like Romeo and Juliet, dead.

What if they could have discovered, under a competent counselor's guidance, the truths in Fritz Perls's *Ego, Hunger and Aggression* or in Leo Madow's *Anger?*[15] They could have named some of their destructive demons and, hopefully, overcome their awesome power. Effective counseling addresses both intrapsychic conflict and interpersonal tension. The pastor thus becomes a minister of tension reduction, conflict management, and a harbinger of change for the better.

5. *Pastoral counseling provides information.* Many counselees do not know what to do or where to go for help. They do not want to repeat old mistakes. An individual may need money, a job, a transfer; may suspect his mate of infidelity; may not know how to relate to a rebellious son or daughter; or where to locate a state school for a retarded child. Some decisions cannot be reached without more knowledge.[16] The pastor's "data bank" of information can be enhanced by collaborating with helping professionals in community agencies or institutions.

For example, a person anticipating divorce may not have reviewed some of the complex legal, financial, physical, and social changes that are involved in the dissolution of marriage. The pastor might suggest that a counselee contemplating divorce read Esther Fisher's *Divorce: The New Freedom,* or that a formerly married person read Roger Crook's *An Open Book to the Christian Divorcee.* [17] Comprehensive pastoral care suggests systems planning and expertise in providing community resources to persons with varied needs. Giving information does not change a person's character; yet, data may provide new perspectives or practical assistance.

6. *Pastoral counseling may improve insight, self-understanding, and self-acceptance.* Insight involves the mind and the heart. It is more than knowledge; insight is emotional-spiritual wisdom. New understanding of a situation involves taking risks. The professional man mentioned earlier, for example, came to see how angry he was with life: at his father for betraying his mother years before, at his wife for her high-handed manipulation and rejection, at the church for failing to live up to his expectations of religious perfection, and at God for permitting him to develop diabetes. But his depression, jitters, and abundance of repressed feelings made sense when he finally confronted it. He was capable of something desperate: either a messiahlike act to set things straight, or demonic actions to punish his enemies. We can only hope an individual will act appropriately after counseling, for insight alone is not enough. New self-knowledge can be painful or threatening, as well as eye-opening and exhilarating.

Most individuals long for a fulfilling life. This is what the late Abraham Maslow called self-actualization—a kind of ultimate need or life thrust. Counselees want to feel that they have a place, a purpose, and chance for a productive life. Thus, pastoral counseling deals not only with conflict management, but with attainment of one's full potential.

7. *Pastoral counseling aids persons in decision making.* This goal is akin to others already mentioned, like learning to live and seeking information. It is unique, however, in that many persons turn to a pastor when they face difficult decisions. The counselor facilitates rebirth in a person who has sat in darkness and seeks redemptive light for a new start. People seek advice about educational needs and opportunities, marriage adjustments, family conflicts, sexual frustrations, treatment of enemies (frequently in their own households), approaches to aging, or negotiating freedom from a manipulative parent. Although such conversations may

involve only one interview, people place great stock in what the minister says.

When folks finally turn to a pastor during a decision making process, events may be rather far down the road. They may be double-checking their previous, though unwise, words or deeds, or may be asking for God's blessing on some unforgiveable behavior in the past. It is essential, therefore, that a minister not place himself on a pedestal, even as Jesus Christ declined to become a "judge or divider" over people (Luke 12:13–15). Jesus spoke the truth, in this instance in a parable about covetousness, and then assured his disciples of God's generosity (Luke 12:32–34). He linked the ultimate treasure with one's heart—being the kind of individual God can bless, not demanding one's way. The pastor serves as a catalyst, facilitating changes; as a broker, putting decision makers in touch with new options; and as a prophet, confronting counselees with divine reality.

8. *Pastoral counseling encourages persons to build on strengths.* By the time deeply troubled people seek out a pastor, they may have gotten widely amiss of life's mark. They do not enjoy being miserable. A severe inner struggle may be going on. Part of the person says, "I'm too bad to help; leave me alone." Another part cries out for companionship and power to break the vicious cycle. It is a question of "having some compassion" for themselves, as well as seeking God's help in the struggle.[18] Both the Old and New Testaments beckon persons to believe in God. "They who wait for the Lord shall renew their strength" (Isa. 40:31); and Moses' promise to Asher was: "As your days, so shall your strength be" (Deut. 33:25). The apostle Paul's faith was a source of strength: "I can do all things in him who strengthens me" (Phil. 4:13). His claim was neither boastful nor grandiose. Paul did not evade tragedy or dodge despair. Like believers through the centuries, he found strength for life and prayed that his followers would be empowered by Christ's spirit (Eph. 3:14–17).

Charles F. Kemp, of Brite Divinity School, holds that "the pastor by virtue of his position builds on strengths."[19] Far too many pastors seek a fatal flaw in their counselees, with the attitude that people will someday pay for their weakness and perversity. Jesus' example helps us here. He came "not to condemn the world, but that the world might be saved through him" (John 3:17). According to Kemp, for pastors to build on strengths does not mean that they ignore weaknesses, or that they must eradicate evil or correct error. When a person is strengthened in faith, hope, and love, difficult situations can be endured and may be overcome.

Strength comes from many sources. When people turn to the church for counseling, they may have focused on their failures so long that they are unaware of their strengths. Strengths vary from one person or family to another. An individual or family in counseling can be encouraged to inventory sources of support: worship, prayer, service to others, common values, encouragement and support from family and friends, recreation and leisure, participation in community affairs, sense of humor, patience, positive attitudes, and so on. Kemp cites research reported in the *Canadian Journal of Mental Health* from three family counseling agencies.[20] They asked family members to identify their strengths, "those factors or forces which contribute to family unity and solidarity and which foster the development of the potentialities which are inherent in the family." Then participants were asked to specify sources of strength in their lives. To help other people gain a sense of strength or mastery in life may well be one of the minister's most important tasks.

9. *Pastoral counseling points persons beyond themselves to greater causes in the social order.* Too many people live in rooms with mirrored walls. They are surrounded on all sides by images of themselves. Life to them is like residing in the Hall of Mirrors at the Palace of Versailles. I have referred to the social bond—one's tie with "Mankinde," as Donne called it. God's person recognizes that he is part of the larger historic process and that many lives are at stake in the common ventures of existence. A homicide, hijacking, or rape affects not only those involved, but us. Graft, political corruption, crime, environmental issues, medical research, welfare, and education of future generations is our concern. It is liberating to discover "the others" through counseling, to find compassion for important causes, and to confront one's own weaknesses.

10. *Pastoral counseling opens life to a future with hope.* It is the pastor's privilege to participate in the dreams, decisions, desires, dreads, and often confused loves of people. The pastor's promise to people is not some unrealistic objective which, unattained, provokes added failure, confinement, and despair. In fact, "pastoral counseling as trust in God prevents the counselor's agenda from getting in the way of growth."[21] One should seek faith, hope, and love for counselees, rather

than any specific thing. This is akin to aspiring first to God's kingdom and his righteousness, with confidence that all things will be provided within God's providential bounty (Matt. 6:33).

Christian growth is not the mere addition of something new to one's frail spirit. Rather, it is the transformation of one's entire outlook. The inspiration of hope, based on God's eternal promise of deliverance, prompts growth rather than change alone. The Bible calls this transformation the "renewing of one's mind" and "proving" the power of one's surrendered life by service to God (Rom. 12:1–2). Life so altered must take on a new shape and style; the old outlook is replaced by faith's vision, love's passion, and hope's aspiration. John Cobb holds that growth involves more than working out a pattern we have designed for ourselves. "We cannot grow without surrendering the effort to control the future."[22] To open oneself to the future with hope involves great risk, for we cannot always predict the outcome. Growth involves the emergence of new ways of being, knowing, and doing. Such surrender is not passive however, with life's forces simply shoving us about like ships at the mercy of the sea. That would be the opposite of true faith. Christian living is a process of constant decision, with commitment to the reality of God's presence. Such hopefulness is based, not on a formula for living, but on trust in God's love, expressed through relationships. Paul, having discovered this secret of certitude amid all of life's uncertainties, exclaimed: "If we live, we live to the Lord, and if we die, we die to the Lord; so then, whether we live or whether we die, we are the Lord's" (Rom. 14:8).

The counseling pastor ministers to human growth, resistance, and struggle in each counselee. He praises initiative in each person who seeks to grow. Barriers will inevitably arise during their communication. "Goals will be redefined, progress will be reviewed, issues restated, growing insights clarified, alternatives weighed, and action foreseen . . . as they move forward" in the relationship.[23] In time, they will consider termination of the interviews.

A counselee's needs may lie beyond a minister's ability to help. One can place such a person or family in the care of God, the ultimate burden-bearer. A helper can refer persons to a professional colleague or agency that is equipped to focus on particular problems (as we shall see in chapter 12). One can pray for parishioners, continue to learn and grow in order to become more competent, and manage special problems in the helping process.

8

Recurrent Risks in Pastoral Counseling

AUTHENTIC counseling is hard work. Each session the helper moves into the vortex of peoples' struggles, complexities, and aspirations. The word *session,* which I have used interchangeably with the word *interview,* is from the Latin *sessus,* meaning "to sit." It requires real effort to sit together, sharing emotion-laden experiences, and considering the ramifications of a person's life. Helping demands, not passivity, but active listening and responding to the facts and feelings at hand.

The prophet Ezekiel was described as sitting "for seven days" with exiled Israelites at the river Kebar. He was overwhelmed with their suffering and shame (Ezek. 3:15). Earlier, Jeremiah felt speechless when called to confront people for God: "I cannot speak, for I am a child." The Lord reassured him: "I put my words into your mouth. This day I give you authority over nations and over kingdoms, to pull down and to uproot, . . . to build and to plant" (Jer. 1:6–10, NEB). In caring for and confronting counselees one needs wisdom and power "to pull down and to uproot, . . . to build and to plant."

Gaining access to another person's life space is risky business. Just as the surgeon must know human anatomy and the craft of surgery, the pastor must understand the life processes of the spirit, and the craft of caring. A pastoral counselor has to negotiate certain risks when giving help. These involve authority, vulnerability, and integrity in pastoral practice.

RISKING ONE'S AUTHORITY

In helping other persons, a carer faces the subtle narcissism of wanting everyone else to become like oneself. This is a delusion that threatens all dependency relationships, including that between parent and child. Attempting to make one's counselees over into one's own image is both counterproductive and self-defeating. The counselee is not the only person who changes during the helping process. Counselors too undergo transformations during a shared pilgrimage. One must learn to manage authority and freedom when giving and accepting help.

MANAGING AUTHORITY AND FREEDOM

One night, after a minister in clinical pastoral education (CPE) had talked with an exserviceman in a Veteran's Administration psychiatric hospital, the patient hanged himself. Everyone assigned to the case—psychiatrist, social worker, minister, and vocational rehabilitation therapist—was shocked. The CPE intern felt that he had completely failed, and became depressed and fearful lest he lose another patient. He felt betrayed by his counselee, and feared the loss of whatever pastoral authority he had achieved.

Trusting the persons with whom we work and the process of counseling itself go hand in hand with trusting God. The helpee asks of his helper, in effect: "Will you stand by me no matter what?" That implies, "Even if I do not accept your God, profess faith in Christ, or behave as you prefer?" Autonomous persons must claim the gift of freedom—even the freedom to fail. Thus, from time to time, the counselor should ask himself: "Am I trusting the person, the process, as well as the heavenly Father? Can I grant the person freedom to choose personal goals, bless those choices, and stand with the individual no matter what?" Such risk taking moves the counselor along from amateur standing into the ranks of professional ministry.

Admittedly, some counselees and their families do not progress, even with intensive consultation. Some situations grow worse, not better. I know of a minister who helped a man's wife, but the husband declined therapy. The angry husband purchased a handgun and threatened to kill the counselor who had consulted with his wife. Law enforcement officials suggested that the minister "drop out of sight" for awhile until the man's family could reason with him or get him some psychiatric help.

The amateur wants success. He feels things must turn out right, even though he is not wise enough to feel empathetically all the hopes and sorrows of people. Still, the young minister brings vitality and radiance into caring conversations. You may be encouraged by what psychiatrist Robert S. Glen, of Dallas, once said: "There is something growing in human beings with which you can make an alliance." To achieve that alliance effectively and to see people "grow in grace," a counselor should ask: "Have I freed my counselees to be who they are and to become what they intend?" A helper's way may not be the only way to grow. One's motives in helping interrelate with authority and freedom in counseling.

FACING ONE'S NEED TO BE NEEDED

Ministers should be people who care. Yet, some persons are attracted to one of the healing arts—medicine, ministry, nursing, social work, or psychology—in a lifelong effort to find themselves. I once asked a clinical psychologist why he chose to work with psychiatric patients in a state mental hospital. "There is something in me," he replied, "that is getting help from being here." One's personal needs may take priority over a parishioner's concerns. One's need to be needed can sabotage therapeutic effectiveness. One's craving for clarity about his own compulsiveness, lack of love, or schizoid behavior might, unfortunately, thrust a person into the ministry.

Psychiatrist James O. Malone, who is a consultant in a pastoral care center in Fort Worth, Texas, commented on the healthy side of meeting one's needs in a counseling capacity. "Each time we see a person and, later, reflect on that experience, we learn something about life and ourselves." That kind of learning opportunity clears the air of emotional germs for persons heavily engaged in therapeutic activity. Many health care professionals remain in some level of therapy all of their lives. I am talking not about growth while handling confused, disordered lives, but the resistance to growth that characterizes some would-be counselors.

Does that mean that a counselor must be totally healthy, almost superhuman? Not exactly. God's servants get discouraged, exhausted, impatient, even resentful of the many demands on their time. Helpers need reassurance, too. New York cotherapists Mildred Newman and Bernard Berkowitz state: "It's all right to be immature at times; people who are totally adult are a little intimidating."[1] Counselors should be in touch with both their gifts and limitations. Some aspiring helpers use counselees to satisfy their own ego or erotic needs. Personal psychotherapy should be sought if intrapsychic conflict prevents effective caring for persons. The responsible counselor will refer to another someone he is blocking on, rather than tarnish a life with inadequate skills or endanger a helpee with motives that are suspect.

The counselor's authority is also related to gifts accepted or declined. One's offer to bless may be rebuffed or rejected completely by certain counselees.

THE POWER TO BLESS AND CURSE

A counselor ideally brings blessing, power, and potency to counselees. One speaks a healing, renewing Word from God. Myron Madden, chaplain of the Southern Baptist Hospital in New Orleans, describes pastoral blessing as "the power to beget—renewal of life—growing through acceptance."[2] A less healthy, unconscious process would involve the helper trying to heal others while himself remaining under life's curse. Here, I use curse in the sense of psychic bondage, alienation, shame, coldness, insecurity, and feeling unloved or unlovable.

Who, then, can be a helper? Don't all of us feel the emptiness of missed blessings? Doesn't each of us know the secret sadness of sin? Given the power to bless, how can counselors be sure that people will accept their pastoral blessings?

Those questions may be answered by four positive responses:

1. *In order to counsel effectively a person needs release from childhood bondages.* Most adults carry both pain and inner strength from childhood. Psychiatrist Hugh Missildine was correct: "The child of the past actually continues, with all his feelings and his attitudes, to the very end of our lives."[3] Counselors should have negotiated childhood's developmental tasks, which, according to Erik Erikson, include trust, autonomy, initiative, and a sense of accomplishment. One hung up on distrust from childhood, for example, cannot invest confidence in others or in the counseling process.

2. *Counselors need to feel secure despite their imperfections.* No one's past is perfect; neither is it fatally flawed. The Christian pastor's strength is based not on skill or self-confidence, ultimately, but on a

promise of sufficient grace from God (2 Cor. 12:9). One learns what Robert E. Neale calls *The Art of Dying,* letting go of life while discovering the power of Christian resurrection. Strengthened in the "fellowship of Christ's sufferings," one has a gift to offer people who sit in darkness (Phil. 3:10).

3. *Counselors must believe in what they are doing.* Working with wounded spirits, weak wills, wayward rebels, and willful delinquents is far too arduous a task for those who remain unconvinced of counseling's worth. If one does not believe in oneself and one's calling, it is difficult to establish trust. Self-confidence carries with it the courage to confront manipulativeness, to stand against dependency, and to set limits on actions. Pastoral care must be both tough and tender. Alan Keith-Lucas warns that "the attempt to keep the relationship on a pleasant level is one of the greatest sources of ineffectual helping."[4] Self-confidence need not be the enemy of warmth or closeness. Pastoral authority searches for truth and exerts administrative control in a counseling situation.

4. *With God's help and that of a skilled therapist, a pastor can turn the curse character of his past into tools of ministry for the present.* Many ministers I know have suffered abandonment by a father, economic or emotional deprivation, manipulation by an insecure mother, critical losses by death, or scars of social injustice. With help they have refashioned a sense of the tragic into pastoral sensitivity to bear on private and public concerns. They are better counselors because of personal victories won over suffering.

The pastor and a counselee may have contracted to work together toward a resolution of some nagging concern. Still, one's best efforts may be snubbed, prayers unanswered, blessings refused, and promises unheeded. Such risks compel one to work as a professing professional person.

RISKING ONE'S AUTHORITY AS A PROFESSING PROFESSIONAL PERSON

The term "professing professional" was coined by Wayne E. Oates in a lectureship at the Lutheran Theological Seminary, Gettysburg, Pennsylvania. Since it embodies the notion of preparedness, with commitment to the Christian faith, let us examine the competencies it suggests. Oates used the word *professing* to mean a "continuing, open admission, acknowledgment, and confession of one's calling as a minister."[5] His advocacy of a principled person in pastoral care, versus one wedded to programmed procedures (rules alone), rested on the prior work of James Glasse in *Profession: Minister* and that of Seward Hiltner.

Glasse, president of Lancaster Seminary, suggested that viewing the ministry as a profession is related to the minister's expertise in a field of knowledge, not merely to following certain ideas. The professional minister, he emphasized, focuses on both information and skills appropriate to his work. The minister professes to be an expert in leading God's flock, interpreting God's Word, celebrating services of worship, and caring for souls.

While Hiltner's remarks were addressed to professional planners, his criteria fit the ministry. He says that the true professional person acts representatively of all members of his group, provides a service, accepts the limitations of personal competence, and functions according to principles rather than following rules of thumb.[6] Hiltner's approach separates the competent counselor from the trial and error, semiskilled counselor.

Based on that background, Oates describes some basic principles for functioning professionally as a minister. These would spare the pastor from functioning as a solution-giver, and could open the way for his role in encouraging a mutual pilgrimage with parishioners. He elaborates on some basic notions: inspecting carefully each individual's situation, forming durable relationships with one's people, providing administrative structure and control in caring situations, being emotionally sensitive, holding a process view of human development, distributing responsibility throughout one's church and community, and precise recording and evaluation of one's counseling contacts. These principles, found in *New Dimensions in Pastoral Care*, are not electives, but requirements for responsible counselors.

While only about one thousand of the hundreds of thousands of ministers, priests, and rabbis in the United States participate in the American Association of Pastoral Counselors (AAPC), that organization's standards address the issue of professional competence.[7] The AAPC was organized to advance the education, test the competency, and guard the credibility of counseling clergypersons. The AAPC *Manual* suggests some ideal educational objectives.[8] Basic requirements for members include college, theological education, and three years of pastoral work in a recognized denominational group. Basic CPE, plus 125 to 400 hours of interdisciplinary supervision of one's professional counseling, is required (according to the level of certification sought). Prospective counselors must be skilled not only in understanding and dealing with the psychological dimensions of personality, but they must be devoted to a religious community and know the history and theology of pastoral care.

One of the most significant areas of preparation suggested by this group is the counselor's ethical responsibility. Each applicant must be identified as a pastoral counselor, clarify fee-taking policies, and manifest awareness of the dangers of exploiting counselees. There is always the danger of developing a "priesthood within a priesthood" in such professional organizations. Carroll A. Wise, one of AAPC's founders, has said: "Part of the identity conflict of many pastoral counselors grows out of the failure of the . . . church to present a clear and acceptable identity to them. So, like orphans, they have [had] to forge a kind of private identity. . . ."9 Such a situation can be remedied, in part, by greater acceptance and integration of counseling as a service of the church.

Continuing education, while one serves in ministry, is available through theological schools, professional consultation, peer-group supervision, self-supervision, reading new books and journals, cassettes of taped information, and sabbatical leave for study. Pastoral care for pastors and their spouses is available through ministers' counseling services, provided by various denominations throughout the country. We turn now to some special problems involved in risking one's vulnerability.

RISKING ONE'S VULNERABILITY

TOUCHING AND INTIMACY

James B. Ashbrook, in *Responding to Human Pain*, details his relationship with a young woman, called Rhonda, at the University of Rochester Counseling Center. They had explored intimate experiences from her past, and she had sought to put several pieces of life's puzzle together. Toward the close of one session, after a Gestalt experiment of imagining herself sitting before a fire with someone she loved, Rhonda and her counselor embraced. Ashbrook defended the gesture of tenderness and warmth, shared with his counselee, by explaining that the session took place in a room with a one-way window. They were observed throughout each session by a group of students. He explained that their special space assumed crucial significance, since it "served to protect us from uncontrollable emotion. There [Rhonda faced] what she feared, yet felt shielded from its consequence."[10] In such situations, the pastoral role tends to promote intimacy, even physical closeness, but the risks of sharing private space are high.

Some psychiatrists feel that touching is taboo. It is too sex-laden, too potent, too perilous, sometimes leading to sexual gratification for both partners. Such indiscretions with a counselee are not only at variance with biblical and social standards, but they tend to destroy a minister professionally.[11] The Scriptures speak of a "time to embrace, and a time to refrain from embracing" (Eccles. 3:5). What does that mean with respect to pastoral intimacy with counselees? One must answer for oneself.

Much of a minister's work is on the boundary of human intimacy. One dealing with the secrets of others' souls is admitted to private, inner space only with permission. Such closeness is permitted, most often, when an individual seeks acceptance as a human being or spiritual blessing as God's person. To seek closeness without the counselee's permission violates both good social taste and professional ethics. Familiarity, forced by a counselor's curiosity or sought for one's own pleasure, generates bad feelings and is not true intimacy.

What about touching or embracing a counselee during or following a conversation? Myron Madden relates meaningful pastoral intimacy to the ancient rite of family blessing, transferring potency or life-generating power from father to son. While there is a "no sex" contract in true pastoral intimacy, "in the modern concept of blessing, one person gets close enough to another so as to affirm that person."[12] There are many levels of touching—from a simple handshake to a nuptial embrace after marriage. Physical closeness should not be confused with blessing and support of another person. Pastoral intimacy offers warmth and positive validation, while avoiding the risks of both sexual relationship and social rejection.

Vulnerability raises three additional relationship problems common in counseling.[13] Transference, countertransference, and resistance are unconscious dynamisms at work in human relationships. They are unavoidable in pastoral counseling. Each of these processes implies positive or negative psychic energy, which is projected on others—love objects, authority figures, and so on.

Rollo May and his associates Angel and Ellenberger wrote, in *Existence*, of a person who perceives his "therapist through the same restricted, distorted 'spectacles' as he perceived father or mother."[14] The term *transference* is generally understood as the projection of feelings out of one's past relationships onto significant persons in the present. Transference helps reveal a counselee's psychic world in miniature to the pastor. Feelings like love, hate, ambivalence, or dependence—evident in one's emotional ties with parent figures—are transferred to the counselor. Such projections may be simple and pleasant, or they may be complex and sticky. Transference may be positive during one part of a session and negative before the hour closes.

A counselor manages transference with the counselee by working from unknown motivations to awareness and integrated understanding of one's behavior. Frieda Fromm-Reichmann tells, for example, the experience of a woman who discovered in counseling that she related to her parents, psychiatrist, and lovers in the same unhappy way. This woman reflected a division between hero-worship and submissiveness, on one hand, and a marked attitude of superiority on the other.[15] Through therapy, she recalled the dissociated childhood experiences responsible for the development of this pattern. This intellectual awareness had to be worked through and incorporated into her relationships, before her basic conflicted pattern could change. A wise pastoral counselor will use transference to facilitate growth, without becoming trapped in reciprocal countertransference.

Countertransference implies the counselor's conscious and unconscious responses to a counselee's real or imagined attitudes and behavior. Brammer and Shostrom wrote in *Therapeutic Psychology* that the "counselor must have insight into his own immaturities, prejudices, objects of disgust, anxieties, and punitive tendencies; no counselor is free of these feelings."[16] Unless counselors are aware of their own emotions, responses to a counselee's attitudes or actions will be unduly influenced by personal needs.

How do these feelings show up, and how does the pastor handle them? Once, a counselee—a registered nurse who had been coming for interviews directly from work, dressed in her white uniform—showed up a bit late in a lovely party dress. Her counselor noted a hint of delicate perfume, her erotic body language, and her positive emotions toward him. He decided to work through the transference feelings in order to prevent a sticky situation from developing. He deliberately piqued her emotions with a comment.

REV. BAXTER: I have a feeling that you don't like me for some reason.

MS. SNOW: On the contrary, you've come to mean a lot to me these past few weeks, Rev. Baxter.

REV. BAXTER: How do you account for that?

MS. SNOW: I'm not sure. I just know that I look forward to Friday afternoons with you, when I get off from work [*pause*]. I think you've helped me a lot. . . . You know more about me than anyone in this world, even my parents. My mother would drop dead if she knew some of the things I've done.

REV. BAXTER: What do you think is happening now?

MS. SNOW: What do you mean . . . happening now? You mean, in my life or right now, here with you?

REV. BAXTER: The latter. Can you say what you're feeling now?

MS. SNOW: Well [*a bit uncomfortable now*], ah . . . I was feeling great until you asked. Now, I'm not so sure [*pause*]. I'm finding it harder to talk to you.

REV. BAXTER: Do you feel that I am making it harder for you?

MS. SNOW: Well, yes, maybe; I'm not sure. You just sitting there looking at me kinda bothers me.

REV. BAXTER: When you think of me as a man, are you getting me mixed up with someone you've felt warmly toward in the past?

MS. SNOW: [*Slowly*] I guess that's true.

From Rev. Baxter's approach, we can learn several practical lessons. *Simple acceptance* permits the counselee to share her positive or negative emotions. The nurse recognized that her warm feelings were indeed hers; they did not reside in the counselor. Rev. Baxter asked certain clarifying questions, such as, "Can you say what you're experiencing now?" This permitted his counselee to interpret what was happening. He focused on what her feelings were rather than the reasons behind them. The *what* aspects of transference should always be explored before *why* aspects.

The main goal of transference interpretation is to clarify any connection between a person's past relationships and present feelings and behavior. There is a risk in calling attention to projected feelings. It generally causes the counselee to relate in the opposite manner. Therefore, the counselor should delay bringing transference matters into the conversation unless emotions are interfering with growth or healing. Because of their complexity, transference and countertransference can give an inexperienced counselor great difficulty. Consultation can help one deal more assuredly with such phenomena.

RESISTANCE

Resistance is an unconscious process by which the counselee's ambivalent attitudes toward counseling are dramatized. Like transference, resistance may work negatively or positively in counseling. Resistance may show up in a number of ways: being late for appointments; canceling sessions at the last minute; being pessimistic about the counselor's ability or the process itself; forgetting fee payment (if one is charged); refusing to work, by silence or by introducing irrelevant subjects into the sessions; and making unrealistic demands on a caring person. Resistance may also take less negative forms: clowning or facetiousness; prolonging a dependency transference, blocking progress; pressing for overtime in every session; calling the counselor at home; trying to seduce the counselor; and expressing strong interest in the counselor's personal life.

The experienced counselor recognizes resistance and deals appropriately with it. One can handle resistance by detecting its origins and intensity. If the symptoms are minor the counselor might disregard them and concentrate on the person's need for emotional security. He might lessen the emotional intensity of a session with a change of pace, by shifting the level of discourse, or with the judicious use of humor. Direct confrontation may be required when intensive resistance is encountered.

Thus far, we have examined several procedures and pitfalls in counseling: managing authority and freedom in the growth process, questionable motivation in therapeutic endeavors, improper personal and clinical preparation for counseling, and four special relationship problems. Recognizing such risks in advance provides the opportunity to concentrate on pastoral skills and sensitivity. One risks not only authority and vulnerability in counseling, but integrity as well.

RISKING ONE'S INTEGRITY

A minister naturally likes to achieve success in counseling. The amateur, with little experience to build on, finds that positive feedback from counselees is one of the most satisfying feelings in the world. Experienced counselors have learned valuable lessons along the way, among them that they must work hard to avoid errors. Still, some events arise that distort the counseling process. One risks integrity, for example, through the management of silence, confidentiality in communication, and wise use of time.

THE MANAGEMENT OF SILENCE

Some people do not know what to say to a counselor. They have never before been so hurt, confused, or on-the-spot, and do not know what to expect from counseling. How do you get over the clumsiness of getting an interview started? Perhaps the best way to begin, at least after an initial intake interview, is to inquire about what has been happening in the person's life since the last visit. This open-ended approach permits the person to move about with freedom. There may be a thread of continuity with the previous visit, an assignment to report on, or the counselee may start on a new slant.

Some counselees are too embarrassed to share a secret part of their life history with a minister. They may fear betrayal. So they may pause, change positions in the chair, divert their eyes out a window or toward a picture, cry, or lean forward with head in hands. If they seem uncomfortable, they should not be forced to continue the story or to share more than they intend to reveal. Their body language itself speaks volumes.[17]

One's emotional state makes a difference in verbal quality. Anger, discouragement, tiredness, strain, depression, or a combination of such factors inhibit thought processes. Grief slows a person down. Some individuals reach an emotional point when their voices break, tears flood the eyes, and they appear overwhelmed, as if saying, "Give me a few moments alone, please." Silence, not speech or reassurance, is what they need at such moments.

A counselor who becomes impatient with sluggish sessions should appreciate that silence serves as a plateau, a resting place. It may give an individual time for gathering insight and strength to proceed, not just with one's story but with life itself. A pastor may make good diagnostic use of silence to detect what is going on. The counselor can pray when the very silence of God is deafening. The Christian shepherd pauses with a weary sojourner and leads on according to the person's pace. One might later return to the issue, and make therapeutic progress from the episode.

CONCERN FOR CONFIDENTIALITY

In pastoral care training centers, the confidential nature of counseling services is discussed with each client. Release forms are signed by each interviewee for any records to be kept—written, taped cassettes, or videotape recording. Records are used for purposes of supervision, education, and research. Policies are fully explained and an agreement is reached.

Pastors in local church settings would do well not to tape-record counseling sessions without the explicit permission of counselees. Legal difficulties or an air of distrust might arise if hidden tapes were made of pastoral conversations. Certain records can be subpoenaed, though "privileged communication" laws protect private confessions made to clergymen in many states.[18] Written records should be kept in locked files and indexed so that unauthorized persons will not have access to them.

In order to assure confidentiality, determine with the counselee any other parties who know of the situation and may be involved at some level. Use great caution in the matter of sermon illustrations; do not betray confidences from the pulpit. Assure the individual or family of confidence. Obtain the person's permission prior to releasing any information to consultants. This is where ministers seldom live up to their good intentions. An inquisitive pastor's spouse or curious congregant may probe for data, and later leak information. A town gossip may slander an individual's or a family's character by betrayal of confidences.

Charles F. Kemp suggests that when people are out of touch with reality, permission should be gained from their families to consult with health care professionals.[19] Further, when dealing with minors who become seriously ill, one should consult family physicians and parents, without disclosing confidential details of any problem. When counseling violators of the law, criminals fleeing justice, or prisoners presenting new information in court, a minister should work with the individual and his attorney. In some cases, an individual may turn state's witness and become a "friend of the court" or enter into a plea bargaining arrangement with justice officials.* Such individuals need help but not betrayal at a minister's hands.

TIME MANAGEMENT

Some psychiatrists work on a fifty-minute "hour." That is, they interview patients briefly, dictate impressions and prescriptions to a medical records secretary, and see numerous patients each day. Many pastoral counselors function on a fifty-minute "hour," though there is nothing sacred about this length of time. Experience has shown, however, that after about an hour, a person's words become repetitive, and both helper and helpee become tired. Some counselees hold out until the hour's end, then spring something special or new on the counselor. This is usually a manipulative maneuver, and should be dealt with if the pattern continues.

Life's stresses and strains cannot all be alleviated in one session, though we should never underestimate the value of one conversation. If it has taken a family thirty-five years to "get into this mess," it will not evaporate in thirty-five minutes. True, we can believe in miracles; God can do anything. So often in counseling, however, his gracious help comes in months not minutes. If more time is needed, schedule additional appointments rather than trying to work all day or all night with one individual or family. A pastor comes to resent a manipulative person who monopolizes his private schedule.

It takes time to develop a soul. If additional time is needed, within reasonable limits, perhaps it can be arranged. One's appointment schedule will affect that decision. Should it be more convenient for both parties to reschedule additional time later, that is easily done. God's spirit will continue to work with people between appointments. Surprising bursts of growth can occur in the week's 168 hours, until the next interview. Time is of great value in a professional person's life. To order time is to gain some mastery over it. That, itself, is healing for everyone

* *Plea bargaining* is pleading guilty to a lesser charge in order to avoid standing trial for a more serious one.

concerned and is an added mark of professional competence.

Much work remains to be done in the area of procedural problems and risks in counseling. This discussion is indicative, though not exhaustive, of possibilities for further research. I turn now from consideration of needs and procedures in counseling to a final section on how promise works in various situations of need. The next focus is on microcounseling in crisis situations.

III

COUNSELING AS PROMISE
IN PARTICULAR CIRCUMSTANCES

9

Microcounseling
in Crisis Situations

THIS book has focused on counseling as a revelatory encounter within the framework of God's saving purpose for mankind. Counselors have been viewed as persons of promise—representing the Creator's care in each stage of human development, decision making, problem solving, and spiritual growth. The issues raised in counseling are broad human concerns related in the Scriptures and recognized in life: creation and accountability, bondage and freedom, isolation and community, covenant and disobedience, forgiveness and renewal, passivity and initiative, anxiety and compassion, sexual repression and fulfillment in family commitment, and despair and hope.

Interestingly, the Bible does not sidestep human predicaments, stressors, anxiety states, developmental concerns, precipitating events, and situational crises. The history of Israel and the development of the Church were often stained by sin, darkened by doubt, and threatened by unlikely persons and events. Claiming the Promised Land, for example, was not a series of simple, steady, forward steps for Israel under Moses leadership.

In Deuteronomy, Moses reviewed Israel's previous history in light of God's commands and blessings. He retraced their steps after escaping Egypt and crossing the Red Sea: "And we came to Kadesh-Barnea" (Deut. 1:19). What a crisis that accomplishment provoked! Since God's people refused the generally good report of their twelve tribal representatives and murmured against their leaders, Israel was rerouted into the wilderness for forty years. None of the rebels who resisted God's promise were admitted into the land beyond Jordan.

Moses learned a lasting lesson from the Kadesh-Barnea crisis, not only for Israel, but for everyone. He recognized that promises can be perverted, not only when they are taken too lightly but also when they are interpreted too rigidly. The Amorite enemies in the land appeared too foreboding; the omen of giants portended evil days ahead. Israel wanted divine care without any responsibilities; but God expected complete and autonomous obedience. Israel's perception of Moses' assignment caused them to shrink back in disobedience, to face military disaster, and to falter forty years on the edge of the place God had prepared for them.

Crises come to nations, to worthy causes, to forgotten minorities, to sacred places, and to members of families. I want to direct attention now to the concept of microcounseling in crisis situations, which is here equated with intervention.

THE SHAPE OF HUMAN CRISIS

It is one thing for an academician to explore theoretical aspects of stress and anguish. It is quite another to practice on the "firing line" with hurting people every day. The Christian pastor and his wife are vulnerable to calls for help on a twenty-four-hour basis. Such vulnerability has also been my experience while serving interim ministries in churches.

Consider the following incident. I received a phone call about 11:30 P.M. one Sunday night from someone I had not seen in many years.

"This is Joe Cardwell," explained a man's voice. I shook off sleep and listened. "Our married daughter, Ann, who is thirty-three now, is upset and crying. She's over at our place and has left her husband and children. She doesn't know exactly what's wrong. They've had a fuss. Ann is almost hysterical" [*Pause*]. "What do you suggest we do?"

Having been asleep nearly an hour, I had to double-check the accuracy of what I was hearing. It had been years since I had seen Mr. Cardwell. Though I remembered him, Ann and her family were strangers to me. There was no way of knowing her spiritual-emotional condition. A decision was required in light of the precipitating event; no long case history was available.

I suggested that if Ann could not be comforted (i.e., if she had lost control of her emotions and appeared in an uncontrollable hysterical state) they should take her to the emergency room of a nearby hospital. There she could receive a medical appraisal, sedating medication if needed, and protective care so that she would not harm herself. This was the strategy they chose to follow. In a short time, following this crisis intervention, Ann recovered her equilibrium and returned to her husband and children.

The shape of human crisis is as varied as the complex situations that thrust themselves into peoples' lives. Imagine, for example, a normal couple facing the early weeks of pregnancy when, precipitously, the wife miscarries. We can assume that they have sent news of the coming event to family members and intimate friends near and far. A wave of anticipation runs through their home planning, budgeting, sex relationships, purchases, and so on. Suddenly, while driving down what appeared as a straight stretch of life's highway, the young parents-to-be found themselves cliff-hanging. Their dreams collapsed as a lump of protoplasm was discharged from the young woman's body. Their joy turned into grief, requiring the supportive aid of family, physician, and a community of faith. The depth of crisis experienced by such persons depends on various factors: the nature of their emotional security, spiritual strength, physical health, support community, and possibility of altering the stressful situation.

A crisis may be thought of as a decisive time—a turning point in life, an illness, a period of history, a battle, and so on. Webster indicates that the word *crisis* comes from the Greek *krisis*, meaning "decision." It relates to illness and health. By definition, a crisis is the turning point for better or worse in an acute disease; a time of pain, distress, or disordered function; an emotionally significant event or radical change of status in a person's life; or an unstable time or state of affairs whose outcome will make a decisive difference for better or worse. A crisis thus has potential for regression or renewal, for withdrawal into crippling anxiety or growth in self-esteem and security.

The nature of human crisis forces us to look seriously at the ambiguous feelings and possible actions of persons under stress. Those studying suicide, like Edwin Schneidman and Norman Farberow, have alerted us to the "cry for help" and potential for self-destructiveness of persons facing seemingly insolvable crises.[1]

Joe Hinkle, for example, was an auto assembly plant employee with twenty-six years' experience and four years left until retirement. At fifty-one, Hinkle was injured in an industrial accident and forced to retire, with disability insurance, at a greatly reduced income. He had obligated himself to make large semiannual payments on some rural land and cattle, purchased in anticipation of his retirement years. In an effort to generate income, Hinkle sought to buy and sell cattle. But his company threatened to cut off his disability payments if his income increased from outside sources. Payments on his cattle, land, and farm equipment were coming due. Painted into an economic corner, threatened with the loss of his future security, as well as his failing health, Joe Hinkle shot and killed himself. His wife subsequently declared bankruptcy and lost almost everything that Joe had purchased.

It is because of the torments of people in crisis and their potential for self-destructive acts that some form of intervention is indicated. I view such help as microcounseling, that is, helping persons briefly, on a small scale.

ALTERNATIVE RESPONSES TO CRISIS SITUATIONS

When someone's life has been hurt by some social, organic, or psychological upset, there are several alternative responses open to counselors. They span the range from indifference to intervention.

INDIFFERENCE

Indifference implies, "I'm sorry, but there is nothing to be done for you." The Bible warns against responding indifferently, and says in James 2:15–16: "If a brother or sister is ill-clad and in lack of daily food, and one of you says to them, 'Go in peace, be warmed and filled,' without giving them the things needed for the body, what does it profit?" Ideally, faith's profession must be turned into action.

A woman in her early seventies was called on, along with her two sisters, to care for their ill, invalid, ninety-year-old mother. The woman was at the end of her rope after months of sleep loss; traveling miles to and from her mother's home, a hospital, and a convalescent center; and emotional and physical exhaustion. In fact, she said, only a knot in the rope's end had prevented her from slipping and falling to destruction.

Hearing her cry, a friend who lived almost three thousand miles away —a semiretired social worker—traveled to the mother's home and helped in a loving, practical way with the elderly woman for about three months. This response, in a time of crisis, was far beyond the social worker's usual role. Her aid was precisely the intervening action that was needed to save the woman trapped with the confining care of her aged mother.

INSTANT REFERRAL

A second possible response to any of the above incidents—hysteric housewife, miscarriage, industrial accident, and aging parent's care—is to send people away from the church. "Instant referral" implies that no appraisal is made of an individual's life situation. One trained, for instance, in preaching or teaching, might send a crisis victim out the door and down the street. Without adequate time to tell one's story, and without enough communication for referral to the proper agency, a person could interpret this as a rejection or grudging assistance at best.

Dependency is a key characteristic of a person or family overwhelmed by a tough situation. Like a traveler in a foreign land—who knows neither the language, the customs, the geography, nor the exchange rate—one swept up in a crisis becomes dependent. It is possible to use that dependency as a vehicle for helping persons through intervention, microcounseling, or rapid referral.

SCHEDULING CONCERNS

Many counselors refuse to see persons on a walk-in basis; long-term counseling, by appointment, for a fee may be the only treatment offered. Such talk-oriented, therapeutic approaches have roots in psychoanalytic theory (free association, dream interpretation, and analysis of transference phenomena). The goal is not merely alleviation of specific psychological symptoms, but alteration of the disturbed person's personality.

Pastoral counseling may be multiple-interview, long-term, insight therapy, patterned on the early approaches of Carl Rogers. As an adjunct, in cooperation with a physician, drug therapy may be used in selected cases. If one avoids talking briefly with counselees about such precipitating events as marital infidelity, accident and injury, job loss, fear of cancer, and so on, crisis intervention is jeopardized. There are therapists who ignore surface causes, and push deeper for intrapsychic sources of difficulty. It is counterproductive in crisis work to force persons to schedule concerns by appointment, in every instance, and to follow a depth psychotherapy model in all cases.

ENVIRONMENTAL MANIPULATION

Some crisis situations may be altered by simply modifying the person's environment. That would not be true following a diagnosis of cancer or some other terminal disease. Yet, modifying elements that may contribute to a crisis can alleviate the stress, and provide a way out of trouble.

There is, for instance, an obese, thirty-nine-year-old woman with three children, the youngest of whom is seven. Mrs. Maxine Stuart was diagnosed as having a heart problem by her cardiologist, who later learned that his patient lived in a three-story house.

"Every time I'm in the basement doing laundry," she explained, "I think of some other clothes which need washing and must go up two flights of stairs to get the boys' things." Being about fifty pounds overweight, negotiating the multileveled house, having young children, plus facing the pressures of her husband's government-related job all contributed to Mrs. Stuart's coronary problems. Her physician suggested environmental manipulation to remove at least two stressors: a diet for weight loss, and a one-level residence to avoid excessive exertion. Rather than insisting that his patient undergo psychotherapy, the cardiologist met her crisis head-on. Discernible differences can be produced by confronting and intervening in such stressful situations.

MICROCOUNSELING THROUGH CRISIS INTERVENTION

Webster's defines *micro* as "small, short," from the Greek *mikros* or *smikros*. There are many instances in pastoral work where short-term counseling and crisis intervention are preferable. Such aid may be termed microcounseling.

Many crises, though disruptive, are self-limiting, lasting only a brief period of time. Although there is a hazard of depression, there is much potential for growth while a crucial issue is being faced. A time of turbulence is a transitional period, with both the danger of increased spiritual-psychological vulnerability and the opportunity for personal growth. The goal in crisis intervention is improvement of personal functioning even above the precrisis level.

Crisis intervention grew out of the initial work of psychiatrist Erich Lindemann, in Boston, following the disastrous Coconut Grove fire in 1944.[2] Trained in the disease model of professional psychotherapy, with its assumption of defective personality structure and functioning, Lindemann found the survivors of the Coconut Grove tragedy generally healthy, yet numb with shock, grief, and loss. With the passing of time most individuals facing bereavement regained equilibrium. They required active support during the period they worked through their grief. Some persons, however, veered off reality's course and required extensive psychotherapy.

Lindemann concluded that persons under stress may temporarily succumb to finite and idiosyncratic limitations. Such a state of crisis does not represent an illness, but a need. Supplementing personal resources with microcounseling, plus the passing of time, was sufficient in most cases to restore equilibrium. Helpers were interventionists, not therapists, offering empathy, warmth, and support to the victims' relatives.

Gerald Caplan, who worked subsequently in Boston's community mental health center program, made similar discoveries.[3] These centers were established for primary prevention and early treatment purposes. Caplan and Lindemann became the chief theoreticians for crisis-intervention counseling.[4] They observed that individuals facing similar negative events, like death and grief, react differently. Not everyone experiences a crisis in response to stress or loss. The depth of a personal crisis depends on the time in a person's life when the event occurs, intensity of the experience, as well as the availability of a support community.

What shall be the Christian counselor's response when crises come: indifference, instant referral, scheduling long-term therapy, environmental manipulation, or microcounseling through intervention? Though the response depends on the situation, hopefully it will not be indifference. Each individual requires a specific approach—crisis intervention, environmental change, mobilizing a support community, psychotherapy, or even hospitalization.

MICROCOUNSELING: A CONCEPTUAL MODEL

In pastoral counseling, many personal contacts are made with only one or a few visits or phone calls, or a single screening interview for evaluation and referral. Role induction into a long-term therapeutic relationship is either not achieved or unnecessary. The typical pastor rarely counsels persons for more than five or six weekly, one-hour sessions. Professor David K. Switzer reported that in one fifteen-month period, as a counseling specialist on a church staff, he saw only 15 out of 154 different counselees, for more than six sessions.[5] In Pasadena, California, psychiatrist Warren L. Jones has trained mental health center volunteers in a simple A-B-C method of crisis management. His three-step model provides a useful frame of reference:

A. Achieve contact with the client.
B. Boil down [focus] the problem to its essentials.
C. Help the person cope through an inventory of his own resources and supportive network of family and friends.[6]

Through repeated case presentations, volunteers learn to apply this three-step procedure under varying circumstances.

OCCASIONS FOR MICROCOUNSELING

Assistance provided to panicked persons by volunteers in suicide prevention centers has encouraged care-givers to train for crisis counseling in the church.[7] In addition, there are various programs calling for microcounseling for drug and alcohol abuse, divorce and grief work, and rehabilitation following psychiatric illness or parole from prison. Some centers function as all-purpose agencies for telephone "hot line" calls and walk-in clients, and are staffed by well-trained volunteers.

But how does microcounseling work in a church setting? Part of the pastor's task is to stabilize his church fellowship during turbulent times, like the period following an accident in which several young people or members of a single family are killed.

A pastor recalled a multiple funeral service for five members of a family killed in a private plane crash. "Bill Leverett was our church treasurer. Libby was a key leader with our women. The young people loved their kids. It took months for healing of memories of those five caskets at the front of the sanctuary. We never really replaced that family." Sermons on divine providence and the mystery of suffering, and numerous conversations with congregants, where issues could not be dodged or addressed vaguely, were needed to work through the trauma of the Leveretts' deaths.

The experienced pastor knows that, just as one bad apple spoils the entire barrelful, so a deeply disturbed individual can create generalized chaos in a congregation. That is certainly true of a schizophrenic person, whose anxious, sometimes hostile, attitudes hurt family members and social associates. In such instances, the pastor should counsel immediately with parishioners, and seek appropriate help for the deeply disturbed member. Psychic suffering should be addressed, not avoided, in order to minimize hurt and prevent problems from mushrooming. Psychiatrist Charles W. Tow reminds ministers that many psychological symptoms are not necessarily of psychogenic origin, and that many organic illnesses can reflect symptoms of emotional disturbance. We should be alert to such "red flags" in parishioners' behavior. Counseling on a small scale and intervening to help follows the example of Jesus Christ in healing (see Luke 7:21, 8:26–40, 13:13, 17:14, 22:51).

Some years ago, a minister visited with a family whose teenage son, Jamie Kerkoff, had been critically injured in a motorcycle accident. The parents and their daughter were notified that Jamie had been taken to a medical center emergency room. When the minister arrived, Jamie was in surgery. The doctors said that he had massive brain damage and had little chance to live. The counselor's contact with the Kerkoffs was established early. Their feelings were mixed: guilt for having given in to the boy's request for a motorcycle, grief that he was now near death, relief that he was in excellent medical hands, and anxious hope that Jamie might live.

A sickness model—treating their feelings as if they were unhealthy, requiring psychotherapy—was not applicable to the Kerkoffs. Their feelings were ambivalent, idealistic, terrified, and strong. Their son was no longer in their control; he was in the hands of God and the neurosurgeons. They needed to cope with what life had brought their way, including the possibility of Jamie's death.

Pastoral strategy with the Kerkoffs included befriending, listening, praying, and supporting their Christian hope. The goal was to restore functioning in a small family devastated by an accident and impending death. Equilibrium was unsteady. In such a situation, the pastor's role shifts from responder to pain, to analyst of anxiety, confidant of secrets of the spirit, father confessor of human guilt, companion in distress, comforter in grief, catalyst of faith, and clarifier of meaning within the divine providence. One collaborates as a Christian brother, not as a superior elitist. In cases like the Kerkoffs', a pastor shares his peoples' pain, hope, and anxious longings within a larger Christian fellowship. Such ministry is possible only because of God's eternal promise to care for his creation both in travail and tranquility (Rom. 8:22–28).

APPRAISAL IN MICROCOUNSELING

Part of the well-intentioned pastor's quandary is that his left hand does not always know what his right hand is doing in sharing stressful human events. Just getting an individual or couple out of one's office or off one's hands oversimplifies the crisis intervention process.

The first task is to determine whether or not a crisis actually exists. David Switzer poses three questions in *The Minister as Crisis Counselor,* and says that when the person seeking help can answer "yes" to all three questions a crisis exists: (1) Are the troublesome feelings or behavior recent (within the last few weeks)? (2) Have they tended to grow progressively worse? (3) Can the time of onset be linked with some external event or change in the person's life situation?[8] A "yes" response to all three calls for crisis intervention. The carer then evaluates how well the crisis victim is coping in light of his resources, creates realistic hopefulness, and assists in making decisions and building relationships.

Second, what kinds of crises are distinguishable in pastoral practice? The counselor must distinguish among various cries for help.

1. *Some cries for help emerge as one negotiates a passage from one developmental stage to another.* Erik Erikson's psychosocial stages of development have become part of our common lore.[9] Most readers are familiar with these hypothesized stages in the development of the human psyche, and with the conflicts that relate to each stage of growth. Erikson and his revisionists have taught us to observe the predictable crises of infancy, childhood, youth, and adulthood. A theologically based summary of this process was offered earlier by Lewis J. Sherrill in *The Struggle of the Soul,* and Shakespeare captured similar stages in Jacque's "all the world's a stage" speech in *As You Like It.*[10]

Interpreting the Eriksonian view that stages overlap and interpenetrate, his biographer Robert Coles has said: "We do not acquire trust and forever rid ourselves of mistrust or 'achieve' autonomy and thus spare ourselves continuing doubts and hesitations."[11] The primary tasks of each growth period, for instance, achievement of intimacy, are never fully completed and cast aside when the chronological age ends. Continual learning must be incorporated into a full, dynamic tapestry of personality development.

Oftentimes, people can function well when doing what they have grown accustomed to. Moving from one stage to another involves giving up the known for the unknown, with consequent adjustment to new, unpredictable situations. It is not easy to give up childhood for adolescence, youth for adulthood, or middle age to become an old person. Some people can be adolescents quite effectively, but have great difficulty becoming adults. Resistance to giving up one life stage and taking up new tasks can lead to transitional, developmental, intertemporal (between the times) crises.

2. *Some cries for help emerge during specific stages in life.* Stresses arise within childhood, adolescence, young adulthood, middle age, and old age. They may be viewed as maturational or intratemporal (within the times) crises. In Goethe's *Sorrow of a Young Werther* and Erikson's *Young Man Luther* one can see what adolescent crises are about.

Psychologist Daniel J. Levinson, of the Yale University School of Medicine, speaks of "marker events," which denote particular transitions or signal notable changes.[12] The mother whose last child, now six, begins school passes a marker event. Increased alcohol consumption or accident proneness by a depressed person, for example, clues family and associates to problems of coping within a given age period. Marker events are not always present, however, to signal the onset of a crisis.

Investigative reporter Gail Sheehy distinguishes maturational crises of adulthood: pulling up roots, entering the adult world, the age thirty transition, and the age forty crucible.[13] Maturational crises for adults include childbirth (particularly a troublesome pregnancy or birth of a defective child), placing a child in first grade, the high school graduation of one's last (or only) child, facing adolescent trials with a troublesome teenager, enduring adultery after discovering a mate's paramour, problems of aging, loss of health, divorce, death of a spouse or friend, and so on.

3. *Some cries for help are heard when trouble comes.* These may be thought of as situational crises. They occur without reference to a particular period in one's life. Such marker events may precipitate destructive or, at least, debilitating periods. Some crises come like combat fatigue in the midst of life, when illness strikes, a move is ordered by one's company, a promotion is accepted, a job is lost, an accident or

disease, like cancer, touches a loved one, someone we know attempts suicide, or a friend is divorced.

The feeling one experiences may be like stage fright, when anxiety forbids saying a word and fear erases memory of one's lines. The counselor's task is to reduce the intensity of the general anxiety. If there is no evident precipitating event, the counselor must help the counselee face raw anxiety until it subsides.

To label a crisis as developmental, maturational, or situational is not enough. The helper must determine whether or not a person's inner resources and supportive network are adequate. How serious is the person who talks of suicide? It is too risky to handle a suicide threat alone. It is wise to consult with a supervising psychiatrist in all such cases. The psychiatrist may wish to see and temporarily hospitalize a person whose anxieties could push him to self-destruction. Psychological appraisal requires recognition of specific characteristics of human crises.

CHARACTERISTICS OF CRISES IN MICROCOUNSELING

A major feature of crisis intervention work is the relatively fleeting nature of crises. A critical suicide threat may last only a few days. Grief work, in the experience of Lindemann and others, generally passed in the span of a year. Seasons of need will vary with the nature of the marker event, the force of the stressors, and the psychological strength of the individual. Befriending persons during trauma, normally an isolating experience, helping them back on their feet again, and making available a network of supportive friends are the counselor's most important functions.

A second characteristic of crises is that they are usually dyadic, involving two persons. A dyadic relationship implies that two persons— spouses, lovers, parent and child, or boss and employee—are affected by the same event or stress. "It follows that crisis intervention will not work as well as it might unless it involves the 'significant other,'—the other half of the dyad."[14] Seeing a couple or entire family may not be one's usual counseling procedure, but it is the best approach in crisis intervention. The social system that has sent the individual into a tailspin will send him back to the original problem unless it too is changed. An individual described by the person seeking help as the chief source of trouble, may turn out to be an auxiliary therapist. One must assess their dyadic interplay and involve other significant persons, as well as community agencies, in the helping process.

Three, ambiguity marks microcounseling situations, particularly suicidal crises, requiring helpers to work around a client's ambivalence. For those ingrained in the Hegelian logic of thesis, antithesis, and synthesis a crisis victim's lack of logic can be frustrating. A counselor will become aware of affection struggling with animosity, hope with despair, love with fear, and security with anxiety. An individual may seem to love and hate at the same time. A counselee may aspire toward autonomy and manifest dependency in the same conversation. "The paradigm of suicide is a person who cuts his throat and cries for help at the same time."[15] To ask such a sufferer to make up his mind makes no sense in his disordered psychic world. That is precisely the trouble; such people are of several minds at once. They wish both to be dead and to be rescued from death.

Ambiguity is not as evident in crises imposed by natural disasters, accidents, fires, plane crashes, and so on. Clearly, in such cases one wishes to live. People cry for help because they are psychologically impotent or spiritually powerless. The intervention indicated should be attuned to these unique characteristics and available early in crisis situations.

Thus far, I have examined the shape of human crises as they might appear in the day-to-day rounds of pastoral work. I have attempted to show how a crisis can be a significant turning point in life, and have considered alternative responses in stressful situations. A conceptual model of microcounseling has been proposed. It remains now to survey some practical implications of these ideas.

SOME PRACTICAL IMPLICATIONS

This discussion has been restricted to crucial situations in the personal realm. This chapter does not attempt to provide responses to social dilemmas of extremism; liberation for women, minorities, and homosexuals; new family styles; obstruction of justice in government; energy crises; environmental management; war; national budgetary control; hazards of inflation; and unemployment. These social issues do affect persons and thus merit serious attention by churchmen. Yet, they lie at the level of public policy and the political process, rather than in pastoral counseling.

Likewise, I have not alluded to controversial issues that might arise in the local church. The very nature of the gospel and its proclamation can generate controversies in some religious communities. Decisions regarding staff-member selection, buildings, budgets, outreach, and worship styles can provoke crises that require "all the king's horses and all the king's men" to resolve.[16] Issues of human sexuality, the role of women in the church, speaking in tongues, the place of evangelism, and use of electronic technology in music reproduction *could* explode into controversy. Such issues are real, but they are not the thrust of this presentation on counseling.

The microcounseling advocated here refers particularly to personal and family crises. What have we learned? First, a variety of individuals can do crisis intervention: senior ministers, staff members, paranurturers of the official church boards, and trained volunteers. Second, intervention should be practical, and relate directly to the nature of the crisis. Microcounseling includes listening and lending support, caring for persons while confronting problems, and avoiding overreactions to problems. A helper mobilizes significant others around a sufferer, and does practical things to alleviate the problem. This is quite different from role induction into long-term therapy. Third, the goal of microcounseling is not merely to reduce tension but to open new paths of action in a network of supportive associates. Some dependency needs, like those of welfare recipients, will be faced over and over again.

To conclude, most people can be helped, and many individuals have an opportunity to aid in crisis work. Youth can help other youth, former drug addicts can aid abusers, formerly married persons can assist new divorcees, and so on. Involving diverse people in mutual caring may threaten the authority of some ministers. But ultimately, it should help us all.

IO

Counseling for Marriage and Family Enrichment

NOTHING gives a Christian minister more joy than seeing family members grow in mutual commitment, competent citizenship, and concern for God's kingdom. Part of his privilege in working with a congregation is helping persons through various life situations: preparing for a lasting marriage, evolving husband-wife commitment, dealing with marital and family stress, or helping a formerly married person cope with being single again. Any minister who enjoys preaching feels drawn to the challenges of family living. His sermon themes—creation and accountability, human perversity and suffering, vocation and time, marital mutuality and negotiation, decision making and conflict resolution, loneliness and community, piety and power, faith and forgiveness, tragedy and hope—often reflect a family emphasis. When crises crush family members and hope falters, the concerned pastor is drawn into counseling conversations with them.

Few things concern a minister more than the weakening of family life in Western culture. Clergymen—along with physicians, attorneys, domestic court judges, law enforcement officials, therapists, and educators—are in a position to observe what is happening to families. We know that traditional marriage, while still preferred by a majority of Americans, is torn and fragmented. One survey revealed that 43 percent of American families reflected a new mentality.[1] The nontraditionalists surveyed considered religion and formal marriage as "not important," and stated that they were more self- than child-oriented. Life-styles of young people today differ widely from those of their parents. In the last decade, the number of Americans living together, without formal matrimony, has jumped from 286,000 to 1,300,000 couples. According to the U.S. Census Bureau, the divorce rate has climbed to more than one million a year. Homosexuals, now "out of the closet," seek legitimation of their alternative life-styles and full civil rights.

Everything from automobiles to health fads to travel is sold using sexually seductive advertising. While publishers of certain pornographic magazines have been accused of illegalities, sales of such magazines soar. Hugh Hefner's *Playboy* empire, begun on a $3,600 shoestring, is now valued at $200,000,000. Youth question and challenge a hypocritical moral code that holds that sex before marriage is taboo. They observe that the ideal of sex only within marriage has been endlessly violated.

Yet, there is an encouraging side to today's marital picture. Recent studies indicate that young people have a high regard for the idea of being married. Studies done for the Institute of Social Research at the University of Michigan show that marriage and family life are the most satisfying parts of most people's lives. Being married is one of the most important determinants of satisfaction with life. Eighty percent of Americans over age eighteen list "a happy home life" as their number one goal.[2] Although the family is changing, its cohesiveness remains a top American priority.

What seems to be happening is that young people are giving more thought to marriage. The women's movement has encouraged many women to enter and continue careers, and current economic instability has made it necessary for many women to enter the labor market. It is also more acceptable to be single and to remain unmarried longer than before. Another factor is that the spiraling divorce rate has made many persons think twice about the pain and heartache of a bad marriage. "Two of my closest friends have divorced since our trip to Europe last summer," observed a single schoolteacher. "I'd much rather remain single than face that kind of sorrow."

The current divorce rate may be reaching a peak because of recent social, economic, and legal changes in divorce. Many states have adopted some form of "no-fault" divorce laws. It has become easier for an unhappy couple to end a marriage than it was a few years ago. Because it is so common, less stigma is attached to being divorced. Also, nearly four-fifths of all formerly marrieds remarry.

Stress and distress may upset a family's equilibrium just as a crisis complicates an individual's state of mind. At such times marital partners and family members may become more sensitive to each other, open about needs, and accepting of outside assistance. At such times pastors are often sought for counsel. What wisdom should the counselor possess before assisting couples who need help? Certainly one should know what marriage was meant to be in God's original intent (see Gen. 2:24; Deut. 24:1–4; Matt. 19:3–12; 1 Cor. 7). Here, we can only survey other basic concepts: marital styles and adjustment, expectations and conflict, and therapeutic approaches.

MARITAL STYLES AND ADJUSTMENT

Marriage is essential to human survival. While many persons do not live well with marriage, they find they cannot live without it. All societies regulate behavior of the sexes and point persons to union in marriage. Through marriage, basic requirements for group survival—social, sexual, economic, and educational—are met.

I see marriage as a lasting relationship between a man and a woman who need and cherish each other, who are committed to a union that can grow, develop, and adapt as it is affected by changing life forces. I believe that God intended marriage to be mankind's basic social relationship. The Creator shaped sexuality into selfhood and fashioned fidelity to bless the human venture on earth. Marriage is practiced in all cultures; it is universal. Even where there is no knowledge of the true God, persons marry, create a home, have children, and seek to educate their children in the rules, customs, and skills of society. A healthy marriage bond provides support, discipline, care, and security for the couple and their offspring.

As in any close relationship, the differences between husbands and wives lead to occasional conflicts. The needs of one spouse may be overlooked by the other, and one's personal needs may be hidden from the other. When such lack of communication threatens our self-esteem, we often respond with hurt or hostility. Ideally, a marriage reflects a sequence of needs, conflict, negotiation, and resolution. But the behavior of some spouses toward each other resembles rather a sequence of needs, hurt, hostility, and detachment. Couples who communicate in a Christian spirit of love are far ahead of those

142   *Counseling as Promise*

who must guess what their partners are thinking (see Eph. 4:15). Here is where honesty, sincerity, and timely communication pay off in marital health.

THE MARITAL SYSTEM

Marriage is more than a union of two persons. A man and woman bring their whole beings and personalities into a total union. Together they form a new identity—a marital system—as their lives become joined. Husbands and wives expect to keep their own identities intact, while investing in the new relationship they are creating.

The marital pair forms its own unique personality out of the two streams of family experiences, sexual differences, definite (though often hidden) needs, and distinctive nature each person brings to the relationship. Figure 1 illustrates what is involved when two people come together in marriage and initiate a family.[3]

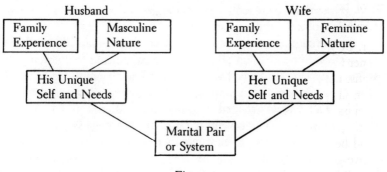

Figure 1

A couple brings unique attitudes, values, and actions to a union, which give it content and shape. The process that guides their behavior and relationship, however, is common to most marriages. Newlyweds do not live in a closed system; they interact with the families, institutions, and structures around them. Marriage as an institution doesn't always work, as Zane Alexander wrote in *Till Death Do Us Part or Something Else Comes Up* (Philadelphia: The Westminster Press, 1976). Husbands don't last forever, he claims, and, given our "no-fault" divorce laws, wives don't either.

Some patterns of marriage produce great satisfaction for both spouses. Other patterns may be frustrating and cause spouses frequent disagreement. Many researchers view conflict between unhappy partners as an indication that the couple is dissolving their relationship and heading toward eventual divorce. I believe, in contrast, that stress and conflict are characteristic of any marriage, just as they are a part of all other human relationships. The task of couples, their children, and their friends is to improve communication and encourage one another to provide an environment of trust.

TASKS OF RELATIONSHIP FORMATION

What is to be accomplished by a couple if they are to have a satisfying relationship? How can they be saved from a closed, rigid, unproductive, and unsatisfying marriage? George Bach and Peter Wyden reported five essentials all couples must learn to handle in forming good relationships.[4] I have adapted their ideas in the following list of tasks basic to relationships. Counselors can use these tasks as checkpoints to help couples who feel constricted by their commitment.

1. *Basic trust and self-revelation.* Marital relationships require one partner to trust the other and to discuss openly how he views life. The issue is, how far can I go in letting the other person really know me? When first attempts at honesty are met with acceptance and affirmation, a person learns to trust and risk more. Responses that are negative, rejecting, or belittling lead to defensiveness and anxiety. Every effort should be made to keep faith with one's spouse and to point toward positive growth.

2. *Privacy and intimacy.* Marriage requires both closeness and distance if one mate is not to become lost in the shadow of the other's personality. There must be "spaces in their togetherness," as Kahlil Gibran wrote in *The Prophet.* Each partner must ask, How much can you be different, from me and similar to me? Some wives, for example, resent that they are expected to give up their individuality in submission to their husbands. It is essential to have open and direct discussion of expectations and boundaries. Sexual relationships are not a guarantee of intimacy, just as sex and love are separate, though intertwined, life forces. Therapists Masters and Johnson acknowledge that "sexual functioning is not sufficient in itself to establish enduring friendships."[5] The

focus of their sex therapy moves beyond performance, technique, and orgasm for their own sake to "becoming committed" over time as a couple.

3. *Leadership and power.* Conventional models of marriage accept the man as head of the household and responsible for final decision making. In a marriage based on companionship, partners are equal, and decision making is shared by the husband and wife. The question is, who leads and who follows under various circumstances? Ideally, leadership is shared by both partners.

"Your vote always overrides everyone else's vote" is a complaint the leader of any family must take seriously. "Why do you always make the big decisions?" is more than an inquiry from a frustrated wife. It is a demand for recognition as decisions are being made.

Partners in complementary marriages can reinforce each other in decisions in different areas of understanding and skill. Power is balanced when marriage partners feel free to agree, disagree, or negotiate in the decision making process. The way a couple resolves fights over money, in-laws, vacations, sexual initiative, and discipline of children is a direct result of negotiation in areas of leadership and power.

4. *Role clarification.* Marriage roles are changing. No longer are men the only breadwinners and women the only homemakers. An attorney, for example, may work at his law firm during regular hours, then join his wife in her direct sales organization in his free time. Is a woman's place in the home, as traditionalists hold? Or is her place wherever she wants to make it—as wife, career woman, or mother? Superficial manipulation of one's mate through sexual gymnastics, like those described in Marabel Morgan's *The Total Woman* and *Total Joy*, fails to clarify fundamental issues of roles and responsibility.

5. *Our family and the others.* The initial separation of each spouse from his or her family of origin must be definite, so that neither partner is a "Daddy's girl" or a "Momma's boy." Newly married individuals are susceptible to envy, hostility, and hurt in relating to those outside the immediate, new relationship. Both individuals must decide who is acceptible to see, separate from one's spouse, and under what circumstances? Does one keep a few best friends from school or work, who might leave the spouse playing second fiddle? A bond of intimacy, fidelity, and enduring friendship must be forged and continually re-forged between marriage partners.

FROM INSTITUTION TO COMPANIONSHIP

A couple striving for healthy adjustment in marriage needs to know what style or model of marriage they seek. In the United States, several types of marriage are common. These are traditional, companionship, and alternative styles—each with variations.

Traditional marriage, represented by the dominant male and submissive female in rigid roles, is under attack. This model assigns an instrumental (outward, job-directed) role to the husband and an expressive role (directed inward toward family relations) to the wife. The wife's contribution is seen as enhancing the home, though both spouses may be employed. In this model, the husband is head of the house in all areas.

In the mid-forties, Ernest W. Burgess, a family sociologist, suggested that marriage was moving from institution toward companionship. His published findings in *Studies of the Family* distinguished companionship marriage as "democratic and permissive" rather than authoritative and autocratic (the conventional view). Companionship marriage relies on internal values, such as love and a growing mutual identification, rather than on external constraints. It differs from orthodox, institutional marriage in being innovative rather than static with respect to the marital relationship, in emphasizing personal happiness rather than duty and respect, self-expression rather than subordination, and negotiation rather than accommodation as a means of resolving conflict. Burgess stressed the need for both mates to retain their own autonomy, and for the couple to make decisions together. He saw marriage's twin goals as healthy personality growth and individual fulfillment for both persons. Companionship, a relationship between persons rather than roles, is the chief objective of this style of marriage.

Monogamous legal marriage is being supplanted in modern societies with alternative living arrangements. These vary: ad hoc arrangements, in which partners live together until they decide to split up; trial marriage, where a man and woman live together without a license for sexual pleasure and to determine whether or not they are suited for each other; singleness, in order to maintain autonomy and integrity; single parenthood, usually because of divorce or the death of one's mate; child-free marriage, in which a couple enjoys sex but wishes to avoid the responsibilities of parenthood; and mate swapping, also known as swinging or group sex, and akin to both communal living and group marriage.[6] In gay marriage, two partners of the same sex commit themselves to a long-term homosexual union.

There are other variations on the nuclear family, which currently comprises 44 percent of the United States population. Roommates of the same sex may occupy a house or apartment for status, safety needs, companionship, and shared expenses without sexual contact. Several families may live together in a shared-dwelling union for social, religious, or economic purposes, without sharing group sex. There is an increasing number of reconstituted or blended families—involving formerly married spouses—including a wife's or husband's children from a previous union, plus any children born into the new family circle.

Those who counsel in marriage and family life can ill afford to confine their ministry to conventional couples with children. Neither, on the other hand, must one approve all of the alternative arrangements practiced today. Biblical ideals place creative tension on all human relationships. Change comes slowly in male/female roles; yet, changes do occur. The shape of things to come points to coprovider marriages, in which major marital roles are interchangeable rather than specialized according to sex. A husband's rights and obligations shift as his wife gains new freedom in the world of work, affirmation of her worth, and a sense of accomplishment beyond bearing and rearing children. The husband gains new income, shares his duties to provide, and participates in household tasks and management.

While the remainder of this discussion addresses pressures most common to spouses in companionate, coprovider, and dual-career unions, readers can apply the principles to parties in other family arrangements.

The Christian pastor presides at the gates of entry into marriage: through family ministry to one or both sets of parents, preaching, confirmation of youth into the family's faith, marriage preparation, and the exchange of wedding vows. He helps newlyweds make the most of their marriage if they turn to the church for guidance and support. The biblical conviction of promise and hope leads Christian helpers to deal with marital hurts and heartaches when they come.

WHEN CONFLICT COMES

A pastor reported his ministry with Mrs. Jane Hollis, a young wife about twenty-one. She and her husband, Ron, had married almost immediately after graduation from high school about two and a half years earlier. Both Jane and Ron were active in a Presbyterian church, which they had attended since childhood. The couple had no children.

Early one evening, pastor Ted Williams called the Hollises to confirm plans for a visit. It was during his conversation that he learned that Jane and Ron had been fighting, and that Ron had gone to live with his parents. Because Jane began crying during the call, Rev. Williams offered to drive over and listen face to face. The pastor had been to the Hollises' house a number of times before. When Jane answered the door he noted that her eyes were swollen and that she had been crying. It seemed as if she might start crying again at any moment. He felt almost overwhelmed by the seriousness of the occasion. He did not want to fail the Hollises as a pastor, yet felt ill-experienced to deal with their marital conflict.

This telephone conversation had preceded the house visit:

JANE:　Hello.

PASTOR:　[*Cheerfully*] Jane Hollis! How are you?

JANE:　I am fine.

PASTOR:　This is Ted Williams. How are you folks enjoying this vacation? [*He knew that Ron was on vacation.*]

JANE:　I don't get a vacation.

PASTOR:　Oh. It's just Ron who gets off free this week! You have to work! [*She assents*] Listen, I wanted to check on our plans tonight. How do things look?

JANE:　[*Starts crying*] I'm sorry [*continues to weep*].

PASTOR:　That's all right, Jane. Go ahead and cry. [*Pause*] What's the matter?

JANE:　Ron has left me.

PASTOR:　I see. [*Pause*] Jane, would you like me to come over there now?

JANE:　[*Still crying*] Yes.

PASTOR:　I'll be there as quickly as I can. Good-bye, Jane.

JANE:　Good-bye.

The pastor drove directly to the Hollises' frame house. As he turned down the street where they lived, he saw Ron driving away as though he had just left their place. He knocked and was admitted by the tearful young wife.

PASTOR: Hello, Jane.

JANE: [*Clearing her throat*] Won't you come in? [*They sat across the room from each other.*]

PASTOR: Was that Ron I saw driving away?

JANE: Yes. He came to tell me not to bother about his clothes, that he would be back tomorrow to get them.

PASTOR: He came back, then?

JANE: Yes. [*Pause*] I don't know. . . . He said it wasn't a snap decision about leaving . . . that he's been thinking about it for a long time. He just now got the courage to tell me.

PASTOR: It surprised you?

JANE: Well, he's been quiet all week. I started noticing something different—I mean about the way he acted—the first part of the week. He just wasn't like himself. He just sat around moping, pacing back and forth. He's always been real moody, but . . . well, the other night we were over at John and Marcia's [*another couple in the community*], and he acted like he wasn't even there. He wouldn't say anything. He wouldn't do anything. He just sat there and watched TV. [*She was more in control of her feelings by now.*]

PASTOR: Ron doesn't usually act that way?

JANE: Sometimes he gets that way. He usually gets over it fairly soon, but this time . . . I didn't know what was the matter. [*Pause*] Then, I came home from work Thursday, and there he was, sitting on the couch. I didn't expect him home from work so early.

PASTOR: What happened then?

JANE: Well, I thought he was sick or something. I asked him why he was home from work so early. He told me to sit down. He said that he had something he wanted to say. He told me how he'd been thinking about it all week and he wanted a divorce. [*She began to cry.*] I'm sorry.

PASTOR: That's okay.

JANE: He said it was no sudden thing with him. He's been thinking about it a long time.

PASTOR: Did Ron seem angry?

JANE: No, he wasn't angry. He was more . . . nervous, but not angry. He still seems concerned about me. He just came back, you know, to see about me. He was afraid I might do something to hurt myself.

PASTOR: Well . . .

JANE: [*Laughing nervously*] No, I wouldn't do anything like that.

PASTOR: Have you and Ron ever had any serious trouble before?

JANE: The biggest problems we've ever had were over little things. Ron always wants me to wait on him hand and foot. He doesn't seem to understand that I work, too, and maybe he should help me more— like with the dishes or taking out the trash.

PASTOR: Have you ever confronted him about this?

JANE: Oh, we've talked about it a lot. He gets mad, and I get mad. We've even threatened to leave each other.

PASTOR: Only threats?

JANE: Ron left one time, but he came back in a few minutes.

PASTOR: Jane, how do you feel about Ron now?

JANE: I still love him. [*Pause*] I didn't love Ron when I married him. Mama was just crazy about him. She thought I ought to marry him even though I didn't love him. So we got married, and since then I've learned to love him.

PASTOR: Does Ron know that?

JANE: He knows I didn't love him when we got married.

PASTOR: What about now?

JANE: You mean, does he know that I love him now?

PASTOR: Yes.

JANE: Yes, I've told him a million times.

PASTOR: Then you still want your marriage to work out.

JANE: If it can. I really do. [*She looked down.*]

PASTOR: I'm going to do everything I can to help you and Ron. Of course, it will take both of you. [*He asked whether she would mind his calling Ron. She gave him Ron's parents' telephone number.*] I'll call Ron. If you need anything, feel free to contact me. I'll be in touch.

Ted Williams was uncertain how competently he could relate to the crisis in the Hollises' marriage. Though inexperienced and lacking supervision, he felt a growing sense of pastoral identity and strength as he helped them in their distress. He offered a durable relationship to Jane and Ron, having called Ron that night and early the following day. Though their conflict took various shapes throughout the crisis, within a brief time Ron and Jane had renewed their commitment to each other.

Upon reflection, Ted Williams felt that he had erred in not interviewing Ron and Jane together. Such an interview, he felt, might have helped sustain their marriage through the symbolic presence of the larger Christian community, which the pastor represented. Most of his sensitive responses to Jane were probes, opening the way for her to reveal hurt or ambivalent feelings. Pastor Williams supported Jane and made her feel understood and prized. Taking more initiative than many ministers would have, he became more than a listener. In the biblical sense, he became a reconciler, creating new pathways of communication between alienated lovers (Matt. 5:9). Because of the crisis nature of the situation, Williams felt that action was indicated. A more severe incident was averted and the young couple was reunited.

Not all pastoral counseling with couples in conflict is of such a brief, informal, or crisis nature. Often, a helper clarifies his role as counselor and continues with multiple interviews. This allows the participants in the counseling relationship to form an alliance toward a common goal. Such orientation also permits participants to focus on realistic goals in intensive marital counseling.[7]

Concerning procedure, the pastor returns telephone calls, consults with counselees in at least an evaluative interview, and agrees to see some individuals and couples on a longer term basis. Several therapeutic approaches are open to persons performing more extensive, formal counseling.

THERAPEUTIC APPROACHES

My own style is to vary counseling procedures after an initial screening interview with an individual or couple. In some cases it seems wise to do conjoint family therapy, where an entire family system comes under the counselor's care. Popularized by John Bell and Virginia Satir on the West Coast, the goal of conjoint counseling is improved self-image and strengthened communication for all members of a family system.[8] Since families live, talk, work, plan, vacation, and worship together—and sometimes become quite unhealthy as a unit—it makes sense to treat the whole system. Family members may be healthy and open; somewhat structured; or highly disturbed and closed. They alone can make decisions related to that marriage-family constellation and move toward health. Such an interdependent system may be symbolized by the interlocking circles in Figure 2.

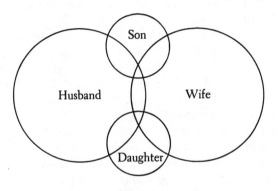

Figure 2

Seeing the family as a whole has a number of advantages over individual sessions: (1) one decides whether or not a deeply disturbed member merits psychiatric evaluation in addition to pastoral conversations; (2) a counselor hears everyone's story in perspective, without missing pieces and relying on guesswork; (3) it reflects the unique feelings toward the marriage bond and filial ties that each family member holds; (4) it saves time over extensive individual interviews; and (5) family sharing often prompts new growth by ventilating and resolving old problems.

Family problems can be extremely complex, in light of various family structures. Psychiatrist Robert Beavers has pictured three general levels of family functioning: seriously disturbed, midrange, and open and healthy—all on a dynamic continuum. He distinguishes various types of families and therapies in *Psychotherapy and Growth: A Family Systems Perspective.*[9]

1. *Closed and seriously disturbed families.*

a). Family seems queer, odd, strange; socially shunned.

b). There is a lack of individual boundaries.

c). Little vital interchange with the outside world.

d). There is a poor parental coalition; a child often leads the family or divides and conquers his parents.

e). One person frequently speaks for others, while denying attitudes, convictions, or feelings of fellow members.

f). Separate identities are impossible; the passage of time is obliterated; and relationships remain unclear.

Such a family appears trapped in quicksand, unable to respond favorably to a helper's efforts. Predictably, any family member in such a quagmire who attempts to achieve autonomy is excluded or destroyed. One growing up in such a closed system feels that it is impossible to be an individual and to feel acceptance or companionship. It fosters a black-sheep syndrome, schizophrenia, and socially unacceptable behavior. Feeling rejected at home, one enters social situations and relationships, then asks (often unconsciously) for rejection.

A pastoral counselor rapidly senses the precarious position of families in such a predicament. While open anger is rare (that would imply hope for change), joy, warmth, and laughter are absent. The counselor's inclination would be to consult with some specialist in the city or region, and to refer these families to a mental health center for evaluation and therapy. Supportive care may be indicated when crises arise, but there is limited hope of major alterations in the family structure. A crisis viewed as a growth opportunity, however, may revolutionize an entire system and free family members for change and growth.

2. *Midrange, partially closed, rigidly structured families.*

a). These families produce children with a constricted, often guilt-laden, low self-image, and limited interpersonal skills. They are the primary seekers of help.

b). The pervading view in rigid families is that persons are essentially evil; hence there is a constant effort to control actions and inhibit attitudes. Behavior is overcontrolled.

c). While social and moral absolutes are imposed on family members, usually by one dictatorial parent, ambivalence is an ever-present quality. Love is infrequently expressed and usually has strings attached. Rebellion is inevitable in a milieu with no successful coalition of parents, no model for negotiation, and no alternatives for compromise. This leaves the growing child extremely crippled in later relationships.

Counselors drawn into the orbit of such a brittle system discover limited autonomy for family members. The general tone or family mood is one of sadness, depression, and repressed anger, with little warmth or humor. Beavers traces the symptoms of constricted family members to neurotic and behavioral disorders, and offers therapeutic suggestions for various needs.[10] Neurotic family members deal with the situation with prescription drugs (tranquilizers, amphetamines, and sleeping medications), all considered socially acceptable. They use denial of needs and repression of destructive feelings in order to cope and survive. Families with character disorders, on the other hand, may have runaway children, and experience violence and alcohol abuse—all of which dramatize the lack of love and the internal disorder at home.

3. *Open, healthy, and flexible families are characterized by:*

a). High self-esteem of each member; positive goodwill.

b). The overall tone is positive, constructive, and hopeful.

c). Each member feels like a real person, is open and receptive to outsiders, is trusting, and is task-efficient.

Such families are the most easily adaptable of any of the groups discussed. Parents have an effective coalition of power and leadership, and children are granted autonomy, with less power. There is a relatively clear and flexible family rule system, with clear rewards and fair punishments. Expression of attitudes and convictions is permitted without reprisal, feelings are freely vented, and negotiation is used to work through thorny issues. Such family systems are relatively free of punitive control patterns, damaging intimidation, and destructive rivalry. Family members are permitted strength, shared decision making, and mutual accountability in goal-setting and achievement.

The pastor's time will be spent, for the most part, with open, healthy families, but crises like illness and death will also come to them. Some disruptions are inevitable in any human system, vulnerable to the pressures and hazards of living. Such families possess greater resources, of spirit within and support without, when trouble does come. Still, they need the pastor's strength and care (just as he needs their understanding when crises crush his own family).

Family members who are open to change and growth have captured Thomas McGinnis's secret of "open family living." They will be accessible for marriage and family enrichment programs, and will carry major responsibilities in the life and mission of the church.[11] In addition to conjoint family counseling, there are other valid therapeutic approaches.

Individual and group counseling may follow the model suggested by transactional analysis, with Gestalt experiments.[12] The theoretical framework for transactional analysis (TA) is relatively simple. Founder Eric Berne holds that each person has three separate ego states, or sources of psychic energy, feelings, and behavior.[13] These ego states are:

1. Parent ego state—includes attitudes and behavior copied from external sources, primarily parents. One is in a parent state when he responds, supportively or punitively, as a parent figure toward others.

2. Adult ego state—implies the ability to relate and respond in a rational manner. An adult acts on the basis of facts, not feelings or unchecked opinions alone, yet may not always make wise decisions. The goal in analyzing transactions is to become aware of which aspect of one's self is operative at a given time, and to move from gamesmanship to creative relations.

3. Child ego state—implies the natural, unchecked impulses with which a person is born. One is in a child state when he feels, talks, thinks, or acts as one did when a small child.

Structural analysis is the term used for analyzing parent, adult, and child ego states, their contamination, plus the drama of life scripts from one's past. This technique permits people to detect the sources of their feelings, attitudes, reactions, and behavior. It helps people change things about themselves they wish to alter. A helper well instructed in structural analysis can sort out predominant ego states in given situations, and assist people in moving toward game-free behavior.

Robert L. Goulding, a psychiatrist who, with his wife, Mary, directs intensive week-long workshops in transactional analysis at their hillside estate near Carmel, California, speaks of *redecision* as a therapeutic objective. In the Gouldings' version of TA (of which there are many), redecision is the point at which a sufferer breaks through an impasse and consciously opts for happiness and fulfillment. "In psychoanalysis you don't make a decision for five years," holds Goulding. "In T.A., you're encouraged to make a decision right away."[14] The Gouldings encourage dramatic Gestalt-style experiments in which old relationships are exposed and shattered, as when a patient pounds a pillow until it is "dead." The pillow represents a person with whom the patient feels conflict, anger, frustration, or rage. This dramatic action prompts relief of pent-up emotions, insight into repressed wishes, and offers an opportunity for change.

One needs taste for, temperament, and training in the use of TA before starting such a group in a church setting. It has much appeal: the language is simple, and TA seems to have theological moorings or, at least, moral overtones. Thomas A. Harris, one of the foremost populariz-ers of TA methods, has been criticized for his commercial approach. TA therapists contract with counselees to change behavior and attitudes, and expect self-discipline in achieving goals. In the course of therapy, Harris sometimes writes out on a regular prescription pad a "prescrip-tion," such as, "John, I want you to smile and greet ten new people every day, by name if possible, and report back."

An investigative reporter asked Harris about his claims of success, to which he replied: "We have thousands of letters—these are all validat-ing. I take these letters at face value, and when an individual in Missouri pours out his soul to me and tells me what happened to him while he was reading the book, why I sense that something really did happen."[15] Such testimonials do not impress analytically oriented psychiatrists. They see TA as simplistic and reductionistic in offering the parent-adult-child paradigm as an explanation for the complexities of human person-ality. Critics also sense that there is limited conscious control of destruc-tive impulses, like suicide. They see the entire project as more of a popular commercial venture than a classic treatment of personal and family disorders.

Along with extended *insight counseling*, focusing on intrapsychic forces as well as interpersonal relations, I use *values clarification* tech-niques and *rational emotive* approaches. Clarifying values helps one in decision making and life planning. I suggest that an individual or couple approach any area of concern, crisis, or conflict through a values grid. At the left, I write down various issues of concern: premarital chastity, parental approval of spouse, abortion, husband/wife equality in decision making, desired number of children, enjoyment of sex, and so on. Then, at the right, I ask the individual or couple to compare values, using seven steps devised by Louis Raths and expanded by Sidney Simon, and their associates:[16]

1. Are you proud of (do you prize or cherish) your position?
2. Have you publicly affirmed your position?
3. Have you chosen your position from alternatives?
4. Have you considered the consequences of your position?
5. Have you freely chosen your position?
6. Have you acted on (done anything about) your beliefs?
7. Have you acted consistently (repeated a pattern) on this issue?

The goal is to move beyond values clarification to self-affirmation; validation of one's spouse, parents, children, or friends; and behavior consistent with one's values.

Similarly, a couple can use rational emotive techniques with the *memo method* to improve communication. Memos, systematically devised by therapist Paul Hauck and family physician Edmund S. Kean, help open blocked communication.[17] The "plaintiff" in a marital squabble notes items on a piece of paper under three headings: the problem, understood causes, and suggested solutions. A memorandum provides a way of expressing a grievance or making a suggestion without fighting about it. Hauck and Kean instruct the "defendant" to take a piece of paper and respond to the same issue in an identical way: problem, causes, and solutions. After tempers have cooled, they suggest getting a cup of coffee and calmly discussing such sensitive complaints as, "I can't stand your drinking anymore," or "You're going to fire your secretary now." Memo-writing holds out the hope of reaching a compromise. Such a method implies equality in conversation, openness to one another, and a conscious desire to improve blocked communication. While listing problems, causes, and solutions may appear easy, self-diagnosis and treatment is not easy to attain. In some cases, a calm atmosphere for discussion is unattainable. In no instance is the memo method a substitute for deeper levels of counseling if that is indicated.

Tests, such as the Taylor-Johnson Temperament Analysis, are used by some marriage counselors in predicting success and in locating problems.[18] This personality test is specially designed for use in premarital and marital counseling.

Most marriage counseling techniques are variations on classical or more traditional listening approaches, conceived by Freud and altered a generation ago by Carl Rogers. I would caution Christian counselors against two extremes: using secular methods in church settings without careful analysis and critical reflection, and rejecting all but one's own homespun theories as unsuitable in the parish. Both extremes are in error, and are misguided counseling approaches.

THE GOAL OF HUMAN GROWTH

As in other forms of counseling, the helper's ultimate goal is to help people become confident and creative members of the fellowship of Christ. The most desirable counseling process follows the paradigm of a child learning to walk—from helpless dependency to full autonomy. A crisis may force a person or couple to seek pastoral counseling, where they find confession and catharsis. To pour out one's hurt, frustration, anger, and confusion will take time. With a model of life provided by the healer-counselor, education occurs; new integration of conscious and unconscious forces is at work. Then, as Jung suggested, a transformation can happen, whereby the person seeking help becomes a therapist-teacher, and the counselor becomes the learner.

The Bible speaks of "becoming as little children"; again, the prophet promised "a little child shall lead them" (Matt. 18:3; Isa. 11:6). Paul spoke of being "children of God" and "children of light," while the apostle John wrote of God's persons walking "in truth" (Rom. 8:16; Eph. 5:8; 3 John 4). Above all, "the children of the promise are reckoned as descendants" of Abraham, and are people of faith (Rom. 9:8; Gal. 4:28). God's child is a person of unvarnished spontaneity, transparent openness, and obvious joy. One moving in harmony with God's design can become an authentic lover, teacher, and carer of the world for which Christ died. That is the promise of counseling.

II

Counseling in Depressive Reactions

COUNSELING is an aspect of pastoral care that personalizes and authenticates a pastor's public ministry. One does not have to wait for a crisis before becoming a counselor. There are always people in a congregation who need to draw strength from God and find fresh power for living. There is an essential unity and evangelical thrust to all that a minister does. Early in the course of ministry, a pastor will discover that depressive reactions happen occasionally to some of the strongest church members. It is no surprise that people have occasional bouts with the blues. People may feel mild discomfort to major discontent, vague dissatisfaction to deep despondency, or they may find themselves discouraged and depressed.

"Depression, along with its associated symptoms," wrote Robert Woodruff, M.D., "is probably the single most frequent problem with which psychiatrists deal."[1] When individuals hurt badly enough, their behavior reflects it. Depression's painful symptoms prompt many sufferers to seek counseling and careful medical diagnosis. Psychic suffering can result in significant growth in one's personality or change in one's life situation, or both. Conversely, the sharp stab of despair drives all too many sufferers to suicide. As many as half of the estimated 50,000 to 70,000 suicides in the United States annually occur among persons suffering from depression. In terms of disability, the toll is equally alarming. One in eight Americans will suffer a bout of depression serious enough to need counseling during his lifetime. According to the National Institute of Mental Health, 125,000 Americans are hospitalized each year with depression, while another 200,000 are treated in physicians' offices.

"A lot of depression is unrecognized," says Dr. Nathan Kline of New York's Rockland State Hospital. "It's the chronic underachiever, the fatigued housewife, the sort of person Churchill described as snatching defeat from the jaws of victory."[2] There is evidence that depression is spreading most rapidly among the nation's youth, due to confusion over social values, cultural disorientation, and existential anomie. Whatever the reasons, figures from the Los Angeles Suicide Prevention Center show that the suicide rate among persons in their twenties has more than doubled in recent years. Drug and alcohol abuse is viewed by some researchers as a kind of self-medication for depression.

Though psychological suffering has reached epidemic proportions, depression is not a new malady. Job, in the oldest book of the Bible, struggled against symptoms of despair. He reasoned with his Maker: "I am allotted months of emptiness, and nights of misery are apportioned to me. When I lie down I say, 'When shall I arise?' But the night is long, and I am full of tossing till the dawn. My days . . . come to their end without hope" (Job 7:3-4, 6). Job's resentment, sleeplessness, pained physical condition, withdrawal into self-pity, and hopelessness characterize depression. Hippocrates, the ancient Greek physician, diagnosed the illness as melancholy, attributing it to an excess of "black bile."

Dr. Aaron Beck of the Depression Research Unit at Philadelphia General Hospital has traced the medical history of depression. He cites Plutarch, a second-century Greek biographer, who ascribed religious reasons to melancholia: "He looks on himself as a man whom the gods hate and pursue with their anger. A far worse lot is before him; he dares not employ any means of averting or of remedying the evil, lest he be found fighting against the gods."[3] Such a despairing person, noted Beck, would drive his physician and friends away so that he might suffer due punishment for breaking spiritual laws. Such a person feels that he has done something that the gods disapprove, is filled with remorse, and is deluded into thinking that he has committed the unpardonable sin.

Many persons of great genius throughout history have been subject to this painful state. Sir Winston Churchill, who rallied the Allied cause during World War II and made famous the challenge: "Never, never,

never give up!" was often crippled by discouragement. He wrote about the "black dog" that haunted him throughout life and finally immobilized him in old age. Abraham Lincoln experienced melancholy periods and dreamed of viewing his own coffin. Low moods do not affect persons of privilege and prominence alone, though the list of artists and literary geniuses plagued with gloom is long. Ordinary people—black and white, rich and poor—taste bittersweet. If the mood swing is exaggerated to the degree of impaired function, or grief is abnormally prolonged for months, the clinical diagnosis is depression.

My purpose here is to examine cases of depression that a pastoral counselor might expect to see in parish practice, including its causes, chief categories, and cures. How does one recognize and diagnose depression? What part does a person's religious viewpoint play in this malady? Is depression a disease, a sin, or both, and does God have a cure for it? How should one react to a threatened suicide? Is it true that depressive episodes may last for months and then spontaneously clear up? It is to these issues that I direct attention in this chapter.

THE AFFLICTION CALLED DEPRESSION

By definition, depression is a painful affect, a subjective feeling state, characterized by feelings of sadness, discouragement, loneliness, and isolation. This malady is more than the Monday morning blahs. People who have been functioning normally, even with excessive demands, may suddenly find themselves in the grip of insomnia or uncontrollable periods of crying. A dark night of the soul sets in. To tell someone who is depressed to "snap out of it" is like ordering the sun to shine on a gray afternoon. In time, with help, support is regained, stress subsides, and new morale is mustered for life's activities.

Depression has many forms. There is, for example, a high school student named Jane Truman. Since Jane's father was out of the city working for weeks at a time, her mother was the rule maker and disciplinarian. Mrs. Truman tried to prepare meals and keep house for Jane, as well as Jane's younger sister and two younger brothers. As head of the household, Mrs. Truman had full responsibility for managing the budget, transporting her children to school, buying groceries, and maintaining the house and yard. Since Jane was sixteen, the eldest, her mother continually stressed that she depended on Jane and "simply couldn't get along without her." Mrs. Truman turned to Jane for companionship, assistance with child care, and household chores.

Jane liked the feeling of being needed for awhile, but in time she resented her parents for entrapping her in heavy housekeeping and child rearing chores. Her feelings of disappointment with her father (for his absenteeism and abandonment), and displeasure with her mother (for her heavy dependency and discipline) drove Jane into an intense relationship with Danny Nelson, a boyfriend at school. Mistaking sexual intercourse for true intimacy, she was attracted to Danny in a search for love. When Jane's indiscretions were discovered, her mother dragged her to their family doctor for a pelvic examination. The physician assured Mrs. Truman that Jane was no longer a virgin. The fact that the doctor did not keep her confidence made Jane feel further betrayed and deserted. That was when she turned to a pastoral counselor for help.

"You don't know what it's like to be depressed," she told the counselor, "scared that you'll miss your period every month, afraid someone will find out." She was angry with her boyfriend for pressing her to go all the way. "Finally, after an argument," she noted, "I gave in." She had been on a moral and emotional skid ever since. "We were all right until we got close. Now, I can't stand him."

An adolescent in American culture experiences fantasies of omnipotence and indestructibility. This is the "land of plenty," where everything—including love, sex, money, energy, work, and leisure—is available. A sixteen-year-old girl is neither a child, nor a woman ready for the full risks and responsibilities of adulthood. Jane's fantasy of parents she could respect, siblings she could feel close to, and friends she could trust clashed with the harsh reality of human limits. Her anger at home drove her to seek consolation from a boy, who, in turn, exploited her needs for warmth. She discovered herself using sex to "hold onto Danny," yet despising the entrapment her promiscuity provoked. Feeling trapped in a topsy-turvy world, Jane poured out her confusion, hurt, and disorder to her counselor. What was to become of her?

When persons turn to a counselor, feeling in utter disarray, discouragement, even despair, this requires diplomacy, tact, and compassion. Their conversations provide a vehicle to convey the hurt, despondency, betrayal, and confinement counselees feel. Jane was exhausted; she was tired of running. She longed for love, self-esteem, and forgiveness, and resented being viewed as a sex-object by Danny. Jane feared that God would punish her behavior with destructive anger, not forgiveness. She even dreamed that something awful was about to happen.

The counselor helped Jane sort out her emotions, explore ways of handling various facets of her predicament, dismiss unrealistic fears, accept divine pardon, and defend herself against inappropriate behavior in the future. By befriending, listening, supporting, guiding, and modeling healthy relationships, along with the passage of time, the counselor can help restore morale. In this instance, with Jane's knowledge and permission, the minister consulted with a psychiatrist friend in the event medication or hospitalization were indicated. The counselor was sharing responsibility for the diagnosis and care of her difficulty.

According to Anthony D'Agostino, M.D., psychiatrists, as well as laymen, are undecided whether "depression is a disease, a scapegoat phenomenon, a problem in living, a conditioned response to a series of more or less accidental environmental contingencies, an . . . existential awareness of the futility of man's struggle against the inevitability of death, or all of the above."[4] Reflecting on Jane's experience, we might be inclined to say, "all of the above," since she was sick with worry, and had experienced suicidal thoughts, insomnia, crying spells, loss of self-esteem, inability to concentrate, and minor somatic symptoms. Jane was not driven to attempt suicide. She felt that she had "a lot of living to do." Yet, the thought of death had crossed her mind, as a way of escaping from an intolerable situation.

How can a helper become sufficient to deal with depression? To respond, one recalls war pictures of the wounded caring for each other. Those who were casualties of grim battles reached out, on an elemental level, to care for those more injured. For better or worse, the pastoral counselor is a "wounded healer" who bears in his own body "the marks of Jesus'" redemptive suffering (Gal. 6:17). Neither the counselor, his family, his congregation, nor his fellow citizens are immune to depression. Thus, we begin close to home.

EXISTENTIAL INVOLVEMENT

Psychiatrist D'Agostino, quoted above, was driven to examine depression subsequent to his father's hospitalization, the year after his son's graduation from medical school.[5] The young doctor went into a psychiatric residency and, at the same time, saw his fifty-two-year-old father, go in and out of four different mental hospitals. His father, normally a compulsive man, became almost helpless. Friends covered for his father at work; yet, his doctors advised early retirement and application for social security benefits. His father was taking a drug containing reserpine for elevated blood pressure. After three previous medical teams had failed, using a combination of drugs and psychotherapy, a fourth doctor insisted on electroconvulsive shock therapy (ECT) and withdrawal of reserpine.

D'Agostino's father, who had lost over twenty pounds, became anxious and agitated. He would ruminate over what he felt were bad judgments on his part. He was a difficult patient to treat, since he did not have a long, sordid story to tell his doctors. Six weeks after his first ECT treatment his father went back to work. He was cured, and saw his psychiatrist only once afterward. He had no insight or awareness of what caused his depressed state. He just had had no motivation (psychoanalytically) to get well. His cure was facilitated by somatic therapy (ECT) and removal of reserpine, rather than counseling.

To date, the cause and cure for depression remains mysterious. A feeling of loss, real or imagined, lies behind most kinds of depression. *Endogenous* depression seems to come from within the person, and is caused biochemically rather than by trauma or loss. *Exogenous* depression (also called reactive or secondary depression) seems to be triggered by outside events, like the loss of a love object. In most cases the lost object—person, position, power, and so on—is viewed with ambivalence. There may be feelings of anger, and a lack of hope that things will ever change.

Healers themselves may occasionally need healing. Students preparing for the ministry sometimes become despondent, attempt suicide, or seek medical help. Harry Emerson Fosdick, one of the foremost preachers and most effective counselors of his generation, wrote of his own bout with depression in *The Living of These Days.*[6] The account of that dreadful time, when he withdrew temporarily from both Union Theological Seminary and Columbia University, where he was working on degrees in theology and philosophy, has helped many young ministers.

Fosdick, who was pastor of Riverside Church in New York, wrote that it was not trouble that threw him but happiness—the excitement of the most exhilarating opportunities for study and ministry he had ever had. While pursuing two advanced degrees, he worked in the city's slums, did not rest or eat properly, and defied the laws of good health. Suddenly, one night in late November, he could not sleep. "It was the beginning of the most hideous experience of my life." Fosdick retraced his steps—his agonizing trips home, four months of rest in a sanitarium in Elmira, New York, and a six-week vacation by steamer to Europe. He returned to school the following September, inched along by alternating study with walking every half-hour, and was gradually able to carry on.

Looking back years later, the famous pastor noted that his experience in an emotional wilderness helped to prepare him for the ministry. For the first time in his life, he had faced a situation too difficult to handle. He descended into the depths, where he lost his self-confidence. The harder he struggled, the more desperate his plight became. One who viewed himself as strong—a giver, not a receiver—was unable to cope with outward circumstances or inner feelings. Depicting his illness as a deeply religious experience, Fosdick said:

I learned some things about religion that theological seminaries do not teach. I learned to pray, not because I had adequately argued out prayer's rationality, but because I desperately needed help from a Power greater than my own. I learned that God, much more than a theological proposition, is an immediately available Resource; that just as around our bodies is a physical universe from which we draw all our physical energy, so around our spirits is a spiritual Presence in living communion with whom we can find sustaining strength. Without that experience I do not think I would have written one of my early books, *The Meaning of Prayer.* And I learned as well much about human nature that academic courses in psychology leave out.[7]

Years later, in his counseling office, when people described the inner hell of their endless waves of melancholia, obsessive anxieties, and desire for suicide, Fosdick might interrupt a story, saying, "Don't you tell me, let me tell you how you feel." One wide-eyed man exclaimed when Fosdick was through, "My God, how did you know that?" The pastor's congregation at Riverside did not realize that occasional references to depression and despair in his sermons were autobiographical. Having been in the pit of deep spiritual need and having won a victory, with God's help, Fosdick was able to help multitudes of fellow human beings.

In order to help persons facing depression, one must first know how to detect and diagnose its symptoms, then decide what to do about them.

DETECTION AND DIAGNOSIS

As a pastor, one of the things I observed about people who became depressed was their misuse of religious beliefs. Some parishioners attempted suicide by overwork, a few under the guise of automobile or hunting accidents. Others consumed varying amounts of alcohol between Sunday worship services. Some church members groveled in self-pity over their misfortunes. Other individuals nursed their hurts privately, with marvelous courage and compassion for fellow strugglers.

CONFUSED RELIGIOUS IDEAS

One pastor recalls a woman approaching fifty who experienced a serious emotional downturn during her climacteric. Menopause is a major turning point for women and men, during which physical energy and sexual activity are reduced. Some individuals attempt to defy middle age by adopting a "swinging" life-style during this period. There are those who seek younger sex partners, who need intense proof of potency, and divorce partners after a quarter century or more of marriage. In order to prove their sexual vitality to themselves, they deceive themselves about the realities of aging.

Confused religious ideas mark the case of Julia Dunn, who became deeply depressed one March. Spring is the season of the year when most suicides occur, when the earth is young and green again, though one's spirit seems old and gray. Ms. Dunn came to the pastor's attention because she believed that she had fallen from grace and was guilty of committing the unpardonable sin. She had left her family and moved in temporarily with her sister, a registered nurse. (The anguish and separation itself was a cry for help.) No theological truths could console her. The death of Jesus Christ upon the cross for her sin was not adequate. What she had done in a delusional state was far more problematic than God's all-sufficient grace.

One night, her sister discovered that Julia had slipped quietly out of the house. She was found some blocks away lying prostrate across some railroad tracks. Julia felt that she had disgraced her family and deserved to die. Without saying good-bye to relatives or friends, she had experienced the psychological severance of one who was unforgiveable. She claimed that she wanted to die—to remain on the tracks until crushed beneath the churning wheels of a giant locomotive.

How is it possible for one to admit the core of pride beneath an unpardonable personality? Though it may not seem logical, one's tears for sins too big for God to handle reflect a subtle stubbornness. "I am too much for heaven to help," goes the lament, "so I must administer my own torment." A person like Julia Dunn ignores Christ's death, and climbs upon a cross of her own choosing. Because it sounds so strange and sick, the family rallies around one in such a pathological state, giving them love and attention, and seeking medical help. In Ms. Dunn's case, hospitalization under a physician's care, rest and medication, time, understanding of her metabolic and hormonal changes by her family and herself, and a fresh sense of God's unqualified acceptance helped to renew the joy of her salvation (Ps. 51:1–12).

SELF-MEDICATION WITH ALCOHOL

Many ministers view the consumption of alcoholic beverages as a central life problem. While liquor provides the scenario for self-destructive practices, it may be secondary to depressive reactions. There is a businessman, for example, who floundered for months after being betrayed by a trusted colleague in his company. Joe Lester had shared confidences for several years with Millard Bell. They had staff planning sessions and sales meetings together, traveled to conventions and shows, and worked together for bigger sales volumes.

"When Millard pulled the plug on me and I missed that big promotion, I lost my balance," reported Joe. "There's nothing worse than to have one's faith betrayed." He had increased alcohol consumption for weeks and narrowly escaped death in a collision, when his car struck a truck from the rear. "I must have wanted out of this mess worse than I thought," he confided. "I'd gotten several tickets for speeding violations recently, but hadn't paid that much attention until this happened."

Joe's family recognized his not so subtle death wishes. They saw his return to alcohol, a habit he had given up years before, as a symptom of something worse. Joe's withdrawal from physiological and psychic dependency on his "glass crutch" required extended hospitalization. In time, he was able to resume sales responsibilities with his company; yet he fought the agitation of depression for years. Millard's rivalry and rejection were not the primary causes. Joe's feelings of having been betrayed by his parents, siblings, and teachers years before were transferred to Millard, who caught the brunt of his rage and desire for revenge. It was hurt piled on top of hurt that drove Joe to the edge of despair.

Given another set of circumstances at life's outset—healthy parents, supportive siblings, and encouraging associates—Joe might have faced Millard's betrayal and survived. There is no simple formula for beating depression, though I have met people who claimed never to have been depressed. That is denial, I suspect, rather than dishonesty. One's creative outlets, social support system, vital faith in God, practice of prayer, willingness to forgive, avoidance of grudges, and spirit of goodwill help provide a buffer against depression.

THE VOICE OF HIDDEN HURT

Some pastors overlook what Thoreau termed the "quiet desperation" of many people's lives. There was an elderly guardian, for instance, who was caring for a sick child while the child's parents worked in a nearby city. Without warning, the young lad first appeared listless and drowsy, and then stopped breathing. By the time an ambulance was called and arrived at a hospital emergency room, little Joey was dead. Pneumonia had taken its toll as his lungs filled with fluid and strangled him. The alert pastor observes that a guardian, like Joey's, who feels a deep sense of shame for her apparent carelessness, as well as grief over his sudden death, will struggle with hidden hurt. While consoling family and friends, a sensitive minister will give additional attention in the months ahead to the woman who carries the guilt of a young life lost in her heart.

As one "acquainted with grief," the Christian counselor is alert to persons in the congregation who bear hidden hurts: (1) idealistic adolescents in conflict with, yet enmeshed in, technocracy; (2) divorcees with gaping psychic wounds, dependent children, lowered incomes, heavy schedules, and additional home-management tasks; (3) singles who age alone, work and play, search for social approval, face sexual frustration and temptation, and seek companionship if the right partner appears; (4) persons stuck in jobs they genuinely dislike, with no hope of disengagement because of economic necessity; (5) victims of epilepsy, cancer, stroke, muscular dystrophy, blindness, and other catastrophic conditions, each of whom faces cloudy skies and sinking spirits day after day;

(6) wheelchair patients—wounded by war, accidents, disease, hereditary dysfunctions, aging, and amputations—who must live disfigured, deformed, and unequal in the eyes of society; (7) persons, like Jane, who have violated their religious values, been disloyal to personal or family loyalties, and feel loneliness from sin, perversity, or a conscience turned inward; and (8) retirees who have not planned well for old age, who lack existential worth in their own eyes, face economic hardships, have time on their hands, and wait for death's inevitablity.

All such people in one's congregation or residents of one's neighborhood are apt to experience depressive reactions. They need church contacts, caring, and growth opportunities in order to avoid the undertow of depression. We have seen how Christian persons become isolated by discouragement and despondency. The following descriptions of various depressive reactions will assist the counselor in detection and diagnosis.

A TYPOLOGY OF DEPRESSIVE REACTIONS

We have seen that all depressions are not the same. Just as causes and symptoms vary, treatment should fit the need. One must look beneath the surface and make some basic distinctions in order to help psychic sufferers. The classification that follows will help counselors to make necessary distinctions and to collaborate with physicians in caring for depressed persons.[8]

1. *Normal versus pathological reactions.* Depressive states may be quite appropriate to a particular life situation, such as a normal grief response. Pathology is present when a reaction is of such intensity or duration that it is inappropriate to the precipitating occasion. The severely depressed person may be uncommunicative and gloomy in outlook. There may be motor retardation and a slowing of thought processes. One's appearance and hampered communication reflect dullness, self-reproach, grimness, and hopelessness.

2. *Primary versus secondary reactions.* Depression may be a basic disorder characterized by low self-esteem, self-accusatory feelings, regret, and self-destructive thoughts. Classic depression is accompanied by somatic complaints: fatigue; insomnia; loss of interest in sex, food, and so on; memory blockage; apathy; and anxiety. Depression, on the other

hand, may be secondary to another basic pattern. For example, obsessive-compulsive persons may become depressed when they are not producing or achieving in life. Compulsive neurosis is the more basic disorder, prompting occasional feelings of failure and self-blame.

3. *Neurotic versus psychotic reactions.* Neurotic depressions leave the person in touch with reality, though some counselees may become so unresponsive that diagnosis is difficult. Psychotic patients, on the other hand, evidence delusions (false beliefs), hallucinations (false sensory impressions), or even destructive behavior.

4. *Exogenous versus endogenous reactions.* These terms were introduced earlier, and refer to external and internal causes of depression. Exogenous reactions seem to be triggered by outside events. The victims usually possess dependent or neurotic personalities. In 1917, Freud wrote in "Mourning and Melancholia" that most depressions involve the loss of a love object—like one's spouse, health, job, or part of one's own body in surgery. Exogenous depressions seem more responsive to psychotherapy than to drugs or shock treatment.

Endogenous depression seems to originate from within the individual, and many researchers believe it is caused biochemically rather than by trauma. The victim experiences lows in the morning and improvement toward evening. Its most notable symptoms are loss of self-esteem, apathy, job dysfunction, and sexual impotence. Such depressives are more treatable with drugs than with counseling. Endogenous depression includes the involutional melancholy found in middle-aged men and in menopausal women with endocrine imbalances, as well as in manic-depressives.

5. *Manic-depressive psychosis.* Persons suffering from this syndrome, which is assumed to have a strong genetic determinant, experience highs and lows in a cyclical fashion. Depressive episodes alternate with elation and hyperactivity. Consider the following case.[9]

Carl Schwartz, a sixty-two-year-old New York lawyer, spent nearly forty years swinging between the highs and lows of endogenous manic-depressive illness. "I literally enjoyed the manic phases," he recalls. "I was a big shot, on top of the world. I spent not only my own money, but everybody else's I could get my hands on—I bought six suits at a time, a lot of stupid unnecessary things. But in between the highs, there were frightening plunges into depression. I feared getting out of bed, and was anxious to get into bed at night because I could block out the horror of my daily life." Thanks to daily doses of lithium carbonate, Schwartz has been able to control his symptoms.

6. *Postpartum and anaclitic reactions.* These abnormal states affect young mothers, and newborn infants who are suddenly separated from their mothers. Postpartum depression usually occurs three weeks to three months after childbirth. The reaction is manifested in panic, fear, and feelings of inadequacy in handling the newborn. Although previously thought to be an organically determined disorder, it is now recognized as a functional illness occurring in response to the threat of motherhood.

Anaclitic depressives are infants who lose interest in living as a result of parental loss. One separated from one's mother, by illness or death for example, suffers withdrawal, disinterest in the nursery environment, loss of appetite, insomnia, and apprehension, all of which, if occurring in an adult, would be interpreted as depression. Intensive care of abandoned or isolated infants by parent surrogates is essential to restore zest for life, appetite, and growth.

Given this typology, the explanations for causation from some sources seem incredulous. Some sort of loss is inherent in depressive reactions—either a metabolic loss in biochemical changes or a love object loss in relationships. Some experts attribute despair to early separation from the mother's breast, physical weaning from basic needs for nourishment, and psychic separation from the mother's care.[10] Guilt before God—in cases like that of Jane Truman, Julia Dunn, and the negligent guardian—affects depressives. The more responsible an individual feels or the heavier one's conscience becomes, the greater the difficulty of escaping discouragement.

Tim LaHaye, a West Coast clergyman who has written *How to Win Over Depression,* presents a somewhat vague picture of the origin and remedy of depression. He acknowledges that "most . . . depressed people are not conscious of the fact that their misery emanates from the God-vacuum within them."[11] LaHaye touches on basic theological and spiritual needs by pointing up a God-void deficiency. This, he holds, makes persons vulnerable to a variety of emotional and physical disorders. However, he confesses major personal bouts with depression, linked to pastoral duties and disappointments, without admitting a God-void in his own life.[12] Lacking consistency, he asserts, "At last we have come to the primary cause of depression. In spite of the causes listed previously, nothing produces depression faster or more deeply than self-pity."[13] His argument from that point places too much emphasis on rational thought control as a solution for depression. While mentioning religious conversion as an antidote, LaHaye advocates a positive mental attitude, devoid of self-pity, as the ultimate therapy. I doubt his wisdom in playing down conventional sources of help, while advocating a "ten steps to victory over depression" formula, which many victims can never achieve.[14]

IS THERE A CURE FOR DEPRESSION?

Even with the realities of human disappointment, guilt, anger, and despair, there is a cure for depression. Several sources of help, implied from this discussion, may be summarized. Some depressive episodes may last for weeks or months, then clear up spontaneously without medication or counseling. When a depressed parishioner seeks counseling, there is always the possibility that the person is contemplating suicide.[15] Cooperative counseling with a physician is particularly wise when depression lingers, rendering a person helpless. Referral may become essential.

Because demoralization, shame, and doubt isolate sufferers, befriending becomes urgent. That is why personal and group counseling can significantly help those who are depressed. Given a counselor's supportive relationship, hurting persons can vent anger, ambivalence, shame, secret desires for revenge, and even wishes for death. Such catharsis may bring relief, even in the absence of insight or evidence of religious conversion. Personal and group intervention permit release of long-held frustrations, tears, and heartaches. New outlooks and relationships can be shaped by a counselor. Liberating life-styles may be explored through group interaction.[16] Fresh challenges and new learning can occur, substituting creative for negative behavior, and prompting caring for others rather than self-pity.

Advances in pharmacology have made it possible to modify the intensity of a depressive reaction by the use of antidepressant drugs. Consulting a reliable physician, for shared diagnostic wisdom and professional responsibility, opens the way to other somatic therapies. Electroconvulsive therapy (ECT) may dramatically relieve intense symptoms, though experts are uncertain why the convulsions help. Some investigators suspect the electrical charge alters the brain's chemistry. Patients usually recover after a series of six to eight such treatments, which may be taken on an outpatient basis. Unlike drugs, ECT does not prevent future bouts of depression. Some physicians hold that excessive use of the technique may have permanent ill effects on memory and cognition.

Some psychiatrists advocate action therapies, with attainable goals, designed to restore self-esteem (like controlled weight loss or a new hobby), and which permit patients to expend energies in harmless ways (like painting a room, jogging, or swimming). Altering environmental circumstances, like living arrangements, one's school or job, or changing associates, may be essential. All therapy is made more difficult by the fact that when people no longer feel depressed, they no longer sense much need for personality growth or environmental change.

Some seekers of health and wholeness turn to a Christian pastor, as Nicodemus did to Jesus Christ one dark night in ancient Jerusalem. There is an aching spiritual void in many people's lives; they have no purpose for living. It is essential to bear a faithful witness of how to be born again: "I say to you, unless one is born anew, he cannot see the kingdom of God" (John 3:3). A person apart from God has good reason to feel dejected; he is in spiritual jeopardy, and needs rebirth. "This new birth happens in all kinds of ways," notes evangelist Billy Graham. "It may seem to happen over a period of time or in a moment. The paths which people take to reach that point of decision may be very direct or very circuitous. Whatever the path, we always find Christ at the end to welcome us."[17] A pastor or friend may introduce a seeker to Christ as Savior, yet it is God's grace alone that makes salvation possible (Eph. 2:8–10).

The fact that an individual is God's person does not exempt him from psychic suffering. God's own Son experienced extreme agony, both in Gethsemane and upon the cross, in order to effect mankind's salvation (see Matt. 26:36–27:66; Luke 22:39–23:49). The apostle Paul wrote of his own limits: "We are afflicted in every way, but not crushed; perplexed, but not driven to despair; persecuted, but not forsaken; struck down, but not destroyed" (2 Cor. 4:8–9). According to Paul, Christian courage, in spite of suffering, showed "that the transcendent power belongs to God and not to us" (2 Cor. 4:7). Such unshakable, transcendent resources undergird the promise of counseling.

Psychotherapist Margaretta K. Bowers acknowledges the saving effect of religious rites in depression. She observed a man in his fifties, who realized marked relief from a severe depression when a courageous priest made use of his sacramental authority and baptized him. It was a symbolic realization that he was acceptable to God and loved within a human community. "Both the therapist and the religionist are often prone to undervalue these sacramental acts," writes Bowers. "A devoutly sincere blessing, touching the head with the hands, can comfort a troubled or dying patient."[18] Many pastoral counselors shrink from body contact with suspicious, phobic, explosive, or overly sensitive individuals. Well-trained counselors, noted Paul Pruyser in discussing this subject, "may be unwilling to reveal any practices of blessing for fear that this may indicate psychological naïveté or an unresolved counter-transference problem."[19] Conversely, some counselees might not wish a blessing. A blessing may seem too pietistic or superstitious to certain individuals. I am suggesting its pastoral, not sacerdotal, use. A prayer of blessing has direct human relevance, not sacramental status alone. It should serve, not as a ritual, but in pastoral response to human need.

Blending the best of several therapies will not suit compulsive parish ministers, who try to heal sufferers on the spot, nor those who seek mind control of depressives. Direct expression of one's anger to God in prayer will bother some Christians who become mute in their rage and refuse to pray. Such honest expression is easier for Jews, who have a tradition of talking with God about intimate matters. Releasing one's feelings to God, who understands human hurts, is illustrated in the book of Job, and in many imprecatory psalms, and biblical passages. Paul taught, "Be angry but do not sin; do not let the sun go down on your anger" in an effort to help Christians work through, not repress or suppress, rage (Eph. 4:26).

Having examined counseling approaches in crises, marriage and family concerns, and depression, I turn next to diagnosis, decision making, and responsibility in pastoral practice.

12

Diagnosis, Decision Making, and Responsibility

EVERY professional person makes certain distinctions in order to live and work with integrity. The Christian pastor arranges his work in some order because of preselected priorities. In an effort to manage time, negotiate around interruptions, and achieve goals he must be guided by larger objectives. Decisions about programs, promotion, personnel, preaching, public and private tasks, and local and outside engagements are prudently arrived at through intentional ministry. When demanding crises come, a pastor makes judgments by assessing their relative weight in light of a larger vision. He also needs wisdom to determine what lies in the hearts of persons—the sources of their pain and joy, and their despair and hope.

Making distinctions in ministry does not mean discriminating against certain persons and projects because of favoritism. Assessment is, in part, a value judgment, as in the words of Jesus: "You will know them by their fruits" (Matt. 7:15–20). One can distinguish real from false persons only by studying people's lives. Laws of character, like nature, are immutable. Evaluation is, in part, intuitive wisdom—relying on one's powers of observation and experience in dealing with people. Jesus expressed it thus with his first disciples: "Behold, I send you out as sheep in the midst of wolves; so be wise as serpents and innocent as doves" (Matt. 10:16). Such discriminating powers have less to do with serpentine wiles than with spiritual wisdom. Appraisal also presupposes tough-minded facts as well as hunches and educated guesses.

In pastoral counseling the capacity for making appraisals lies in purity of heart and accurate knowledge rather than in magical powers. Pastoral diagnosis requires distinctions, decision making, and responsibility regarding human pain and growth. There is an axiom in medicine that holds: "Proper treatment is based on correct diagnosis." That rule of thumb accounts for the large amount of time devoted to assessing, rather than prescribing, in medical schools. Correct diagnosis is a matter of life and death in medicine. Should it mean less to one devoted to disorders of the human heart?

I have a friend who once worked in a family treatment center as a cotherapist with a child psychiatrist. "He keeps the diagnostic manual ever before him while dealing with people," said the counselor, "and has a label on them before they get out of his office." Diagnosing is one of the physician's strengths. Though labeling church members is not the pastor's primary task, when plunged into the storms of peoples' lives, pastors should attempt to understand those seeking help. One's desire to help is not always matched with one's ability to facilitate change and growth.

People turn to pastors as counselors for many reasons, as I have alluded to in earlier chapters. Have you ever wondered: "Why precisely is Mrs. Raines seeking help?" The problem as presented may send the fledgling pastor on a "wild goose chase," and mask the person's real concern. If one lives where there are numerous health care professionals, a second diagnostic question arises: "Why did Mrs. Raines turn to me, a minister, for help?" The corollary question is: "Why has this person come for help now?" Susceptibility to pastoral care is greatest at the precise time of need. A marriage threatened with divorce, for instance, is open to being saved for only a limited time span. When legal proceedings are underway, the husband-wife relationship may be beyond healing, and thus not be open to counseling efforts.

A sharp clinical eye looks beneath the surface for signs of hope amid despair; detects body language, voice tone, test results; and assesses one's willingness to find solutions beyond mere token investments in conversations. A diagnostician wonders and inquires about any other healers Mrs. Raines may have seen before turning his way, and what she expects from him. Pressure increases if the counselee's situation appears critical, as in a threatened suicide, and one feels responsible for what may happen to her. Since the first priority in helping is diagnosis, we need to understand this concept in pastoral practice.[1] In this discussion, terms like distinction, assessment, evaluation, discrimination, appraisal, and diagnosis have no moralistic implications.

DIAGNOSIS IN COUNSELING

What is pastoral diagnosis? The word *diagnosis* is rooted in two Greek words: *dia,* meaning between or apart, and *gnosis,* or knowledge. It implies the ability to distinguish between things. In medicine it means the art of distinguishing one disease from another.

A physician's diagnostic skills are crucial, for proper treatment depends on correct assessment of disease. The medical doctor's expertise in diagnosis helps him to understand what is troubling his patient. He makes a tentative diagnosis, based upon all available information, but subject to change with new test data. Until the physician determines the causes of a patient's illness, he treats symptoms with nonspecific types of medications. Given the significance of spiritual concerns, pastors are as obligated as physicians to assess human needs correctly.

Think for a moment about some of the various problems or symptoms people bring to counseling ministers.

1. *A person may be searching for meaning and acceptance.* Doris Huber is a bright, thirty-two-year-old woman with a religious background, whose father was an alcoholic and absent from home much of the time. Her father beat her when he was drinking. Mrs. Huber married to escape a bad family situation, was divorced at nineteen, and remarried at twenty-one. Now with two children, Mrs. Huber has been unfaithful to her husband, a truck driver who is away from home for weeks at a time. She worries about her girls, ages seven and nine, and mistrusts her husband Jim, whom she suspects is "sleeping around" with women across the country.

A neighbor heard Doris's confession of disenchantment with life while they were drinking coffee together one morning. "Why don't you call Rev. Williams, the minister at Trinity Church," she advised, "and tell him what you've just told me. I don't know enough to tell you what's best, but he can help you if anyone can." On the basis of that advice from a friend, Mrs. Huber made an appointment through the pastor's secretary and poured out her confession to Rev. Williams.

"I no longer love Jim; I don't know if I've ever loved anyone in my whole life. I'm so mixed up, I'm not even sure what love is anymore. Things are under a constant strain at home. I snap at the girls; they can tell I'm edgy. . . . They should be in Sunday school. If the rest of my life is gonna be like the past thirty years, it's not worth living."

Where does the minister begin in sorting out Doris's hurt feelings, self-pity, immoralities, and sense of loss? How does Jesus' forgiving spirit of "go, and do not sin again," recorded in the variant John 8:11 passage, shape the minister's observations, responses, and suggestions? He sees a multifaceted search for meaning and acceptance, for forgiveness and community, for worth and vocation. Self-condemned as sexually promiscuous, longing to be someone's number one mate and a decent mother, Doris Huber needs no scolding. She is saying, in effect, "I'm a sinner. Help me to make sense out of life." To overcome the temptation of fleeting sexual pleasure with various boyfriends requires a new sense of being God's person. She needs faith, devotion to God's power and providence, and a sense of vocation and destiny forged within Christian selfhood. That is diagnostic thinking. Counseling with such a person requires extended sessions, as well as bringing her into the worship and work of the church.

2. *A person may long for salvation and health.* Gary Tanner turned to a Christian pastor after trying many substitute, false gods. He had lived in Arizona, Washington state, and California—"just moved around a lot." Vocationally, things were "up for grabs." He had washed dishes, driven a cab, sawed logs, worked in a commercial cleaning establishment, and been on government welfare. He was unmarried at the time but had lived with numerous, nameless women. In an effort to tune out life's realities and escape its responsibilities, Gary had used various drugs for several years. He had been to a musical concert, where a former pusher and noted singer gave his Christian testimony. This gave Gary some second thoughts about his hopelessness, loneliness, lack of creativity, and his counterproductive efforts to reach some goal in life.

A psychiatrist might have suggested Gary was suffering from a severe character disorder, and had a fragile, irresponsible personality structure. Another therapist might have termed him a schizoid personality in light of his lifelong pattern of social disengagement, his inability to express hostile or warm feelings, and his tendency toward autistic (self-centered) thinking.

Rather than viewing Gary through Freudian determinism, a pastor (along with Jung) would see the shackles confining Gary's life. His ministry should help Gary to name his fetters, and, with God's power, remove the sinful manacles. He must part with drugs, deceiving employers, dependending on befrienders, and demeaning women. Hopefully, he will move from bondage to freedom, from despair to creative hope, and from broken dreams to accountability in Christian calling.

3. *A person may need moral reinforcement for a decision already made.* A youth dropping out of college to work awhile may desire the approval of a significant adult. Someone getting a divorce may wish confirmation of the decision and divine acceptance, even though the marriage has failed. A minister is sought, not for a way out, but for a way to proceed.

Morris McClain's wife is dying of cancer. He tells his minister that he has already given her up, in advance of death, and has "moved in" emotionally with another woman. Mrs. Yancey, his girlfriend, understands the pressures he faces, the financial drains on his budget, and his dependency needs. She has been good to him, prepared some meals while his wife was hospitalized, given him small gifts, and opened her house to him by day or night.

Mr. McClain wonders if he can hold out sexually, though he has remained physically faithful to his wife. He asks his minister to help him distinguish the rightness or wrongness of the situation. Is it wrong for him to feel loved by another woman while being drained, in every respect, by his wife's illness? Also, he wonders what he has done to deserve such treatment from the Creator—why cancer struck his wife instead of someone else. How shall the pastor respond—out of his judgmental, prophetic gifts, out of personal guilt over his own past, or as a teacher sent from God? What if, in the process of counseling, the pastor detects he is being misled and manipulated by Morris McClain, who has already been unfaithful to his dying spouse?

There are diagnostic variables for assessing the religious dimensions of Mr. McClain's experience. He swings between devotion toward and deception of his wife; he is trapped between fidelity and vulnerability to his dependency needs. He struggles with the providence of God and human fate. Morris longs for communion; he wants to belong to another human being. Yet, he experiences loneliness. Morris McClain needs moral reinforcement for a value system now being violated, faith to face tragedy, and grace to befriend his wife who is dying. Because he also needs befriending, the pastor might propose a variety of responsible associates in lieu of Mrs. Yancey's special charms.

One senses how significant it becomes to reach a diagnostic decision about what is happening in the counselee and in oneself, in light of countertransference phenomena. Helpers' theological convictions and sense of rightness run directly into the realities of counselees' lives. One sees the power of custom, religion, taboo, logic, habit, and mishandled ethics to repress unacceptable feelings and actions. Seekers of true wisdom may have been teased, scolded, pressured, and deceived into present behavior patterns. Now, in a desperate leap of faith, the socially programmed counselee turns to a minister. The counselee hopes magically that something can be done, even as God's Son helped the tomb-dweller named Legion (Mark 5:1–20). Some pastors, wanting to feel needed, fall into the trap of "playing God" rather than ministering "in Christ's stead."

THINKING DIAGNOSTICALLY

The ministry of Jesus exposed him to every conceivable human need. God's Son distinguished among needs, since he "knew mens' hearts," blessed those with "ears to hear" his saving message, healed "not the well but the sick," and told persons "all that they ever did" (Matt. 11:15, 15:21–28; Mark 4:24; Luke 4:16–44; John 4:29). With accurate knowledge of an individual's needs, he can usually be helped even as Jesus ministered effectively in his lifetime. There are exceptions, of course.

Pastors who are "answer men" think prescriptively, and offer pat answers for deep needs. What is real pastoral diagnosis and how does it work? *Pastoral diagnosis implies one's ability to deal wisely with human personality, to bring administrative control into the relationship, to exercise discriminating judgment in light of diagnostic variables, and to function redemptively according to the person's needs and the pastor's social role in the community.* Diagnostic thinking requires wisdom of the head, heart, and hand. A faithful pastor taps the rich reservoir of scriptural wisdom, clinical observations of health care professionals, and the guidance of true pastors and pastoral theologians in an effort to bless lives.

A minister's accountability in dealing wisely with human personality
has been discussed in prior chapters. We may contrast it with judgments
of laypersons, based on conventional wisdom and common sense. Accountability implies more than mere criticism. The Bible warns against
a censorious spirit, but advocates discriminating assessment in helping
people change and grow (Matt. 7:1, 15–20).

Lynn Matthews, a middle-aged counselee, continued to fall asleep
during conjoint marriage counseling sessions. There are all sorts of
insensitive, even humorous, cracks that could be made about such behavior. Wisdom suggests that he may have been fatigued, on medication, selectively inattentive to protect himself at some unconscious level,
a diabetic patient, or have suffered depression or blood pressure imbal-
ance. Kindness suggests that we should focus on Matthews's behavior
rather than dismissing him. A physical examination by a medical doctor
is indicated if he is not already under a physician's care. Any humor or
concern that avoided a medical evaluation would be ultimately unkind.

ADMINISTRATIVE CONTROL IN THE RELATIONSHIP

Diagnostic thinking suggests that an agreement or contract should
be made between the helper and helpee. After an initial intake interview, at which time much basic information may be gleaned, the counselor should interpret what he has heard to the individual. The first
thirty or so minutes (of a fifty-minute hour) are spent listening and
responding to what is communicated. Feedback permits clarification.
"This is what I understood you to say. Help me to make certain that
I understand you," the counselor might say. He then summarizes the
hour's accomplishments and looks ahead. Matters like initiative and
responsibility—with the counselee being responsible to pursue growth
or therapeutic goals—should be clarified. The counselor and counselee
need to reach an understanding about time and place of future meetings,
fees (if any) charged, records kept, confidentiality of their visits, assignments between sessions (like free writing or reading), any need for
psychological testing, referral for medical examination, and psychiatric
evaluation or consultation.

In such moments of clarification, the pastor should not promise
more than he can deliver. Nor should he take charge of a dependent
person's life and run things for him, or hide from an angry, anxious, or
agitated parishioner. Each counselee must be free to resolve his concerns

and claim his own power under God (John 1:12). In addition, the pastor must decide whether or not he is the best resource for the counselee or whether other help is required. Meanwhile, the pastor collaborates with the person, reassuring him realistically, supporting him with prayer, and helping him face the future.

DISCRIMINATING JUDGMENT IN LIGHT OF DIAGNOSTIC VARIABLES

This is not the occasion to outline an elaborate system of spiritual anomalies, paralleling a psychiatric glossary, with therapies for each malady. That is not my purpose, though ancient Catholic documents, like the Penitentials, influenced diagnosis for many centuries. Under the Roman Catholic system of moral theology, priests practiced casuistry by examining individual cases of conscience. Penitents enumerated their transgressions; the priest's role was to hear the confessions and invoke God's pardon, including the imposition of penances in order to alter behavior. The intent of indulgences and penances was to amend life, but the abuses of these practices played a part in the Protestant Reformation. Protestant pastors divested themselves of the practice of casuistry, and diagnosis experienced a gradual demise.

In counseling, a pastor should note specific items in his confidential records for future reference. The diagnostic eye observes details like the person's dress, posture, mood, promptness, peculiar mannerisms, nervous tics (involuntary contortions of facial or eye muscles are cues of stress), stereotyped gestures, and body language. The sensitive ear may detect a quiet (almost inaudible) voice tone, reflecting low self-esteem, grief, anxiety, or depression. The counselor needs to probe gently to determine what lies behind suppressed speech. Such signs do not necessarily imply that the individual has a disorder. They are merely useful in observation and assessment of a counselee's state of mind.

Since the pastoral diagnostician will assess theological and psychological variables simultaneously, what are some of these phenomena?

AREAS FOR ASSESSMENT

Paul Pruyser, a gifted teacher at the Menninger Foundation, has suggested some criteria for establishing diagnostic variables for pastoral care. He holds that diagnostic criteria "should have phenomenological aptness, richness, and diversity to capture personal idiosyncrasies."[2]

Diagnostic clues should provide empirical distinctions, become obvious
in interview situations, probe conscious and unconscious processes, and
yield a picture of the person, from which pastoral strategies for intervention might be developed. His suggestions lie in the realm of religious
ideas, involving feeling and thoughtful expressions, based on one's past
and present God-relationship. Most of the following areas for assessment
were suggested initially by Pruyser. I have recast them into bipolar
concepts, reflecting the creative tensions at work in human personality.

GOD AND SELFHOOD

A primary focus of interest for the pastoral counselor is the Creator-
creature relationship that man has with God. What is the counselee's
awareness of *mysterium tremendum,* the Holy Other, which Rudolf
Otto called "the idea of the Holy?"[3] Has he ever seen God at any time,
or, like Job, heard God speak? "Then God answered Job out of the
whirlwind: 'Gird up your loins like a man; I will question you, and you
declare to me' " (Job 40:6–7). What is the counselee's source of power,
virtue, good feelings, and creativity? Are there sacred places, holy persons, or untouchable areas in his life? What is taboo—forbidden under
power of banishment from family or clan—or worse, the curse of death?

The pastoral diagnostician observes how one's sense of creatureliness
comes through. Does the counselee use biblical imagery and speak of
himself as a grain of sand, a blade of grass, breath, cloud, or vapor soon
diffused; as a black sheep or prodigal child suffering banishment; or as
a favored person, like Abraham or the Virgin Mary? Is the person who
seeks a way out of grief, guilt, or a bad marriage an appropriately
dependent creature or a pompous, self-inflated egotist? Does he prize
God above all else, "with heart, soul, mind, and strength" (Matt. 22:-
36–38)? Is the language of God used in the interview—with due reverence, profanity, disappointment, or regret? Is talk of God entirely absent?

What lesser deities have been elevated to God's level: physical culture, success, sex, a prior loss, or poor health? "Pastors should be im-
mensely curious about the gods of their clients," holds Pruyser, "not
taking their God-talk for granted but trying to find out what it refers
to in thought and action."[4] Does some modern demonic force hold sway
over the treasure room of a counselee's heart (Luke 12:34)?

PROVIDENCE AND FATE

A pastoral observer will also consider variations on the theme of providence. The Christian doctrine of providence holds that God is in full control of the universe and human destiny. Many counselees wonder, in childlike fashion, whether God has any personal interest in the course of events here on earth? "Can he be counted on to support and undergird our striving after good in the face of so much that is plainly evil in the world we have to live in?" asks Roger Hazelton.[5] Some people today are plainly prejudiced against the notion of providence. They are like primitive tribesmen who experience the world with no principle of order, only fate and magic as buffers for survival. The more sophisticated ones are likely to agree with one of the characters in a play by Christopher Fry: "A man has to provide his own providence, or there's no knowing what religion will get hold of him."[6]

Providence is a shorthand word for several kinds of experience. It lies close to the heart of true reverence, Christian worship, basic trust, prayer, the ability to learn, and openness to care. A counselor should not ask his counselee for a discourse (nor give one himself) on the theme of providence. Rather, he might explore whether or not his counselee lives in a friendly world. "Is your world friendly or miserable?" Or he may comment, "That sounds lonely. . . . Is anyone experiencing this with you?" Or, "Things look rather dark. . . . Is there light anywhere?" Or, "Who responds to your tears when you cry?" One's chosen responses to the notion of God's concern for man demonstrate one's reliance on faith, magic, or fate.

This theme of providence brings us full circle to the promise of counseling. It is a beacon pointing the way toward hope. Providence is the north star for steering one's craft, through sunny skies and shadows, on this long journey. If one lacks confidence in God's care for his creation, one wallows in shallow wishes, haunting fears, and dark fantasies. One may wait magically on fate to save an ailing marriage; to provide a new job, money, rain for dry crops; or to point a way out of trouble. This is the rescue fantasy: "Maybe someone will help." One who believes in God, in contrast, tests reality, makes creative efforts in pursuit of goals, and practices prayer.

God's promise and providence are linked through his wise provision "for good with those who love him, who are called according to his purpose" (Rom. 8:28). Reflections on what a person thinks God has promised to him provide clues to his character. Pastors must be patient with those who are young in the faith, and are trying to make sense out of life. "It takes experience to make sense out of experience," as Myron Madden has said.[7] God will not grant immediate gratification of every desire. Awareness of the divine presence is enough as one "walks through the valley of the shadow" (Ps. 23:4). A counselor can assist the humble seeker to live openly, no matter what comes.

BELIEF AND UNBELIEF

These variables illuminate what Tillich called "dynamics of faith" in tension with doubt. The counselor's concern is less with creeds or objective historical tenets, than with commitment, aliveness, and subjective trust. What does the seeker ultimately discover? What lies behind the loner's sense of disengagement from the human community? Has he been trampled on—more sinned against than sinner—or is he the abuser? One may respond, "My faith is all I've got"; "My prayers aren't getting beyond this hospital room"; or, "My faith teaches. . . ." One's faith either binds or activates, stifles or strengthens, accuses or guides, frightens or frees a person for life. One is ultimately saved by the power of faith. Unlike the constrictions of unbelief, healthy faith opens one to others, to risk, to adventure, to good feelings (like joy and peace), to the management of loss, and to positive action.

GRACE AND VULNERABILITY

Grace, a derivative of the Latin *gratia*, bespeaks the power to bless, gives potency, grants freedom, and opens the way to salvation and health. Its cognates are graciousness and gratitude, matters of spirit and style. Grace denotes God's lavish generosity in freely giving us "all things," including his own Son (1 Cor. 2:12; 2 Cor. 8:9). Jesus Christ became vulnerable (from the Latin *vulnerare*, meaning to wound), open to man's attack and the damage of the cross. Grace is significant in matters like giving and receiving, repentance and forgiveness, helpfulness and dependency. Grace shares, touches, strokes, and sparkles on the just and unjust alike. Grace is charitable, not greedy. Freely it receives; freely it shares. Grace searches our hearts and calls us, beyond selfishness, to vulnerability that redeems the world.

Someone might say, "I know that the Bible says confess your sins and God will forgive, but that cannot include me." Such a person experiences tension between the need for pardon and feelings of unworthiness. Pruyser labels self-rejection as a kind of narcissism, behind which lies a hard core of pride. We have examples, in both the Bible and life, of unforgivingness, holding on to old grudges, impervious to the wounds of others. One incapable of righting a relationship, restoring damage, or extending pardon suffers what the Scriptures call "hardness of heart." Beneath such imperturbability is a spirit, not of serenity, but of smug revenge.

At the heart of repentance lies a sense of accountability to God. One shoulders his share of responsibility in a troubled situation. David confessed: "Against thee, thee only, have I sinned" after seducing Uriah's wife, Bathsheba, then ordering his servant Uriah slain (Ps. 51:4). Some counselees, unlike the king of ancient Israel, claim to have been victims of circumstance. "It seemed all right at the time to do it, but now things have gone against me." One who is rigid assumes no responsibility for consequences and finds nothing in himself to improve. Counselors should resist the manipulativeness of self-indulgent victims, who claim innocence in their plight.

Another disorder of conscience is pseudo scrupulosity, which shrinks at small sins in order to hide bigger ones. "False face must hide what the false heart doth know," exclaimed Macbeth to his wife, who had advised him, "Look like the innocent flower, but be the serpent under't." Some people repent superficially for minor sins, but harbor deep duplicity within. They are full of confessions of worthlessness. Pruyser states: "Since this happens rather often in upstanding citizens and pillars of the church, this hyper-repentance tends to have a phony quality, which bespeaks perhaps a delusional awareness of sin which does not match with the objective facts."[8] Such rigid individuals see sin everywhere, yet are blind to forgiveness. The Bible speaks of a "broken, contrite heart." This quality of genuine repentance is the feeling a counselor should seek in guiding alienated persons toward God's acceptance.

COMMUNION AND LONELINESS

A common thread running through the cases of Doris Huber, Gary Tanner, and Morris McClain was alienation. Each counselee felt cut off from the human community for a different reason. It is not merely that they were out of fellowship, with reference to some local congregation. Far worse, all viewed themselves as discontinuous with the rest of mankind and nature. Doris Huber said that she was a sex machine, neither an authentic woman nor a number one wife. Tanner had attempted relationships with the opposite sex but sensed that he had destroyed women, not loved them. McClain was living with two women, yet felt victimized by both of them. At the outset of counseling, they each felt alienated from true lovers, separated from God, and were cautious about commitment.

Paradoxically, wrote Pruyser, "it is precisely within the faith group or local church that persons may experience a keen sense of alienation."[9] Young persons may feel let down by their choir group or rejected by a certain clique. People sitting face-to-face in Sunday school classes and on church committees are estranged by polarizing tendencies: liberal-conservative views, militant-pacifist views, those split over plush buildings or creative ministry, and so on. Single adults—divorcees, widows, and those never married—may feel alienated by a church's family orientation. Various estrangements—town versus gown, old versus young, charter members versus newcomers—may run deep. Despite its proclamations of brotherhood, the church may breed loneliness. The counselor must listen to angry, alienated individuals, though he may be tempted to defend the status quo. To be effective, he must approach some cases with great warmth, confront some strictly, and approach others with forgiving compassion.

SENSE OF VOCATION AND STAGNATION

Sigmund Freud was once asked what he thought a normal person should be able to do well. The questioner probably expected a complicated response. But Freud simply said, "Lieben und arbeiten" ("to love and to work"). His answer reflects surprising emotional and theological accuracy. Such a notion of vocation comes close to Calvin's sense of "effectual calling." It involves the performance of meaningful work, creative leisure, companionship with one's spouse or friends, and care of offspring within the family circle. The initial area of assessment involves more than going to work. It is the centering sense of identity, calling, and destiny that gives life meaning and fulfillment. Vocation is not merely an abstract theological concept. It involves dealing with the details of everyday life, rubbing shoulders with one's fellow human beings. Loving involves more than pleasurable sexual contact. The principal thing is one's contribution to the ongoing life process—having and rearing children, and sending them forth as healthy citizens of the world.

Some people, like Doris Huber and Gary Tanner, seem unable to take hold of life. Mrs. Huber symbolizes countless individuals who achieve pseudointimacy, without the enrichment of devotion. The counselor saw a woman regressing from true relationships to obsessive sexual games. Absorbed in their alternative contacts, she and her husband had abandoned parental responsibility and suffered stagnation. They remind us that desiring or having children does not in itself qualify persons for parenthood.

Similarly, Gary Tanner had never discovered himself, his unique place, and his purpose in life. Since he found no niche, no love satisfied him. He discovered that a double-minded man is indeed "unstable in all his ways" (James 1:8). Such a "lost" man does not have to wait for the eschatological hell of Scripture. He already suffers torment. He has no integrity with which to withstand the physical and economic threats of life. Like Robert Frost's "hired man," he has nothing to look back on with pride and nothing to anticipate in hope. Denying historical reality, Tanner had cut himself off from the human community, despaired over his life, and dreaded death. For someone like that, salvation is good news.

Women's liberation challenges a young woman to get her act together. Defying past customs, which suggested that a woman should not come on too strongly about some things, liberation challenges women to sexual frankness and vocational openness. One's vocation should not be based on one's sex. Both men and women require satisfaction, and face similar frustrations in their marriages and jobs.

One's sense of vocation has cosmic, as well as personal, significance. Pruyser writes, "Vocation . . . is putting one's talents to work as a participant in the process that moves the universe toward increasing integrity."[10] Pastoral counselors are concerned, not merely with persons who are vocational drifters. They are equally concerned about persons whose absenteeism indicates alcoholic preoccupation, lack of altruism, or meaningless activity. They are concerned with the compulsive man, more dedicated to his calling than to his family, who is an unconscious or avowed "workaholic." Counselors are equally concerned about individuals for whom life has become a boring and fatiguing grind.

With these diagnostic variables in mind, pastors' therapeutic approaches should be tailor-made for each person and situation. They should avoid stereotyped formulas like: "You'll have to get back into church"; "Prayer changes things"; or "You ought to start tithing again." Each case has its own uniqueness and challenges all the wisdom, skill, patience, and love that can be mustered.

PASTORAL RESPONSIBILITY

We must now clarify how to function redemptively in light of the individual's need and the pastor's social role in the community. This takes us to the realm of pastoral treatment. The skilled pastor recognizes the relative health and pathology of the counselee. The counselor must ask himself certain questions.

1. *Is this a developmental growth problem or a destructive personal or family crisis?* A counselor distinguishes, for example, between a healthy, young woman prior to marriage and a young widow whose husband was accidentally killed. Marriage planning and grief work are uniquely different processes. Growth needs require health-maintenance counseling. Preventive ministry is normative in pastoral care, and is clearly distinct from the pathology-therapy approach of counseling in crises.

2. *Does this interview involve crisis intervention on an emergency basis, or long-term rehabilitation of a chronic disorder?* It is one thing, for example, to make a hospital call on a young mother who has miscarried. It is quite another process to listen to the confessions of a woman who never recovered from an out-of-wedlock pregnancy and abortion. The first counselee usually needs one visit; the second may require fifteen sessions.

3. *Is the problem due to intrapsychic conflict in one's personality, or to cultural background, or both?* To aid a man of Italian descent, skilled as a glassworker, to find a job would be distinguished, for example, from counseling a man who is paranoid about his European parentage. One's accumulated values, experiences, language, and religious faith greatly

influence personality formation. Cultural determinants may work for good or ill depending on the individual. It should also be noted that mental illness is treated differently in various cultures.

4. *Is this a religious conversion (evangelistic) interview or one dealing with serious religious problems?* Since a person knows that God is important to a minister, he may discuss his concern, conflict, or crisis in religious terms. For example, someone may be embarrassed to talk about God; he may claim to be an atheist. He may quiz the pastor about evil and death, or war and peace, or engage him in a debate about the occult or speaking in tongues.

A sensitive pastor realizes that such a person may have personal convictions that function for him much as God sustains traditional Christians. The pastor can pick up on the man's "cosmic optimism," and thread a biblical witness into the interview. Or he can detect the person's despair, and offer resources of the Christian faith. Religion, like music, is a universal language that operates at several levels. An individual's religious notions may contain unconscious problems and hidden family conflicts.

5. *How healthy is the person's character or personality?* The counselee may see himself as no one else does. He may think more highly of himself than he should, or denigrate himself because of guilt or depression. The narcissistic person can see no faces except his own, and tends to ignore other's feelings. Such a person is highly manipulative, the opposite of the biblically humble person.

Wayne Oates illustrates in *When Religion Gets Sick* how one's psychological conflicts may be revealed in weird religious dreams, unhealthy attitudes, and odd biblical interpretations.[11] Thus, the pastor should determine the religiocultural background of the person he is counseling, and attempt to learn the unique meanings the person phrases in religious language. A healthy individual, on the other hand, reveals a capacity for creative relationships; is tolerant of traumatic events and stressful situations; expresses feelings, from anger to warmth, in appropriate ways; reflects a clear perception of reality; and relates to God, himself, and others in constructive ways.

6. *At what depth do counselor and counselee work during the session? Is the counselor functioning as pastor, friend, teacher, or therapist?* To function effectively, the wise counselor collaborates with each counselee in evaluating goals and plans as the session ends. Is testing advisable? Should consultation be made with a health care or social work profes-

190   *Counseling as Promise*

sional? Are assignments like free writing or reading a selected book potentially worthwhile? Is referral indicated for psychiatric evaluation or hospitalization?

7. *What investment is the congregant or client willing to make for services rendered?* Whether or not a pastoral counselor charges fees, the question of a counselee's investment in the healing process is unavoidable. Most ministers offer counseling services to their own parishioners at little or no cost. Such services for nonparishioners are viewed as community ministries, and are subsidized wholly or in part by one's congregation. Some pastors suggest making a gift to the church each session as an investment in the counseling process. One minister said: "After I have seen parishioners two or three times I usually send them to a fee-taking person because I think they'll heal quicker."

Logic suggests that what is cheap is of little value and what is dear is valuable. Many counseling centers staffed by ministers use a sliding fee-payment scale, which covers both those who are able and those unable to pay for services. In order to survive economically and to serve constituents ethically, more and more pastoral counseling centers charge all clients equitably on a *cost of delivered services* basis.[12] In cases of financial privation, a financial aid fund, established as a vital aspect of the center's ministry, subsidizes many clients. Some centers request "in-kind payment" from counseled persons, who are asked to do volunteer work in return for the pastor's counseling.

The counselor's goal is not just to meet a person's therapeutic or growth needs. Each person seeking help merits personal recognition on the way to fulfillment, salvation, and health. Hopefully, the counseled person will gain the power to bless and become a helper in-kind, caring for other persons and strengthening the fabric of society. Such hope is the promise of counseling.

The notion of a person seeking help becoming a helper, sharing newfound strength to love with others, is the essence of counseling's promise. Whether one views counseling as a growth process or a therapeutic process, it relates to persons becoming whole. With help from Christian counselors, strugglers learn to care for themselves and the people around them. Treated as individuals, counseled persons can move forward in the mainstream of society. Giving and receiving help calls us beyond ourselves toward a future full of hope, strengthened by the promises of God.

Notes

INTRODUCTION: THE BASIS FOR HUMAN CARING

1. Martin Heidegger, *Being and Time*, trans. John Macquarrie and Edward Robinson (New York: Harper and Row, 1962), p. 370.
2. John Cheever, *Falconer* (New York: Alfred A. Knopf, 1977); see also Joan Didion, "Falconer," *New York Times Book Review*, 6 March 1977, pp. 1, 22–24.
3. Charles L. Rassieur, *The Problem Clergymen Don't Talk About* (Philadelphia: Westminster Press, 1976).
4. See Paul W. Pruyser, *The Minister As Diagnostician* (Philadelphia: Westminster Press, 1976). I acknowledge both the biblical teachings concerning a woman's role in the church (like 1 Tim. 2:8–3:13) and current practices of ecclesiastical endorsement or ordination of women in some communions. Ordination of women in Baptist life, though rare, does occur. The work of laywomen in churches has been indispensable through the ages. Traditionally, *he* has been taken to mean all persons and is so used here. Every effort has been made to avoid sexist language in this discussion of counseling.
5. Gabriel Marcel, *Homo Viator: Introduction to a Metaphysic of Hope*, trans. Emma Crawford (Chicago: Henry Regnery Co., 1951). See also Robert L. Carrigan, "Where Has Hope Gone? Toward an Understanding of Hope in Pastoral Care," *Pastoral Psychology* 25 (1976): 39–53; and Paul W. Pruyser, "Phenomenology and Dynamics of Hoping," *Journal for the Scientific Study of Religion* 3 (1963): 86–97.
6. Church historian Donald F. Durnbaugh has provided seven criteria of the Believers' Church that clarify my own doctrinal roots in *The Believers' Church: The History and Character of Radical Protestantism* (New York: The Macmillan Co., 1968), pp. 32–33.
7. See Donald G. Bloesch, *The Evangelical Renaissance* (Grand Rapids: Eerdmans Publishing Co., 1973); Richard Quebedeaux, *The Young Evangelicals* (New York: Harper & Row, 1974); and David F. Wells and John D. Woodbridge, eds., *The Evangelicals* (Nashville: Abingdon Press, 1975).

8. Dean M. Kelley, *Why Conservative Churches Are Growing* (New York: Harper & Row, 1972, p. 136.

9. Cf. H. R. Mackintosh, *Types of Modern Theology* (London: Collins Fontana Library, 1964); Martin E. Marty and Dean G. Peerman, eds., *A Handbook of Christian Theologians* (Cleveland: World Publishing Co., 1965); Daniel Day Williams, *What Present-Day Theologians Are Thinking* (New York: Harper and Row, 1967); Stanley N. Gundry and Alan F. Johnson, eds., *Tensions in Contemporary Theology* (Chicago: Moody Press, 1976).

10. See Jim Wallis, *Agenda for Biblical People* (New York: Harper & Row, 1976).

11. Sydney E. Ahlstrom, "From Puritanism to Evangelicalism: A Critical Perspective," in *The Evangelicals*, eds. Wells and Woodbridge, p. 269.

12. Cf. George W. Forell, *The Protestant Faith* (Philadelphia: Fortress Press, 1975); Brooks Hays and John E. Steely, *The Baptist Way of Life* (Englewood Cliffs, N.J.: Prentice-Hall, Inc., 1963); Robert McAfee Brown helped to clarify the shared convictions of most Protestants for outsiders in *The Spirit of Protestantism* (New York: Oxford University Press, 1961).

13. E. Y. Mullins, *The Christian Religion in its Doctrinal Expression* (Valley Forge: Judson Press, 1917); W. T. Conner, *Revelation and God: An Introduction to Christian Doctrine* (Nashville: Broadman Press, 1936); idem, *The Faith of the New Testament* (Nashville: Broadman Press, 1940); idem *The Gospel of Redemption* (Nashville: Broadman Press, 1945); Frank Stagg, *New Testament Theology* (Nashville: Broadman Press, 1962); idem, *Polarities of Man's Existence in Biblical Perspective* (Philadelphia: Westminster Press, 1973).

14. Jürgen Moltmann, *The Theology of Hope*, trans. James W. Leitsch (New York: Harper & Row, 1967); idem, *The Crucified God*, trans. R. A. Wilson and John Bowden (New York: Harper & Row, 1974); and idem, *The Church in the Power of the Spirit* (New York: Harper & Row, 1977).

15. David P. Scaer, "Theology of Hope," in *Tensions in Contemporary Theology*, eds. Gundry and Johnson, pp. 197–234.

16. John Macquarrie, *Principles of Christian Theology*, 2d ed. (New York: Charles Scribner's Sons, 1977), p. 338.

17. William Clebsch and Charles Jaekle, *Pastoral Care in Historical Perspective* (New York: Jason Aronson, 1975).

18. William B. Oglesby, Jr., ed., *The New Shape of Pastoral Theology* (Nashville: Abingdon Press, 1969).

19. Seward Hiltner, *Preface to Pastoral Theology*, (Nashville: Abingdon Press, 1958).

20. William E. Hulme, *Pastoral Care Come of Age*, (Nashville: Abingdon Press, 1970).

21. John Patton, "Propositions and Pilgrimage," *Journal of Pastoral Care* 30 (1976): 219.

1. WHEN PEOPLE NEED HELP

1. William Clebsch and Charles Jaekle, *Pastoral Care in Historical Perspective* (New York: Jason Aronson, 1975), pp. 56–64, 253–61.
2. Don S. Browning, *The Moral Context of Pastoral Care* (Philadelphia: Westminster Press, 1976), p. 21.
3. C. W. Brister, *Pastoral Care in the Church* (New York: Harper & Row, 1964). The theological perspective developed in this earlier book is an introduction to the spirit of the present book. I am here filling in details of a counseling method largely implied, but left underdeveloped, in that earlier work.
4. Sam Keen and Anne Valley Fox, *Telling Your Story* (Garden City, N.Y.: Doubleday and Company, Inc., 1973). See also Alex Haley, *Roots* (Garden City, N.Y.: Doubleday and Company, Inc., 1976) for the saga of one man who traced his African heritage through half a million miles of travel and twelve years of work. See Jeane Eddy Westin, *Finding Your Roots* (New York: J. P. Tarcher—St. Martin's Press, 1977), which details how people can trace their ancestors, at home and abroad.
5. Jay E. Adams wrote: "The biblical approach requires giving advice. Nouthetic counselors listen in order to gather the data about which to advise people" (*Competent to Counsel* [Grand Rapids, Mich.: Baker, 1970], p. 91). My quarrel with Adams is not his searching the scriptures for authority, nor his warnings against humanistic therapies (though I disagree with much of his interpretation). Rather, it has been demonstrated beyond question that personality is not transformed by advice. Adams has built, unfortunately, an entire model of pastoral counseling on the restricted concept of condemnation and correction, suggested by the Greek word *noutheo.* See also Jay E. Adams, *The Christian Counselor's Manual,* (Grand Rapids, Mich.: Baker, 1973), chap. 4.
6. Karl Menninger, a respected psychiatrist, wrote in *Whatever Became of Sin?* that the clergy is too preoccupied with disease and treatment, that it is neglecting theological and ethical matters (New York: Hawthorn Books, Inc., 1973), pp. 223–30.
7. Edward E. Thornton suggested this insight in a personal communication with the author. See also Clyde E. Fant's focus on pastoral humanity in *Preaching for Today* (New York: Harper & Row, 1975), pp. 51–52.
8. Warren L. Jones, M.D., "The A-B-C Method of Crisis Management," *Mental Hygiene,* 52 (1968): 87–89; see also Donna C. Aguilera and Janice M. Messick, *Crisis Intervention: Theory and Methodology* (Saint Louis: The C. V. Mosby Co., 1974); and Howard W. Stone, *Crisis Counseling* (Philadelphia: Fortress Press, 1976).
9. Howard R. Burkle, *God, Suffering, and Belief* (Nashville: Abingdon Press, 1977), p. 121.
10. Henri Nouwen, *The Wounded Healer: Ministry in Contemporary Society* (Garden City, N.Y.: Doubleday & Company, Inc., 1972).

2. DISCOVERING GOD'S CARE: A PERSONAL ODYSSEY

1. Daniel Day Williams, *The Minister and the Care of Souls* (New York: Harper & Row, 1961), p. 68.
2. Bel Kaufman, "Letter to a Dead Teacher," *Today's Education* (March-April 1975): 20.
3. Williams, *The Minister and Care*, p. 91.
4. See John Biersdorf, ed., *Creating an Intentional Ministry* (Nashville: Abingdon Press, 1976).
5. Henry T. Close, "On Saying NO to People: A Pastoral Letter," *Journal of Pastoral Care*, 28 (1974): 92–98.
6. Williams, *The Minister and Care*, p. 26.

3. COUNSELING INSIDE OUT AND OUTSIDE IN

1. Wayne Oates, *Pastoral Counseling* (Philadelphia: The Westminister Press, 1974), p. 57. The article by Roy Pearson, president of Andover Newton Theological School, "The Parish Ministry," inspired certain ideas in this section (*Today's Ministry* [October 1975]: 2).
2. Thomas C. Oden et al., *After Therapy What?* The John G. Finch Symposium on Psychology and Religion, 2d ed. (Springfield, Ill.: C. C. Thomas, 1974), pp. 15, 36.
3. Cf. Carl Rogers, *Client-Centered Therapy* (Boston: Houghton Mifflin Co., 1951); *On Becoming a Person* (Boston: Houghton Mifflin Co., 1961); and idem, *Carl Rogers on Encounter Groups* (New York: Harper & Row, 1970).
4. Carl Rogers, *Becoming Partners: Marriage and Its Alternatives* (New York: Delacorte Press, 1972), pp. 213–14.
5. Charles B. Truax and Robert R. Carkhuff, *Toward Effective Counseling and Psychotherapy: Training and Practice* (Chicago: Aldine-Atherton, Inc., 1967); William Glasser, *Reality Therapy: A New Approach to Psychiatry* (New York: Harper & Row, 1965); and O. Hobart Mowrer, *The Crisis in Psychiatry and Religion* (Princeton: D. Van Nostrand Co., 1961).
6. Howard Clinebell, *Basic Types of Pastoral Counseling* (Nashville: Abingdon Press, 1966), chaps. 4–15.
7. Seward Hiltner, "The Minister and the Care of Souls, Revisited," *Union Seminary Quarterly Review* 30 (1975): 215.
8. Seward Hiltner and Lowell Colston, *The Context of Pastoral Counseling* (Nashville: Abingdon Press, 1961).
9. David Roberts, *Psychotherapy and a Christian View of Man* (New York: Charles Scribner's Sons, 1950); Edward Thornton, *Theology and Pastoral Counseling* (Englewood Cliffs, N.J.: Prentice-Hall, Inc., 1964); cf. Wayne Oates, *The Christian Pastor*, rev. ed. (Philadelphia: The Westminister Press, 1964); idem, *Christ and Selfhood* (New York: Association Press, 1961); idem, *The Psychology of Religion* (Waco, Tex.: Word Books, 1973); and idem, *Pastoral Counseling* (Philadelphia: Westminster Press, 1974).

10. Charles F. Kemp, *A Pastoral Counseling Guidebook* (Nashville: Abingdon Press, 1971), pp. 41–42.

11. Edgar Draper, M.D., *Psychiatry and Pastoral Care* (Philadelphia: Fortress Press, 1968), pp. 25–72; and Paul W. Pruyser, *The Minister as Diagnostician* (Philadelphia: The Westminster Press, 1976), pp. 60–87.

12. Seward Hiltner, *Pastoral Counseling* (Nashville: Abingdon Press, 1949); Carroll A. Wise, *Pastoral Counseling, Its Theory and Practice* (New York: Harper & Row, 1951); Anton T. Boisen, *The Exploration of the Inner World* (New York: Harper & Row, 1952); Russell L. Dicks, *Pastoral Work and Personal Counseling* (New York: The Macmillan Co., 1955); and Oates, *The Christian Pastor.*

13. Seward Hiltner, *Theological Dynamics* (Nashville: Abingdon Press, 1972); Oates, *Pastoral Counseling;* and Carroll A. Wise, *The Meaning of Pastoral Care* (New York: Harper & Row, 1966).

14. Abraham Maslow, *Toward a Psychology of Being*, 2d ed. (Princeton: D. Van Nostrand Co., 1968), p. 5.

15. C. Eric Lincoln, *My Face is Black* (Boston: Beacon Press, 1964), p. 75; cf. Calvin E. Bruce, "Nurturing the Souls of Black Folk," *Journal of Pastoral Care* 30 (1976): 259–63.

16. Edgar J. Ridley, "Pastoral Care and the Black Community," *Journal of Pastoral Care*, 29 (1975): 271–276.

17. Charles F. Kemp, *Pastoral Care With the Poor* (Nashville: Abingdon Press, 1972), pp. 72–75.

18. Cf. James B. Ashbrook, *Responding to Human Pain* (Valley Forge: Judson Press, 1975); Edgar N. Jackson, *Coping With the Crises in Your Life* (New York: Hawthorn Books, Inc., 1974); and Wayne E. Oates and Andrew Lester, *Pastoral Care in Crucial Human Situations* (Valley Forge: Judson Press, 1969).

19. Cf. Don S. Browning, *Atonement and Psychotherapy* (Philadelphia: Westminster Press, 1966); and Thomas C. Oden, *Contemporary Theology and Psychotherapy* (Philadelphia: Westminster Press, 1967).

20. See James N. Lapsley, *Salvation and Health* (Philadelphia: Westminster Press, 1972).

21. Harry Emerson Fosdick, *The Living of These Days* (New York: Harper & Brothers, 1956), pp. 83–112.

22. John S. Bonnell, *Psychology for Pastor and People* (New York: Harper & Brothers, 1948).

23. Karl Menninger, *Whatever Became of Sin?* (New York: Hawthorn Books, 1973), p. 188.

24. Jay Adams, *Competent to Counsel,* (Grand Rapids, Mich.: Baker, 1970); and Hobart Mowrer, ed., *Morality and Mental Health* (Chicago: Rand McNally & Co., 1967).

25. Lawrence J. Crabb, Jr., *Basic Principles of Biblical Counseling* (Grand Rapids, Mich.: Zondervan Publishing House, 1975); and Gary R. Collins, *The Rebuilding of Psychology* (Wheaton, Ill.: Tyndale House Publishers, Inc., 1977).

26. Don S. Browning, *The Moral Context of Pastoral Care* (Philadelphia: The Westminster Press, 1976); Thomas C. Oden, *Game Free* (New York: Harper & Row,

1974); Seward Hiltner, *Theological Dynamics*, (Nashville: Abingdon Press, 1972); William B. Oglesby, ed. *The New Shape of Pastoral Theology* (Nashville: Abingdon Press, 1969); John Biersdorf, ed., *Creating an Intentional Ministry* (Nashville: Abingdon Press, 1976).

27. Paul W. Pruyser, *The Minster as Diagnostician* (Philadelphia: The Westminster Press, 1976), pp. 49–50.

4. THE UNIQUENESS OF PASTORAL COUNSELING

1. "The Impossible Dream: Can Seminaries Deliver?" *Christianity Today*, February 4, 1977, pp. 18–21.

2. *Readiness for Ministry*, vol. 1 (Vandalia, Ohio: The Association of Theological Schools in the United States and Canada, 1975), p. 7.

3. Interview with Thomas H. Cole, Chaplain Supervisor, Memorial Hospital System, Houston, Texas, February 8, 1977.

4. John Patton, "Propositions and Pilgrimage," *Journal of Pastoral Care* 30 (1976): 220.

5. *Journal of Pastoral Care* 26 (1972).

6. Hans H. Strupp, "On the Basic Ingredients of Psychotherapy," *Journal of Consulting and Clinical Psychology* 41 (1973): 7–8.

7. Sol L. Garfield, "Basic Ingredients or Common Factors in Psychotherapy?" *Journal of Consulting and Clinical Psychology* 41(1973): 10.

8. Gordon W. Sixty, Basic Counseling Skills Seminar, The Ecumenical Center for Religion and Health, San Antonio, Texas, fall, 1976, unpublished notes.

9. H. Eysenck, "The Effects of Psychotherapy: An Evaluation," *Journal of Consulting Psychology* 16 (1952): 319–24; see also *The Effects of Psychotherapy* (International Science Press, 1966); and Charles B. Truax and Robert R. Carkhuff, *Toward Effective Counseling and Psychotherapy: Training and Practice* (Chicago: Aldine-Atherton, Inc., 1967), p. 5.

10. Jerome D. Frank, *Persuasion and Healing: A Comparative Study of Psychotherapy*, rev. ed. (Baltimore: Johns Hopkins University Press, 1973); idem, "The Demoralized Mind," *Psychology Today* (April, 1973), pp. 22–24.

11. Jerome D. Frank, "Psychotherapy: The Restoration of Morale," *American Journal of Psychiatry* 131:3 (1974): 272.

12. Morris Taggart, "The AAPC Membership Information Project," *Journal of Pastoral Care* 26 (1972): 220.

13. Wayne E. Oates, *Pastoral Counseling, op. cit.*, chap. 1; and see his response to "Do Pastoral Counselors Bring a New Consciousness to the Health Professions?" in *Journal of Pastoral Care*, 26 (1972): 255–57.

14. Edward E. Thornton, personal communication, June 7, 1977.

15. Interview with Thomas H. Cole, February 8, 1977.

16. Jürgen Moltmann, *Theology of Hope*, trans. James W. Leitch (London: SCM Press Ltd., 1967), p. 91.

17. Ibid.

18. Ibid., p. 43.

5. WHAT PSYCHOLOGY CAN WE TRUST?

1. T. N. Weide, "Varieties of Transpersonal Therapy," *Journal of Transpersonal Psychology* 5 (1973): 7–14; cf. A. J. Sutich, "Transpersonal Psychology: An Emerging Force," *Journal of Humanistic Psychology* 8 (1968): 77–79.

2. Erik H. Erikson, *Identity and the Life Cycle* (New York: International Universities Press, 1959), pp. 88–94.

3. Erik H. Erikson, *Childhood and Society*, 2d ed. (New York: W. W. Norton, 1963), p. 277. Emphasis supplied.

4. Myron Madden, *The Power to Bless* (Nashville: Abingdon Press, 1970).

5. Charlotte Buhler, "Life's Basic Tendencies," *American Journal of Psychotherapy*, 13 (1959): 561–81; cf. idem, *Values in Psychotherapy* (New York: Free Press, 1962); and Charlotte Buhler and Melanie Allen, *Introduction to Humanistic Psychology* (Monterey, Calif.: Brooks/Cole, 1972).

6. Gardner Murphy, *Personality: A Biosocial Approach to Origins and Structures* (New York: Basic Books, 1966). See also, Sigmund Freud, *The Claims of Psychoanalysis to Scientific Interest*, standard ed., vol. 13 (London: Hogarth Press, 1955); and Anna Freud, *Difficulties in the Path of Psychoanalysis* (New York: International Universities Press, 1969).

7. Harry Stack Sullivan, *Conceptions of Modern Psychiatry* (Washington: Wm. Allison White Psychiatric Institute, 1948); see idem, *The Interpersonal Theory of Psychiatry*, eds. Helen S. Perry and Mary L. Gawel (New York: W. W. Norton Co., 1953); Gordon Allport, *Becoming: Basic Considerations for a Psychology of Personality* (New Haven: Yale University Press, 1955); idem, *The Individual and His Religion* (New York: Macmillan Co., 1960); idem, *Pattern and Growth in Personality* (New York: Holt, Rinehart, and Winston, 1961); idem, *The Person in Psychology* (Boston: Beacon Press, 1968); Theodore Lidz, *The Person*, 2d ed. (New York: Basic Books, 1976); Erik H. Erikson, *Young Man Luther* (New York: W. W. Norton Co., 1958); idem, *Insight and Responsibility* (New York: W. W. Norton, 1964); idem, *Identity: Youth and Crisis*, (New York: W. W. Norton, 1968; idem, *Gandhi's Truth*, (New York: W. W. Norton, 1969); Abraham Maslow, *Religions, Values, and Peak Experiences* (Columbus: Ohio State University Press, 1964); idem, *Toward a Psychology of Being*, 2d ed. (Princeton: D. Van Nostrand Co., 1968); idem, *The Farther Reaches of Human Nature* (New York: Viking Press, 1971); and Rollo May et al., *Existence: A New Dimension in Psychiatry and Psychology* (New York: Basic Books, 1958).

8. See the seminal correlational works by Wayne E. Oates, *The Religious Dimensions of Personality* (New York: Association Press, 1957); idem, *Christ and Selfhood* (New York: Association Press, 1961); and idem, *The Psychology of Religion* (Waco, Tex.: Word Books, 1973).

9. Sigmund Freud, *Civilization and its Discontents* (London: Hogarth Press, 1930).

10. Margaret Mead, *Male and Female: A Study of the Sexes in a Changing World* (New York: Mentor Books, 1955); cf. her more recent views, idem, *Culture and Commitment* (New York: Doubleday and Co., 1970).

11. Abraham Maslow, *Motivation and Personality* (New York: Harper & Row, 1954).
12. James Coleman, *Psychology and Effective Behavior* (New York: Scott, Foresman, & Co., 1969), p. 18.
13. Carl Rogers in *The Nature of Man in Theological and Psychological Perspective*, ed. Simon Doniger (New York: Harper & Row, 1962), p. 93.
14. Gordon Allport, *The Nature of Prejudice* (Boston: Beacon Press, 1954), p. xiv.
15. Charles K. Hofling, M.D. *Textbook of Psychiatry for Medical Practice*, 2d ed. (Philadelphia: J. B. Lippincott Co., 1968).
16. Wayne W. Dyer, *Your Erroneous Zones* (New York: Funk & Wagnalls, 1976).
17. Juanita H. Williams, *Psychology of Women: Behavior in a Biosocial Context* (New York: W. W. Norton Co., 1977). cf. Jean B. Miller, *Toward a New Psychology of Women* (Boston: Beacon Press, 1976).
18. Helene Deutsch, M.D., *The Psychology of Women*, vols. 1 and 2 (New York: Grune & Stratton, 1944).
19. Joseph Wolpe, *Psychotherapy in Reciprocal Inhibition* (Stanford University Press, 1958); and idem, *The Practice of Behavior Therapy* (New York: Pergamon Press, 1969).
20. Cf. Maslow, *The Farther Reaches of Human Nature, op. cit.;* and Carl Rogers, *On Becoming A Person, op. cit.*
21. Cf. Walter Lowrie, *A Short Life of Kierkegaard* (Princeton: Princeton University Press, 1944); Paul Tillich, *On The Boundary* (New York: Charles Scribner's Sons, 1966); Viktor Frankl, *Man's Search For Meaning* (New York: Washington Square Press, 1963); May et al., *Existence;* and Rollo May, *Love and Will* (New York: W.W. Norton Co., 1969).
22. Paul K. Jewett, *Man as Male and Female* (Grand Rapids, Mich.: Wm. B. Eerdmans Publishing Co., 1975), pp. 141–43. cf. Wilfred Bockelman, *Gothard: The Man and His Ministry—An Evaluation* (Santa Barbara, Calif.: Quill Publications, 1976).
23. *Ibid.* cf. Dana V. Hiller and Robin Ann Sheets, eds., *Women And Men: The Consequences of Power* (Cincinnati: University of Cincinnati office of Women's Studies, 1977).
24. *Life Under Pressure: Dealing With Stress in Marriage* may be obtained from the Materials Services Department, Sunday School Board, 127 Ninth Ave. N., Nashville, Tenn. 37234.
25. Sidney B. Simon, Leland W. Howe, and Howard Kirschenbaum, *Values Clarification* (New York: Hart Publishing Co., 1972).
26. One of the finest theological statements about humanity's paradoxical nature is Frank Stagg's *Polarities of Man's Existence in Biblical Perspective* (Philadelphia: Westminster Press, 1973). My own list of polar tensions was prepared independently of Stagg's helpful discussion.
27. Gary R. Collins, *The Rebuilding of Psychology: An Integration of Psychology and Christianity* (Wheaton, Ill.: Tyndale House Publishers, Inc., 1977).

6. PSYCHIATRY'S OFFER TO HELP

1. John T. McNeill, *A History of the Cure of Souls* (New York: Harper & Row, 1951).
2. H. Meng. and E. L. Freud, eds., *Psychoanalysis and Faith: The Letters of Sigmund Freud and Oskar Pfister* (London: Hogarth Press, 1963).
3. Karl Menninger, M.D., quoted in *Fort Worth Star-Telegram,* June 29, 1975, page 1-F.
4. See the studies in social psychiatry by Jerome D. Frank, M.D., *Persuasion and Healing: A Comparative Study of Psychotherapy,* rev. ed. (Baltimore: Johns Hopkins University Press, 1973); and Ari Kiev, M.D., *Curanderismo: Mexican-American Folk Psychiatry* (New York: Free Press, 1968).
5. Carl G. Jung, *Memories, Dreams, Reflections,* ed. Aniela Jaffé, trans. Richard and Clara Winston (New York: Vintage Books, 1963), p. xi.
6. Henri F. Ellenberger, *Discovery of the Unconscious: The History and Evolution of Dynamic Psychiatry* (New York: Basic Books, 1970).
7. See Michael T. Malloy, "It's the Old-Time Religion," *The National Observer,* May 26, 1973.
8. See Paul W. Pruyser, "Religion and Psychiatry: A Polygon of Relationships," *Journal of the American Medical Association* (January 17, 1966), pp. 35–37.
9. Karl Menninger, *Whatever Became of Sin?, op. cit.,* pp. 94–132.
10. Frank, *Persuasion and Healing, op. cit.,* p. x.
11. B. F. Skinner, *Beyond Freedom and Dignity* (New York: Alfred A. Knopf, 1971).
12. See Frederick S. Perls, Ralph F. Hefferline, and Paul Goodman, *Gestalt Therapy: Excitement and Growth in the Human Personality* (New York: Julian Press, Inc., 1951); and Joen Fagan and Irma Lee Shepherd, eds., *Gestalt Therapy Now: Theory, Techniques, Applications* (New York: Harper & Row, 1971).
13. Thomas S. Szasz, *Manufacture of Madness* (New York: Harper & Row, 1970).
14. Robert J. Havighurst, *Human Development and Education* (New York: David McKay Company, Inc., 1953); Erik Erikson, *op. cit.*
15. I am indebted to Kenneth Pepper, *"The Churches and the Helping Professions," Southwestern Journal of Theology* (Spring 1957): 46–49 for helpful ideas in this section.
16. Lewis R. Wolberg and John P. Kildahl, *The Dynamics of Personality* (New York: Grune & Stratton, Inc., 1970), pp. 12–24.
17. Robert S. Glen, M.D., "The Psychiatrist's Role with Pastors Under Stress," *Pastoral Psychology,* 22 (1971): 27–34.
18. Kenneth R. Mitchell, *Hospital Chaplain* (Philadelphia: Westminster Press, 1972), pp. 73–81.
19. Paul W. Pruyser, *The Minister as Diagnostician* (Philadelphia: Westminster Press, 1976), pp. 80–87. See the helpful resource volume, prepared from the psychiatrist's perspective: E. Mansell Pattison, M.D., ed., *Clinical Psychiatry and Religion* (Boston: Little, Brown and Company, 1969).
20. Lucy Freeman and Karl Menninger, M.D., *Sparks* (New York: Thomas Y. Crowell Co., 1973), p. 259.

7. GOALS OF PASTORAL COUNSELING

1. Eli Wiesel, *The Gates of the Forest*, trans. Frances Frenaye (New York: Holt, Rinehart and Winston, 1966).
2. David K. Switzer, *The Minister as Crisis Counselor* (Nashville: Abingdon Press, 1974), p. 23.
3. John B. Cobb, Jr., *Theology and Pastoral Care* (Philadelphia: Fortress Press, 1977), p. 4.
4. William B. Oglesby, Jr., "Pastoral Care and Counseling in Biblical Perspective," *Interpretation: A Journal of Bible and Theology* (July 1973): 320.
5. Ibid., p. 324.
6. Ibid., p. 325.
7. E. Mansell Pattison, *Pastor and Parish—A Systems Approach* (Philadelphia: Fortress Press, 1977), p. 12.
8. Cobb, *Theology and Pastoral Care*, p. 34.
9. Ibid., pp. 34–35.
10. See Richard A. Gardner, M.D., *The Boys and Girls Book About Divorce* (New York: Jason Aronson, 1970).
11. Cobb, *Theology and Pastoral Care*, p. 47.
12. Seward Hiltner, personal communication, March 30, 1977.
13. Cobb, *Theology and Pastoral Care*, p. 51.
14. Ibid., p. 56.
15. Frederick S. Perls, *Ego, Hunger and Aggression* (New York: Random House, 1969); and Leo Madow, *Anger* (New York: Charles Scribner's Sons, 1972).
16. See Kirk H. Neely and Wayne E. Oates, *Where to Go for Help*, rev. ed. (Philadelphia: Westminster Press, 1972); cf. Waylon Ward, *The Bible in Counseling* (Chicago: Moody Press, 1977).
17. Esther Fisher, *Divorce: The New Freedom* (New York: Harper & Row, 1974); and Roger H. Crook, *An Open Book to the Christian Divorcee* (Nashville: Broadman Press, 1974).
18. Mildred Newman and Bernard Berkowitz, *How to Be Your Own Best Friend* (New York: Random House, 1971), p. 13.
19. Charles F. Kemp, *A Pastoral Counseling Guidebook* (Nashville: Abingdon Press, 1971), p. 46.
20. Ibid., p. 47.
21. Cobb, *Theology and Pastoral Care*, p. 53.
22. Ibid., p. 52.
23. Paul E. Johnson, *Person and Counselor* (Nashville: Abingdon Press, 1967), p. 163.

8. RECURRENT RISKS IN PASTORAL COUNSELING

1. Mildred Newman and Bernard Berkowitz, *How to Be Your Own Best Friend* (New York: Random House, 1971), p. 35.
2. Myron Madden, *The Power to Bless* (Nashville: Abingdon Press, 1970), p. 144.

3. W. Hugh Missildine, M.D., *Your Inner Child of the Past* (New York: Simon & Schuster, 1963), p. 25.
4. Alan Keith-Lucas, *Giving and Taking Help* (Chapel Hill: University of North Carolina Press, 1972), p. 48.
5. Wayne E. Oates, *New Dimensions in Pastoral Care* (Philadelphia: Fortress Press, 1970), pp. 47, 49–66.
6. Seward Hiltner, "Planning as a Profession," *Journal of the American Institute of Planners* 23 (1957): 162–67.
7. Address membership applications to American Association of Pastoral Counselors, 3 West 29th St., New York, New York 10001.
8. *American Association of Pastoral Counselors Manual*, 1965–66, pp. 18–20; cf. *Standards for . . . the Certification of CPE Supervisors* (from ACPE, Interchurch Center, 475 Riverside Dr., New York, N. Y. 10027), 1977, pp. 33–37.
9. David M. Moss III, "Pastoral Psychology in a Historical Perspective: An Interview with Carroll A. Wise," *Pilgrimage: The Journal of Pastoral Psychotherapy* 4:2 (1976): 24.
10. James B. Ashbrook, *Responding to Human Pain* (Valley Forge: Judson Press, 1975), p. 57.
11. Charles Rassieur, *op. cit.*, pp. 17f.
12. Myron Madden, "Meaningful Pastoral Intimacy," *Pastoral Psychology* 25:1 (1976): 38.
13. Cf. Lawrence M. Brammer and Everett L. Shostrom, *Therapeutic Psychology* (Englewood Cliffs, N.J.: Prentice-Hall, Inc., 1968), pp. 232–66; Frieda Fromm-Reichmann, *Principles of Intensive Psychotherapy* (Chicago: University of Chicago Press, 1950), pp. 65–66; Lewis R. Wolberg, M.D., ed., *Short-Term Psychotherapy* (New York: Grune & Stratton, 1965), pp. 41–42.
14. Rollo May et al., *Existence: A New Dimension in Psychiatry and Psychology* (New York: Basic Books, 1958), p. 79.
15. Frieda Fromm-Reichmann, *op. cit.*, pp. 104, 143.
16. Brammer and Shostrom, *Therapeutic Psychology*, pp. 232–66.
17. See Julius Fast, *Body Language* (New York: M. Evans and Co., Inc., 1970).
18. Ronald A. Wilkins II, chaplain, St. Joseph's Hospital, Houston, "Appropriate Use of Pastoral Confidences and Privileged Communication: A Survey of Articles," October 16, 1970, unpublished manuscript.
19. Charles F. Kemp, *A Pastoral Counseling Guidebook* (Nashville: Abingdon Press, 1971), p. 81.

9. MICROCOUNSELING IN CRISIS SITUATIONS

1. Edwin S. Schneidman and Norman L. Farberow, *The Cry for Help* (New York: Blakiston Division, McGraw-Hill Book Co., 1961).
2. Erich Lindemann, "Symptomatology and Management of Acute Grief," *American Journal of Psychiatry* 101 (1944): 141–48.
3. Gerald Caplan, *Support Systems and Community Mental Health* (New York: Behavioral Publications, 1974); cf. *Principles of Preventive Psychiatry* (New York: Basic Books, 1964).

4. Cf. Erich Lindemann, "The Meaning of Crisis in Individual and Family," *Teachers College Record*, 57 (1956); and Gerald Caplan, *The Theory and Practice of Mental Health Consultation* (New York: Basic Books, 1970). The historical development of crisis intervention methodology is traced in Donna C. Aguilera and Janice M. Messick, *Crisis Intervention: Theory and Methodology*, 2d ed. (Saint Louis: The C. V. Mosby Co., 1974), pp. 1–10.

5. David K. Switzer, ed., *The Minister as Crisis Counselor* (Nashville: Abingdon Press, 1974), p. 31; cf. Howard W. Stone, *Crisis Counseling* (Philadelphia: Fortress Press, 1976), pp. 1–11.

6. Warren L. Jones, "The A-B-C Method of Crisis Management," *Mental Hygiene* 52 (1968): 87–89.

7. See Howard J. Parad, ed., *Crisis Intervention: Selected Readings* (New York: Family Service Assn. of America, 1965); Robert R. Carkhuff, *The Art of Helping* (Amherst, Mass.: Human Resource Development Press, 1972); idem, *The Art of Problem Solving* (Amherst, Mass.: Human Resource Development Press, 1973); David Lester and Gene Brockopp, *Crisis Intervention and Counseling by Telephone* (Springfield, Ill.: Charles C. Thomas, 1973); and Glenn E. Whitlock, *Preventive Psychology and the Church* (Philadelphia: Westminster Press, 1973).

8. Switzer, *The Minister as Crisis Counselor*, p. 54.

9. Erik H. Erikson, *Identity and the Life Cycle* (New York: International Universities Press, 1959), pp. 50–100.

10. Lewis J. Sherrill, *The Struggle of the Soul* (New York: The Macmillan Co., 1952).

11. Robert Coles, *Erik H. Erikson: The Growth of His Work* (Boston: Little, Brown and Co., 1970), pp. 132–39.

12. Daniel J. Levinson's book is in press, with the working title *The Seasons of a Man's Life*.

13. Gail Sheehy, *Passages: Predictable Crises of Adult Life* (New York: E. P. Dutton & Co., 1976), pp. 34–284.

14. Edwin Schneidman, "Crisis Intervention: Some Thoughts and Perspectives," in *Crisis Intervention*, eds. Gerald A. Specter and William L. Claiborn, vol. 2 (New York: Behavioral Publications, 1973), p. 13. cf. Mansell Pattison, M.D., *Pastor and Parish-a Systems Approach* (Philadelphia: Fortress Press, 1977).

15. Ibid.

16. See "Baptists Deal with Controversial Issues," a series of articles in *Southwestern Journal of Theology* 19 (1977).

10. COUNSELING FOR MARRIAGE AND FAMILY ENRICHMENT

1. Daniel Yankelovich and associates Skelly and White, *The Baptist Standard*, May 11, 1977, p. 6.

2. Institute of Life Insurance survey, "No. 1 Goal of Americans: A Happy Family Life," *Memphis Mirror*, January 24, 1975, p. 2.

3. C. W. Brister, *Life Under Pressure: Dealing With Stress in Marriage* (Nashville: Sunday School Board, 1976), p. 6.

4. George R. Bach and Peter Wyden, *The Intimate Enemy* (New York: William Morrow, 1969).

5. William H. Masters and Virginia E. Johnson, *The Pleasure Bond: A New Look at Sexuality and Commitment* (Boston: Little, Brown & Co., 1974).

6. See John Scanzoni, "A Christian Perspective on Alternative Styles of Marriage," in *Make More of Your Marriage*, ed. Gary R. Collins (Waco, Tex.: Word Books, 1976), pp. 157–68.

7. William J. Lederer and Don D. Jackson clarify what one may expect from marriage counseling in *The Mirages of Marriage* (New York: W. W. Norton & Co., 1968), pp. 441–49.

8. John E. Bell, *Family Therapy* (New York: Jason Aronson, 1974); Virginia Satir, *Conjoint Family Therapy*, rev. ed. (Palo Alto: Science and Behavior Books, 1967); and idem, *Peoplemaking* (Palo Alto: Science and Behavior Books, 1972).

9. Robert Beavers, M.D., *Psychotherapy and Growth: a Family Systems Perspective* (New York: Brunner/Mazel, Publishers, 1977).

10. Readers interested in how unhealthy persons misuse religion and affect entire congregations should read Wayne E. Oates, *When Religion Gets Sick* (Philadelphia: Westminster Press, 1970).

11. Cf. Thomas C. McGinnis and John U. Ayres, *Open Family Living* (Garden City, N.Y.: Doubleday & Co., 1976); Howard J. Clinebell, Jr., *Growth Counseling for Marriage Enrichment* (Philadelphia: Fortress Press, 1975); Myron and Mary Ben Madden, *The Time of Your Life* (Nashville: Broadman Press, 1977); and Herbert A. Otto, ed., *Marriage and Family Enrichment: New Perspectives and Programs* (Nashville: Abingdon Press, 1976).

12. Cf. Muriel James and Dorothy Jongeward, *Born to Win: Transactional Analysis with Gestalt Experiments* (Menlo Park, Calif.: Addison-Wesley Publishing Co., 1971); Frederick S. Perls, *Gestalt Therapy Verbatim* (Lafayette, Calif.: Real People Press, 1969); and Joen Fagan and Irma Lee Shepherd, eds., *Gestalt Therapy Now* (New York: Harper Colophon Books, 1971).

13. Eric Berne, *Games People Play* (New York: Grove Press, 1964); and *Transactional Analysis in Psychotherapy* (New York: Grove Press, 1961).

14. Kenneth Lamott, "The Four Possible Life Positions: 1. I'm not O.K.—you're O.K.; 2. I'm not O.K.—you're not O.K.; 3. I'm O.K.—you're not O.K.; 4. I'm O.K.—you're O.K.," *New York Times Magazine*, Nov. 19, 1972, pp. 42–45.

15. Ibid.; cf. Thomas A. Harris, M.D., *I'm OK—You're OK: A Practical Guide to Transactional Analysis* (New York: Harper & Row, 1969).

16. Cf. Louis Raths et al., *Values and Teaching* (Columbus, Ohio: Charles E. Merrill, 1966); Sidney B. Simon et al., *Values Clarification* (New York: Hart Publishing Co., 1972); and Roland and Doris Larson, *Values and Faith* (Minneapolis: Winston Press Inc., 1976).

17. Paul A. Hauck and Edmund S. Kean, M.D., *Marriage and the Memo Method* (Philadelphia: Westminster Press, 1975).

18. Workshops for counselors in the Taylor-Johnson Temperament Analysis are scheduled periodically in various parts of the country. Address inquiries to: Psychological Publications, Inc., 5300 Hollywood Boulevard, Los Angeles, California 90027.

11. COUNSELING IN DEPRESSIVE REACTIONS

1. Robert A. Woodruff, M.D., Samuel B. Guze, M.D., and Paul J. Clayton, M.D., "Is Everyone Depressed?" *American Journal of Psychiatry*, 132:6 (1975): 627.
2. "Coping With Depression," *Newsweek*, January 8, 1973, p. 51.
3. Aaron T. Beck, *Depression: Causes and Treatment* (Philadelphia: University of Pennsylvania Press, 1967), p. 5.
4. Anthony M. D'Agostino, M.D., "Depression: Schism in Contemporary Psychiatry," *American Journal of Psychiatry* 132:6 (1975): 629.
5. Ibid., pp. 629–32.
6. Harry Emerson Fosdick, *The Living of These Days* (New York: Harper & Row, 1956), pp. 72–76.
7. Ibid., p. 75.
8. Shervert H. Frazier, M.D., and Arthur C. Carr, *Introduction to Psychopathology* (New York: The Macmillan Co., 1964) pp. 9–22.
9. "Coping With Depression," *Newsweek*, January 8, 1973, p. 53.
10. Frazier and Carr, *Introduction to Psychopathology.*
11. Tim LaHaye, *How to Win Over Depression* (Grand Rapids, Mich.: Zondervan Publishing House, 1974), p. 79.
12. Ibid., pp. 12, 120–23.
13. Ibid., pp. 97–99.
14. Ibid., pp. 83, 201–8, 229.
15. E. E. Levitt and Bernard Lubin report in *Depression: Concepts, Controversies, and Some New Facts* (New York: Springer, 1975), pp. 6–7, that suicidal thoughts and threats appeared as a symptom of depression in thirteen selected sources of authority.
16. James A. Peterson and Barbara Payne report in *Love in the Later Years* (New York: Association Press, 1975), that group intervention proved to be a saving factor in the lives of numerous depressed retirees, pp. 34–43.
17. Billy Graham, *How to Be Born Again* (Waco, Tex.: Word Books, 1977), preface.
18. Margaretta K. Bowers, M.D., "Psychotherapy of Religious Conflict," in *Clinical Psychiatry and Religion*, ed. E. Mansell Pattison (Boston: Little, Brown and Co., 1969), p. 239.
19. Paul W. Pruyser, "The Master Hand: Psychological Notes on Pastoral Blessing," in *The New Shape of Pastoral Theology*, ed. William B. Oglesby *op. cit.*, p. 357.

12. DIAGNOSIS, DECISION MAKING, AND RESPONSIBILITY

1. Until the publication, in 1976, of Paul W. Pruyser's *The Minister as Diagnostician* (Philadelphia: Westminster Press, 1976), the concept of pastoral diagnosis was rarely mentioned in literature. Brief references occur in Howard Clinebell, *Basic Types of Pastoral Counseling* (Nashville: Abingdon Press, 1966), pp. 58–59, 67; Charles F. Kemp, *A Pastoral Counseling Guidebook* (Nashville: Abingdon Press,

1971), pp. 41–44; and a chapter in Edgar Draper, M.D., *Psychiatry and Pastoral Care* (Philadelphia: Fortress Press, 1968), pp. 25–72.

2. Pruyser, *The Minister as Diagnostician*, p. 61.

3. Rudolf Otto, *The Idea of the Holy*, trans. John W. Harvey (New York: Oxford University Press, 1928).

4. Pruyser, *The Minister as Diagnostician*, p. 64.

5. Roger Hazelton, *God's Way with Man* (Nashville: Abingdon Press, 1956), p. 5.

6. Christopher Fry, *The Dark Is Light Enough* (New York: Oxford University Press).

7. Myron and Mary Ben Madden, *The Time of Your Life* (Nashville: Broadman Press, 1977), p. 136.

8. Pruyser, *The Minister as Diagnostician*, pp. 72–73.

9. Ibid., p. 75.

10. Ibid., p. 78.

11. Wayne E. Oates, *When Religion Gets Sick* (Philadelphia: Westminster Press, 1970), pp. 177–99.

12. See John E. Hinkle, Jr., "The 'Robin Hood' Policy: Ethical and Practical Issues Growing Out of the Use of Fee Scales in Pastoral Counseling Centers," *Journal of Pastoral Care*, 31 (1977): 119–24; cf. R. J. Ross et al., "In-Kind Payment as Therapy in Pastoral Counseling," *Journal of Pastoral Care* 31 (1977): 113–18.

Index